Brian Catchpole, formerly Dean of Faculty and Head of the School of Teacher Education, Hull College of Higher Education, is now a Dorset-based freelance writer and lecturer in International American schools and colleges.

He has examined at O level for the Cambridge board and is the author of numerous textbooks on history. His books include *Pan Revision Cards: History 1 and 2* and *History 2: Britain and Europe since 1700*, also available in the Pan Study Aids series.

Pan Study Aids for GCSE include:

Accounting
Biology
Chemistry
Commerce
Computer Studies
Economics
English Language
French
Geography 1
Geography 2
German
History 1: World History since 1914
History 2: Britain and Europe since 1700
Human Biology
Mathematics
Physics
Sociology
Study Skills

PAN STUDY AIDS

HISTORY 1:
World History since 1914

Brian Catchpole

A Pan Original
Pan Books London, Sydney and Auckland

First published 1987 by Pan Books Ltd,
Cavaye Place, London SW10 9PG

9 8 7 6 5 4 3 2 1

© Brian Catchpole 1987

ISBN 0 330 29983 2

Text design by Peter Ward
Text illustration by M L Design
Photoset by Parker Typesetting Service, Leicester
Printed and bound in Spain by
Mateu Cromo SA, Madrid

This book is sold subject to the condition that it shall not, by way of trade or otherwise, be lent, re-sold, hired out or otherwise circulated without the publisher's prior consent in any form of binding or cover other than that in which it is published and without a similar condition including this condition being imposed on the subsequent purchaser

CONTENTS

Acknowledgements 7
Introduction to GCSE 8
Preface 10

1 ▶	The First World War and its aftermath	13
2 ▶	Options and topics	41
3 ▶	Peace-keeping 1919–39: the League and the international treaty systems	69
4 ▶	Aggressive nationalism: Japan and Italy	81
5 ▶	The United States to 1941	99
6 ▶	The Second World War, 1939–45	119
7 ▶	The United Nations, international alliances and arms limitations to 1986	153
8 ▶	Independence in Africa, Asia and the Caribbean	179
9 ▶	The Arab–Israeli conflict	213
10 ▶	Race relations: contrasts between the United States and South Africa	233

11 ▶	Asian contrasts: China, Vietnam and Japan	261
12 ▶	Science and technology	293
	Index	318

ACKNOWLEDGEMENTS

The author and publishers would like to thank the following people for kind permission to reproduce the illustrations on the following pages: the Trustees of the Imperial War Museum, pages 18, 21, 128; the Evening Standard Co. Ltd., and thanks to the Centre for the Study of Cartoons and Caricature, Canterbury, for supplying the print, page 60; Edward Arnold, page 93; the BBC Hulton Picture Library, pages 72, 266, 269; Photo Source, page 110; United States Information Service, pages 172, 173; UPI/Bettmann Newsphotos, page 172 (Berlin Wall); *The Times*, pages 176, 278, 284; Camera Press Ltd., pages 188, 189, 201, 230; The Mansell Collection Ltd., page 197; Kevin Kallaugher, page 257; John Hillelson Agency, page 271; Popperfoto, page 284; Col. R. Sage (Lagonda 16/80, 1934), page 299; the Pakistani Embassy, London, page 200.

For kind permission to quote extracts from various other publications, the author and publishers would like to thank the following people: *Dunkirk – the Necessary Myth*, © Nicholas Harman 1980, reprinted by permission of Curtis Brown, page 127. *All Quiet on the Western Front* by Erich Maria Remarque, translated by A. W. Wheen, reprinted by permission of the Bodley Head, page 27. Thanks to Laurence Pollinger for permission to quote from *A Soldier's story* by General Omar Bradley (Holt, Rhinehart & Winston, Inc.), page 155; and to Peter Farrar for permission to quote from *The Diary of Private James Tait*, page 20.

INTRODUCTION TO GCSE

From 1988, there will be a single system of examining at 16 plus in England and Wales and Northern Ireland. The General Certificate of Secondary Education (GCSE) will replace the General Certificate of Education (GCE) and the Certificate of Secondary Education (CSE) In Scotland candidates will be entering for the O grade and Standard Grade examinations leading to the award of the Scottish Certificate of Education (SCE).

The Pan Study Aids GCSE series has been specially written by practising teachers and examiners to enable you to prepare successfully for this new examination.

GCSE introduces several important changes in the way in which you are tested. First, the examinations will be structured so that you can show *what* you know rather than what you do *not* know. Of critical importance here is the work you produce during the course of the examination year, which will be given much greater emphasis than before. Second, courses are set and marked by six examining groups instead of the previous twenty GCE/CSE boards. The groups are:

Northern Examining Association (NEA)
Midland Examining Group (MEG)
London and East Anglian Group (LEAG)
Southern Examining Group (SEG)
Welsh Joint Examinations Council (WJEC)
Northern Ireland Schools Examination Council (NISEC)

One of the most useful changes introduced by GCSE is the single award system of grades A–G. This should permit you and future employers more accurately to assess your qualifications.

GCSE	GCE O Level	CSE
A	A	–
B	B	–
C	C	1
D	D	2
E	E	3
F	F	4
G		5

Remember that, whatever examinations you take, the grades you are awarded will be based on how well you have done.

Introduction to GCSE

Pan Study Aids are geared for use throughout the duration of your courses. The text layout has been carefully designed to provide all the information and skills you need for GCSE and SCE examinations – please feel free to use the margins for additional notes.

N.B. Where questions are drawn from former O level examination papers, the following abbreviations are used to identify the boards:

UCLES (University of Cambridge Local Examinations Syndicate)
AEB (Associated Examining Board)
ULSEB (University of London Schools Examination Board)
SUJB (Southern Universities Joint Board)
O&C (Oxford & Cambridge)
SCE (Scottish Certificate of Education Examination Board)
JMB (Joint Matriculation Board)
SEB (Scottish Examining Board)
ODLE (Oxford Delegacy of Local Examinations)
WJEC (Welsh Joint Examinations Council)

PREFACE

You should understand that the examiners in GCSE History want to test you in very specific skills, not simply your ability to recall basic historical facts and dates. Of course, the ability to have events and dates at your fingertips is vital when coping with any written examination or project activity. But the examiners also hope that, as a result of your study of History, you have begun a real enthusiasm for the past; you know how to use the 'raw material' of history – historical sources; you know the difference between historical causes and historical results; you can detect bias, analyse data and construct, verbally as well as on paper, a reasoned argument about a particular historical issue or event.

The examiners will therefore set questions that present you with various kinds of evidence, e.g. a politician's speech, a public notice dating from the 1930s, some extracts from an international treaty, a photograph of an aeroplane, some opinions, judgements and examples of pure bias. You will have to put the evidence into its correct context and add to it your own comment and opinion. For example, you might be given several descriptions of a battle uttered by people who were directly or indirectly involved. Your task will be to use your knowledge and understanding to match the speaker with his or her description. As you work through this study aid you will find lots of examples of the sort of question examiners will set in GCSE History examinations.

You should also know that every examination board has selected some aspect of Twentieth-Century World History as a basic examination subject. However, they don't all use the expression 'World History'. The NEA (Northern Examination Association) deals with events after 1914 under very specific headings. For example:

1 Conflict and Conciliation includes The First World War, the Treaty of Versailles, the Second World War, peace-keeping processes such as the League of Nations, the United Nations and the process of détente between the superpowers; and in particular the long-standing Arab-Israeli conflict and the conflict between Iran and Iraq.

2 Government in Action covers the Russian Revolution and the work of Lenin and Stalin, the history of Germany between the two World Wars, how China became a communist country and, in total contrast, the history of two western democracies, Britain and the USA. The Northern Ireland and Welsh GCSE boards have adopted a 'modular'

Preface

approach and encourage GCSE candidates to select special topics such as the Soviet Union, Hitler's Germany and China after the Long March. The Midland Examination Group entitles its syllabus *The Modern World, 1914 to the Present Day* with a core content covering the period after 1918 and optional topics such as the First World War, Soviet Russia, Hitler's Germany, Race Relations in America and South Africa and South East Asia's independence movements. The Southern Examination Group (SEG) emphasises technological change as well as the history of the superpowers and the liberation of colonial peoples. SEG's special topics include Lenin, Hitler, China, the Arab-Israeli conflict, though some are limited in time-span. For example, the USA is studied between 1945 and 1976 only. The London and East Anglian Group requires you to choose widely differing sections from its *Modern World History Syllabus*, e.g.

Section A: Asia, beginning with the story of Japanese aggression in the 1930s.
Section C: The Middle East and North Africa, with special emphasis on the Arab-Israeli conflict, the Iranian Revolution and the Gulf War.
Section F: Western Europe including Britain, from the Versailles Treaty to the Second World War, plus the changes in Europe since 1945.

All of these topics and more are described and tested in this Study Aid. For success in the GCSE History examination you will also need a history textbook covering your period or option together with a good map history.

CHAPTER ONE

THE FIRST WORLD WAR AND ITS AFTERMATH

CONTENTS

▶ **The origins of the conflict** — 15

▶ **The nature of the war and civilian involvement** — 17
The Western Front   19
The war at sea   23
The campaigns in Africa   31
War and the civilian populations   35

▶ **The Versailles Peace Treaty** — 37

The First World War and its aftermath

1 ORIGINS OF THE CONFLICT

The immediate cause was the unprovoked German attack on Belgium (3 August 1914). That this should have happened astonished most Europeans. Belgium was a neutral country, her neutrality guaranteed by the great powers. Germany was Europe's leading industrial nation and one of the most civilised and cultured nations in the world.

Understandably, historians have sought the underlying causes of the 'Great War' 1914–18.

Colonial rivalry? Germany was seeking 'a place in the sun'.
Economic rivalry? German exports were selling worldwide.
Naval rivalry? This had been more apparent after Germany suffered humiliation during the 1911 Agadir Crisis.
The arms race? The Europen powers were locked into an arms race and it is usual to date this from the launch of Britain's HMS *Dreadnought* (1906).

All of these causes are significant but the main problem besetting historians is: why did European diplomacy suddenly fail to operate at the crucial moment in 1914? After all, diplomats had prevented conflict over Agadir (1911) and had managed to contain the two Balkan Wars (1912–13, 1913). Yet the threat of a major European war had existed for many years. Its roots go back to 1871 when the German Chancellor Bismarck defeated France and called into being the united German Empire. Bismarck protected Imperial Germany with a system of defensive alliances:

    1879 Dual Alliance with Austria
    1882 Triple Alliance with Italy
    1883 Reinsurance Treaty with Russia

Kaiser Wilhelm II, Emperor of Germany, failed to renew the Russian Treaty. Consequently, Russia formed an alliance with France (1894–5). In 1904 Britain came to a friendly understanding with France (Entente Cordiale) and three years later (1907) made a similar Entente with Russia.

By 1907 two power blocs existed in Europe
    The Triple Alliance: Germany, Austria, Italy
    The Triple Entente: France, Russia, Britain

Their armies and navies were ready for war even though their politicians proclaimed they were working for peace, particularly in the Balkans.

First Balkan War (1912–13), settled by Treaty of London (1913).

Second Balkan War (1913) settled by Treaty of Bucharest (1913). Then came the assassination of Archduke Franz Ferdinand of Austria in Sarajevo (28 June 1914), an event that led directly to the First World War.

How did this happen? Read the following extract:

> Serbia was a Slav nation. Millions of Slavs living within the Austrian Empire were agitating for the right to form their own breakaway Slav state. On 28 July, after making some impossible demands on Serbia, Austria declared war. Why? Her motives were mixed – partly to solve her own domestic Slav problems and partly to further a longstanding ambition to reach the Mediterranean. But Russia was also a Slav state and promised to honour Serbia's sovereignty. On 30 July Tsar Nicholas II ordered the mobilisation of his Imperial armies – virtually a declaration of war on Austria. Under the old 1879 Dual Alliance, Germany was now bound to help Austria and to do this she put into operation her famous Schlieffen Plan. This was Germany's solution to the threat of a war on two fronts, something the Kaiser deeply feared. The essence of the Plan was that the German army could afford to wait up to six weeks before meeting the Russians as they lumbered across the Polish plains; and that in the interval it could invade France via Belgium, turn the French northern flank and then sweep round to attack Paris and the fortress system stretching between Verdun and the Swiss frontier – from behind! Only then, with France at its feet, would the German army clamber into troop trains, set off for the east and there engage and defeat the advancing Russians.

1. Why did Austria oppose the Slav nationalist movement?
2. Why did the Tsar order his armies to mobilise?
3. What problem was the Schlieffen Plan supposed to solve?
4. How long were the Russians supposed to take to reach Germany?
5. Why did the Germans choose to attack through Belgium?
6. What form of transport would the German troops use to move between the two fronts?

THE OUTBREAK OF WAR

This was so rapid that international diplomacy had no time to operate. This timetable shows how quickly events developed:

    28 July Austria declared war on Serbia.
    30 July Russian armies began to mobilise.
        Germany objected to Russian mobilisation.
    1 August Germany declared war on Russia.
    3 August Germany declared war on France.
        GERMAN TROOPS INVADED BELGIUM.
    4 August Britain declared war on Germany.

The First World War and its aftermath

Now contrast the attitudes of the rulers of Imperial Germany and Great Britain in 1914.

1 The Kaiser Wilhelm II

'If His Majesty the Emperor Franz Josef of Austria makes a demand, then the Serbian government must obey. If not, Belgrade must be bombarded and occupied until his wish is fulfilled. And rest assured that I am behind you and ready to draw the sword whenever your action requires.'
(Speaking to the Austrian Foreign Minister earlier in the year)

*'Now thank we all our God
With heart and hand and voices.'*
(Leading the German people in song, August 1914)

2 King George V

1 August *Germany declared war on Russia this evening . . . whether we shall be dragged into it God only knows.*

3 August *Public opinion that we should not allow Germany to pass through the English Channel and that we should not allow her troops to pass through Belgium has entirely changed and now everyone is ready for war and helping our friends.*

4 August *Warm, showers and windy. I held a Council at 10.45 to declare War with Germany; it is a terrible catastrophe but it is not our own fault . . . Please God it may soon be over.*
(Extracts from the Diary of King George V)

1. What evidence is there that the Kaiser was not prepared to consider a diplomatic settlement of Balkan affairs?
2. What evidence is there that King George V regretted the onset of war?
3. Who were 'our friends'?
4. Did George V regard Britain as being in any way responsible for hostilities?
5. Do you think that the two monarchs fairly reflected the mood of their respective countries?

2 THE NATURE OF THE WAR AND CIVILIAN INVOLVEMENT

No Board neglects the importance of the First World War but the methods of examination vary considerably. MEG, for example, regards the conflict as a major topic in its own right; while NEA treats the two World Wars, as well as other conflicts such as Vietnam, as part of the changing nature of warfare in the twentieth century. It is important that you have an overview of the major campaigns on land and sea, the remarkable changes in military technology and the involvement of civilians.

*Maps relating to the fighting on the Western Front are on pp. 28–29

THE GERMAN ADVANCE INTO BELGIUM*

Source A

Within a few days of the outbreak of war it was obvious that every man, woman and child, as well as the soldiers, were in the firing line. As the Germans advanced in the glorious summer sunshine, any Belgian who showed signs of resistance was put to death; while they simply set fire to a village if they felt it had harboured hostile civilians.

Source B

As we shot the Germans down, the fallen were heaped on top of one another in an awful barricade of dead and wounded that threatened to mask our guns.
(A Belgian officer who took part in the defence of Liège)

Source C

Before long the Germans brought up their siege guns and these huge howitzers pulverised Liège and Namur, wiping their defence systems off the face of the earth. A holocaust of high explosive had arrived in the west. Artillery, with its high explosive shells, shrapnel and mortar bombs, would be the greatest killer in the First World War and far more deadly than gas and machine-guns.

Source D

Source: Charles Roetter, *Psychological Warfare*. Batsford 1974

1. In Source A, what evidence is there that German soldiers did not always respect Belgian civilians?
2. To what extent do you think that Belgian refugees influenced British attitudes, an example of which can be seen in Source D?
3. Does Source B suggest that the German leaders had a lack of respect for the lives of their own men?
4. Source C identifies the major killer of the First World War. What was this?
5. Did the Belgian officer quoted in Source B have to face the German siege guns?
6. Two of the howitzer types used in the Belgian campaign were named 'Big Bertha' and 'Slim Emma'. Identify the German and Austrian manufacturers of these weapons.

THE WESTERN FRONT

THE BATTLE OF THE MARNE, 1914

By September the German front line was dangerously extended and the tired soldiers were unable to advance on Paris, a mere 24 km away. The French commander, General Joffre, forced the German General von Moltke to pull back to prepared defences along the River Aisne. At this river, both sides tried to turn the other's flank. A series of bloodthirsty battles resulted (Picardy, Artois, Yser, Ypres) and then both sides began to 'dig in'. The British Expeditionary Force covered the line from Ypres to Armentières; the French held the rest of this new front. From the Swiss frontier to the English Channel a line of trenches and fortifications grew into a static defence system that men would call the Western Front.

THE IMPORTANCE OF THE WESTERN FRONT

It was the key battle zone of the First World War – just as the Eastern Front was during the Second World War. It predominated because the bulk of the German armies operated on this front; and because the Allies were forced to concentrate their main effort in Belgium and North East France in their efforts to dislodge the Germans. For nearly three and a half years the European nations tried to annihilate one another's armies in set-piece battles on the Western Front. In 1916 alone over two million European soldiers died in the 'mincing machine' of Verdun and on the 'killing ground' of the Somme. Both the Allies and the Central Powers believed that victory would come through attrition – the wearing down of resistance by the sheer weight of firepower and superior numbers.

*P. N. Farrar, *Malet Lambert Local History Originals* Vol. 8. p. 6, p. 8.

CONDITIONS ON THE WESTERN FRONT

The following extracts are from the diary of Private James Tait* who joined the East Yorkshire Regiment in 1915 – at the age of fifteen! He fought in the early battles of 1916 and in the final battles of 1918.

20 April 1916 Source 1

Dawn of an eventful day. At 5 p.m. the Germans play hell with us. A grand bombardment is directed against our lines and communication trenches. Whizz-bangs, high explosive shells and trench mortars play havoc with our trenches . . . I spend the night in the listening post – lying in water. In a dazed condition when relieved . . . Everybody is absolutely whacked.

2 May 1916 Source 2

On permanent day working party to continue for fifteen days. Back early and spend enjoyable evening rambling through some woods . . . Hark to the cuckoo! How the thursh makes the woods so gay with its clear song! As in the firing line the larks mock the efforts of men whose object is slaughter . . . we think how absurd it is to be at war, and how the folly of it all is brought home to us!

4 June 1916 Source 3

Shortly after 12 o'clock the British commence a terrific bombardment. After ten minutes the Germans reply . . . and we are all compelled to stand to. No one who has not been through such a hell can possibly conceive any idea of its devastation. It was a very hell upon earth. The shells screech overhead, creating a weird sensation . . . and we had many narrow escapes. You hear an approaching shell screeching through the air. It comes overhead and then one calls up one's utmost nerve power to withstand the shock. There is a flash across the eyes, then a deafening report, followed by part of the parapet tumbling on top of us. I think several times that it is the last time I shall see daylight. The strafing was appalling. This lasted for an hour and then immediately afterwards we rushed down to the front line to dig the poor fellows out. What a sight! Dead and wounded are strewn everywhere. The front line is blown to hell.

Source 4

This was one of Britain's most famous recruiting posters in which an appeal is made not only to a man's natural patriotism but also to his sense of concern for the welfare of his wife and family.

The centre-piece depicts Britain's most senior Field Marshal with his finger pointing summarily at the reader – a device first drawn by Alfred Leete.

Source 4

Source: Charles Roetter, *Psychological Warfare.* Batsford, 1974

1. Is James Tait describing the Battle of the Somme in Source 3?
2. In Source 1 what was James Tait's role during the night?
3. Was he in danger of suffering from 'trench-feet'?
4. In Source 2 what does he mean by the statement that 'the larks mock the efforts of men whose object is slaughter'?
5. What does the word 'parapet' mean in the context of Source 3?
6. Did Tait expect to survive on 4 June 1916?
7. What was the minimum call-up age when Tait joined up in 1915?
8. To what age was this later lowered?
9. Source 4 depicts a famous British Field Marshal. How did he die?

10 The flags in Source 4 are those of the Allies. Name the ally whose flag appears on the far right.
11 Source 5 depicts one of Germany's most famous wartime posters. What evidence is there that the German is a front-line soldier?
12 What evidence is there in Source 5 that the poster must have been issued after April 1915?

Source 5
A German appeal to the civilian population:

> *Help us to Victory!*
> *Subscribe to the War loan.*

Source: in author's collection

1917: ANOTHER YEAR OF ATTRITION

Despite the lessons of 1916, the generals used their usual tactics in vain attempts to break the deadlock on the Western Front. Yet despite the use of immense artillery bombardments it was impossible to dislodge the enemy from defences protected by barbed wire, trenches

The First World War and its aftermath

and machine-gun nests. The Canadians tried at Vimy Ridge; the British, Australians and New Zealanders at Messines. The culmination came during the Third Battle of Ypres, 1917.

Read this extract:

> Marked by a flooded terrain and the use by the Germans of mustard gas, the fighting for Passchendaele Ridge began to lose all meaning and seemed to be helping no one, certainly not the Italians or the Russians. The British suffered 244,000 casualties at 'Third Ypres' and when Canadian troops eventually captured the little village of Passchendaele there was nothing to see there apart from a 'brick-coloured stain on a watery landscape'. How could such a war be ended? Not by sea battles between the fleets of dreadnoughts built up by Britain and Germany before the war.

1 On whose side were the Italians and Russians fighting in 1917?
2 What disaster did the Italian armies suffer in 1917?
3 Name the event that effectively removed Russia from the war in 1917.
4 Why could the war not be resolved by the huge surface fleets?

THE WAR AT SEA

The role of the Royal Navy was twofold:

- to maintain control of the oceans so that help could flow in unimpeded from the Empire and from neutral countries;
- to blockade the German people, to prevent food and war supplies reaching them via the sea.

Germany challenged the Royal Navy with

- Surface raiders;
- U-boats.

The U-boat war began on 20 November 1914 when a British merchant ship was sunk in the north Sea.
   On 4 February 1915 Germany declared the seas around Britain to be a War Zone and in the first unrestricted campaign (February–August 1915) U-boats sank 0.75 million tons of shipping.

1 Explain the meaning of the term 'War Zone'.
2 Name the most famous victim of U-boat attack in 1915.
3 Why did the captain of U-20 attack this target?
4 He 'had sown the seed, slow in germinating as it might be, which would essentially grow into America's entry into the war.' (William Jameson).
Explain.
5 What did the German High Seas Fleet do during the first unrestricted campaign?

THE BATTLE OF JUTLAND 1916

The German commander Admiral von Scheer (1863–1928) had no

intention of fighting the entire British Grand Fleet. His plan had been to lure the lightly armoured battle cruisers out of Rosyth and destroy them with the full force of the High Seas Fleet. The British commander Admiral Jellicoe (1859–1935) intercepted German transmissions and guessed that Scheer was planning a major operation. He therefore steamed out into the North Sea with the entire Grand Fleet.

Losses at Jutland 1916		British	German
Battleships (Dreadnought)		0	0
Battleships (pre-Dreadnought)		0	1
Battlecruisers		3	0*
Armoured cruisers		3	0
Cruisers		3	4
Destroyers		8	5
	Killed	6,000 men	2,500 men

*The Lutzow sank on the way home.

1. What was the obvious design defect in the British battlecruisers?
2. On the statistics shown above, which side appeared to have won the Battle of Jutland?
3. Why is Jutland claimed as a British strategic victory?
4. 'Its value as a battle was in every sense negligible.' Do you agree?
5. Did the German High Seas Fleet ever leave port again before the Armistice in 1918?

THE SECOND UNRESTRICTED U-BOAT CAMPAIGN

In 1917 the Germans decided to break the deadlock on the Western Front by means of a second unrestricted U-boat campaign.

Source A

> '. . . the prospect is that we shall have England at our mercy by the next harvest. The experiences of the U-boats in recent months, the increased number of boats, the bad economic situation in England, certainly form a reinforcement for luck. Taking it all round the prospects for the unrestricted submarine campaign are very favourable . . .'
> Chancellor Bethmann-Hollweg, January 1917

Source B

> 'We need the most energetic and ruthless action possible. Therefore the U-boat war must begin not later than 1 February 1917.'
> Field Marshal von Hindenburg

The First World War and its aftermath

Source C

The aim is to force England to make peace and thereby decide the whole war . . . each boat should fire her entire outfit of ammunition as often as possible . . . Short cruises, short visits to the dockyard, curtailment of routine practices . . .
Instructions to 111 U-boat commanders, 1917

Source D

Sinkings by U-boats, February–June 1917

February		464,599 gross tons
March		507,001 gross tons
April		834,549 gross tons
May		549,987 gross tons
June		631,895 gross tons
	Total	2,988,031 gross tons

Source E

'. . . we have lost command of the sea.'
Classified statement by Lord Digby (Secretary of State for War)

Read all the sources A to E and then answer the following:

1. Source A: How long did the German Chancellor expect it would take to defeat England?
2. Source B: Why was the Field Marshal so anxious to begin the second unrestricted U-boat campaign?
3. Source C: Implicit in this source and in Sources A and B is that the defeat of England would be the key factor in an ultimate German victory. Why was England seen as a more dangerous enemy than, for example, Russia and France. (Remember that Germany always used the expression 'England' rather than 'Britain'.)
4. Source D and E: Look at the tonnage sunk by the U-boats. When do you think Lord Digby made his statement and why, in your opinion, was it never released to the British people?
5. Clearly, Germany did not win the second U-boat campaign. Write an essay explaining the reasons why the British survived the German onslaught, mentioning:
    Lloyd George
    Convoys
    Echo-sounders, depth charges and Q-ships
    The Zimmerman Telegram
    The action of the US Congress, 6 April 1917.

To score high marks in this essay you should emphasise how narrow the margin of victory was. US warships were invaluable as convoy escorts in 1917 and helped to sink some of the 60 U-boats destroyed that year. Germany still had 142 U-boats in January 1918. The Allies sank 69 but German shipyards provided 70 replacements. Admiral Scheer admitted defeat in October 1918 and recalled all U-boats.

THE FINAL GERMAN OFFENSIVES, 1918

German and Allied commanders still believed in the 'Big Push' – smashing through the enemy trenches to bring a rapid end to the war. Germany's final offensives began in March 1918 (Operation Michael) and lasted until June. This was the Kaiserschlacht or 'Emperor Battle'.

Germany put her faith in the Kaiserschlacht for the following reasons:

- She had a temporary 4:3 manpower advantage over the Allies ever since Russia's surrender (for details, see page 34).
- American troops were not expected to arrive in Europe until the summer.
- German commanders hoped to smash the British Fifth Army and capture the Channel ports to end the war by early June.

1. Who were the two German commanders?
2. How far did their troops manage to advance?
3. Who was the Allied Commander-in-Chief?
4. Who were the 'boy conscripts' sent to serve in France in 1918?
5. How many US troops were in France by July 1918?
6. By then, what was Germany's main problem?
7. Of the British Imperial troops, who bore the brunt of the fighting for the rest of 1918?

Why did it take so long to end the war? Read the following extract:

> The infantry relied on the creeping barrage when they advanced under cover of artillery shells bursting just a few yards ahead of the assault troops. And even when they reached their objective they might be pinned down by carefully concealed machine-gunners who had survived the barrage. Many an infantry officer then prayed for help from a low-flying Camel or a noisy Whippet tank. Sadly, aircraft were often out of range while tanks were either knocked out or incapable of negotiating the muddy terrain during the rain-swept autumn of 1918. Booby-trapped bridges, cratered roads and twisted railway tracks made it hard to supply the 6.5 million fighting men, especially as the lines of communication grew longer every day. Above all, the advancing troops had to contend with German machine-gun squads, amply supplied with ammunition belts, who wrought fearful havoc during the last few weeks of war. These terrible losses hardened the hearts of politicians in Paris and London. They would exact very harsh terms when the final surrender came.

1. What was a 'creeping barrage'?
2. Why were infantry officers unable to summon aircraft to help them?
3. What climatic conditions hindered the allied advance in 1918?
4. Why was there a supply problem in 1918?

The First World War and its aftermath

5 The Germans carried out a skilful fighting retreat. What weapon did they use to slow down the Allied advance?

THE GERMAN SURRENDER

Source A

We have no more meat in Berlin. We can't deliver potatoes because we are short of trucks. Fat is absolutely unobtainable . . . It's a mystery to me how the workers of Berlin manage to live. They are inclined to say, 'Better a horrible end than an endless horror.'

Source B

I urge you to abdicate. The great majority of people believe you to be responsible for the present situation.

Source C

Canadian troops of the First Army have captured Mons.

Source D

For every one German plane there come at least five English and American. For one hungry, wretched German soldier come five of the enemy, fresh and fit. For one German army loaf there are fifty tins of canned beef over there. We are not beaten, for as soldiers we are better and more experienced; we are simply crushed and driven back by overwhelmingly superior forces.

Who do you think uttered these words?

	A	B	C	D
Field Marshal Haig	☐	☐	☐	☐
Chancellor Max of Baden	☐	☐	☐	☐
Erich Remarque in *All Quiet on the Western Front*	☐	☐	☐	☐
A Berlin Social Democrat leader	☐	☐	☐	☐

MAP WORK

Study the four maps A, B, C & D depicting the Western Front 1914–18.

History 1: World History since 1914

Map A

Map B

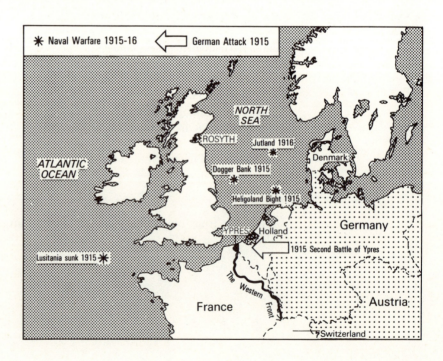

The First World War and its aftermath

Map C

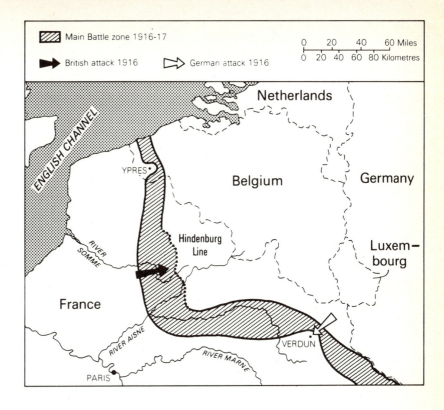

Map D: the last German offensives, 1918

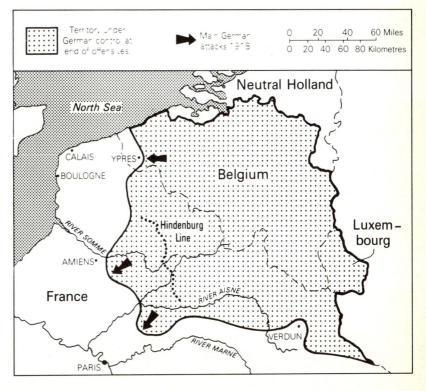

	Which map	A	B	C	D
1	Might be fairly entitled 'The Race to the Sea'?	☐	☐	☐	☐
2	Marks the battle where tanks were first used?	☐	☐	☐	☐
3	Marks the battle where gas was first used?	☐	☐	☐	☐
4	Shows the 'Miracle of the Marne'?	☐	☐	☐	☐
5	Shows the German attack known as the Kaiserschlacht?	☐	☐	☐	☐
6	Shows where the German attack on Verdun and the Battle of the Somme took place?	☐	☐	☐	☐

THE 'SIDESHOWS'

Important military campaigns were fought in Italy, Serbia, the Middle East, at Gallipoli and in Africa.

Map A depicts the strategic significance of the Gallipoli campaign.

Map A: the strategic importance of Gallipoli in the Allied plan to help Russia, 1915

The First World War and its aftermath

1. List three objectives in the Allied attack on Gallipoli. (Consider Russia's needs: such an attack would at least reduce pressure in the Caucasus, might open up a new supply route to Russia through the Black Sea and perhaps even lead to the capture of Constantinople and the removal of Turkey from the war).
2. Give three reasons why the Allies had little chance of success. (Perhaps the most glaring were the lack of intelligence regarding Turkish defences and the lack of accurate maps of the peninsula.)
3. Name (a) the German general and (b) the Turkish general who led the defending forces.
4. Who were the Anzac troops?
5. Comment on the statement that the evacuation from the Dardanelles was the most successful part of the Gallipoli campaign.

LAWRENCE OF ARABIA

Write an account (about twenty lines) to show the importance of T. E. Lawrence (a) in the defeat of Turkey in the Middle East and (b) in the support of Arab nationalism.

Plan your answer to show:

- the special qualities of T. E. Lawrence (1885–1935);
- his role as specified by British Military Intelligence;
- his special relationship with the Arab leadership;
- his guerrilla style warfare against the Turks, e.g. raids on the Medina Railway and the capture of Akaba;
- his contribution in 1918, working with Allenby and capturing Damascus.

Conclude your answer with a reference to Lawrence's contempt for the terms of the Versailles Treaty (1919) and his belief that the Allies had betrayed the Arab cause.

THE CAMPAIGNS IN AFRICA, 1914–18

Map B shows the major campaigns against the German colonies in Africa. Study this map and then read the following extract:

> Neither the Germans nor the Allies had ever contemplated conflict between white armies in Africa. Indeed, the Germans actually hoped that their African colonies would remain neutral and that the 'Great War' would be confined to Europe. However, Britain and France were determined to carry the struggle to every German colony. But victory was not immediately forthcoming and had it not been for the physical endurance and fighting skills of African troops the Allies might have suffered far more serious reverses in German-held parts of Europe. As it was, only the campaign in German East Africa lasted until 1918.

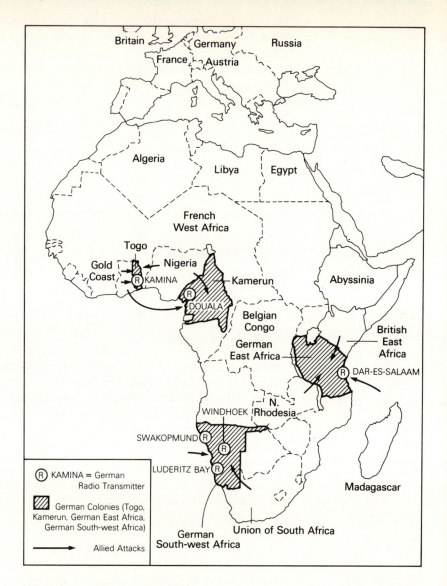

Map B: German colonies under attack

1. Note the presence of radio transmitters in each German colony. Why did the Allies want to destroy these? (When you answer this question bear in mind that U-boats were roaming the Atlantic and Indian Oceans).
2. Why did the Allies and the Germans depend so heavily on African soldiers? (Bear in mind the climate and tropical sicknesses, especially during the campaign in Kamerun.)
3. Why were the Germans able to hold out so long in East Africa? (Emphasise the leadership qualities of General Paul von Lettow-Vorbeck and the loyalty of his askaris.)

The First World War and its aftermath

4 Why do you think the Union of South Africa refused to use African troops in the attack on South-West Africa, 1914–15?
5 Where did the Union troops suffer defeat in 1914?
5 What was the result of the Union victory in South-West Africa?
7 Did Germany retain any of her African colonies after the war?

TECHNOLOGICAL INNOVATION DURING THE FIRST WORLD WAR

Source A

The First World War pushed forward technological innovation at an unprecedented rate. There were two significant new dimensions of warfare: in the skies and under the seas. It is sometimes said that, had technological change been even faster, the ghastly losses in the trenches and during each 'Big Push' might have been avoided. This is wishful thinking.

Source B

The German Army and Navy had the use of 130 airships during the war. They proved to be slow and unwieldy and prone to destruction at the hands of the elements or the incendiary bullets of fighter aircraft. Above all, because of their huge size and (from the ground) their apparent silence, they could strike terror into the hearts of civilian populations. Aircraft proved to be far more effective as weapons.

Source C

'The new technology made the submarine the most dangerous single weapon of the First World War . . .'

Source D

I felt the action of the gas upon my respiratory system; it burned my throat, caused pains in my chest and made breathing all but impossible. Spat blood and suffered from dizziness. We all thought we were lost . . .

Source E

Both sides desperately needed a bullet-proof machine, powered by an internal combustion engine, armed with quick-firing guns, to traverse enemy trenches, crush barbed wire entanglements and destroy machine-gun nests. In 1916 Britain's Ministry of Munitions authorised the construction of such vehicles.

Source F

Drawings of four aeroplanes labelled 1, 2, 3 and 4

1 Source A dismisses the idea that even more rapid technological change might have reduced the huge casualty figures of the First World War. Do you think this is correct?
2 Source B emphasises the use of airships as a means of striking terror into civilian populations.
   (a) Why were these airships called Zeppelins?
   (b) When did a Zeppelin first attack Britain?
   (c) Why did Zeppelins fall victim to 'incendiary bullets'?
   (d) When did Zeppelin raids on Britain cease?
   (e) Did German air attacks on Britain continue?
3 The new technology that made submarines so dangerous included the following:

	Yes	No
Diesel engines	☐	☐
Depth charges	☐	☐
Electric batteries	☐	☐
Periscope optics	☐	☐
Magnetic mines	☐	☐
Accurate torpedoes	☐	☐
Compressed air	☐	☐

The First World War and its aftermath

4 This is a doctor's description of the first gas attack in 1915 (Source D)
  (a) What sort of gas is he describing?
  (b) Would he have had access to a gas-mask?
  (c) Name *two* even more powerful gases used during the war.
  (d) Why did politicians expect that gas would be used in any future conflict against civilian populations?
  (e) What steps did the British take to combat this before the outbreak of the Second World War?

5 Source F depicts four military aeroplanes labelled 1, 2, 3 and 4.

		1	2	3	4
(a)	Which was flown by the German ace Richthofen?	☐	☐	☐	☐
(b)	Which aeroplane bombed London?	☐	☐	☐	☐
(c)	Which aeroplane was not used during the First World War?	☐	☐	☐	☐
(d)	Which aeroplane was outstanding in ground attack as well as in aerial fighting?	☐	☐	☐	☐

6 Sources B, C, and D show that the Germans were leaders in military technology. Source E indicates that Britain took the lead in developing a 'bullet-proof machine'.
  (a) Why was it called a 'tank'?
  (b) Were there any major battles between tanks during the First World War?
  (c) Did the Germans make use of tanks on a large scale?
  (d) Did the use of tanks have a significant effect on German military thinking after the war?

WAR AND THE CIVILIAN POPULATIONS

RATIONING

Source A

Food rationing was more stringent in Germany than in Britain or France and by January 1915 bread rationing was general.

Source B

We are all gaunt and bony now . . . and our thoughts are chiefly taken up with wondering where our next meal will come from.

Source C

Whoever first peels potatoes before cooking wastes much. Therefore cook potatoes with their jackets on.

1 What was the main cause of food shortages in Germany?
2 Did Britain introduce rationing?

3   (a)   What nationality was the writer of Source B?
   (b)   Do you think food shortages had wider psychological effects on German civilians?

4   Source C is taken from Germany's 'Ten Food Commandments'. Did it make good nutritional sense?

THE EMPLOYMENT OF WOMEN

One of the most important social developments during the First World War was the mobilisation of women to fill the vacancies caused by the mass-conscription policies from 1916 onwards. In France, Britain and Germany women secured work in munitions factories and acted as railway porters, lift attendants, farm workers, nurses, bus and tram conductors. Unlike the situation that existed in Britain, German and French women seemed to distrust uniforms other than that of the Red Cross.

Write an essay describing the importance of women workers during the First World War.

Plan your essay so that you can set the story of the unprecedented feminist take-over against the background of rapid social and political change. In France, for example, four million reservists were called up after the 1914 German invasion. This dislocated industry and brought instant hardship to millions of families.

The importance of women workers in Britain must be considered against the background of a rapidly changing society:

(a)   Censorship and suspension of many civil liberties (Defence of the Realm Act 1914 – 'DORA').

(b)   Radical change in the British way of life as it abandoned a peacetime economy in order to out-produce and outgun the enemy.

(c)   Women workers learnt new skills overnight in newly constructed factories and thus contributed to yet another step forward in the process of industrialisation.

(d)   Some paid a very heavy price:
      (i) workers on 14½ hr shifts in aircraft factories sometimes contracted lung diseases from inhaling aircraft dope
      (ii) women who filled shells contracted eczema from handling TNT.

(e)   Note that women who served in the WRNS, WAACS and WRAFS were always non-combatants.

Conclude your essay so that you can stress that:

◊ the entry of women into war work in Britain was of profound importance to the war effort and to ultimate victory;
◊ it also influenced women's social and political aspirations;
◊ it began to change the normal balance of the sexes in British industry.

NAVAL BOMBARDMENTS AND AIR RAIDS

All the boards test your empathy with the past, i.e. your ability to project yourself into the past and so more fully understand it. Could you, for example, project yourself into Whitby, Scarborough and Hartlepool under bombardment from German warships; or into London, under attack from German Gotha bombers? Consider this question: You are in London on 13 June 1917 and witness the worst German air raid on the city. Write a description suitable for inclusion in the local paper next day. Your material could include (although some might be deleted by the editor because of censorship regulations):

> The sight of 14 Gothas flying over the East End;
> The failure of RFC fighters and anti-aircraft guns to shoot any of the above down;
> Bombs on the docks and Liverpool Street;
> At least 162 people killed, including children at a school in Poplar;
> Thousands of prounds' worth of damage;
> Ambulances, fire-engines, police vehicles;
> People's opinions of the situation.

3 THE VERSAILLES PEACE TREATY

Germany surrendered on 11 November 1918. On 28 June 1919 her representatives signed the Treaty of Versailles.

Source A

> *Vengeance! German Nation!*
> *Today in the Hall of Mirrors, the disgraceful Treaty is being signed. Never forget this. With unceasing labour the German people will press forward to regain the place among nations to which she is entitled. Then will come vengeance for the shame of 1919.*
> Deutsche Zeitung, 28 June 1919

Source B
The terms in brief are:

> *Disarm Germany.*
> *Give France Alsace Lorraine and the Saar Coalfield. Set up Poland and Czechoslovakia as new states.*
> *Take all Germany's overseas possessions.*
> *Compel her to pay £1,000,000,000 as a first instalment of her total bill.*
> *Appoint a trial of the ex-Kaiser and the war criminals.*
> *Establish the Allies' right to ton-for-ton of sunk ships.*
> *As a guarantee the Allies hold the left (west) bank of the Rhine for 15 years.*
> Daily Mail, June 1919

Source C

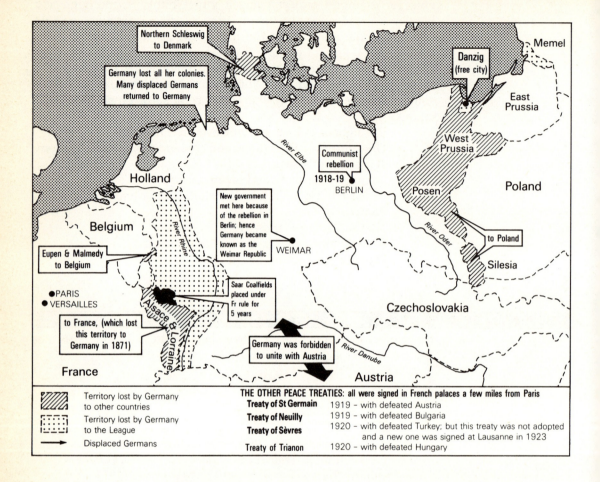

Source D
The 'war guilt' clause Article 231 of the Treaty of Versailles:

> 'The Allied and Associated Governments affirm and Germany accepts the responsibilities of Germany and her allies for causing all the loss and damage to which the Allied and Associated Governments and their nationals have been subjected as a consequence of the war imposed upon them by the aggression of Germany and her allies.'

1. Where is the Hall of Mirrors, mentioned in Source A?
2. Source A calls the Versailles Treaty 'disgraceful'. By what term was the Treaty known in post-war Germany?
3. Source B shows that the Allies wanted to try the ex-Kaiser.
   (a) Where was he in 1919?
   (b) As he was no longer Emperor, what sort of government had been set up in Germany?
   (c) When did the Kaiser die?
   (d) Name *two* other new states created after the First World War.

4 Study Source C.
(a)   Name the four countries that acquired parts of German territory.
(b)   What effect did the loss of West Prussia have upon post-war Germany?
(c)   Was the Weimar Republic allowed to station troops west of the Rhine?
(d)   Was the Treaty of Sèvres a lasting agreement?

5 Read Source D
(a)   Why do you think the German people resented this clause more than any other in the Versailles Treaty?
(b)   Bearing in mind this source, and Sources A and B, do you think that Germany was punished too severely at Versailles?

CHAPTER TWO

OPTIONS AND TOPICS

CONTENTS

▶ **Study techniques** 43

▶ **The Soviet Union** 43
War Communism, 1918–20 45

▶ **Nazi Germany** 53
Adolf Hitler, 1889–1945 55

Options and topics

STUDY TECHNIQUES

First read a simple textbook that covers your chosen subject in a few pages. Make sure that you have access to an atlas or Map History.

Now check that you have a sound knowledge of:

◊ the chronological order of the main events;
◊ the leading historical personalities;
◊ the major geographical features that influence events in your option, e.g. the location of Petrograd (Leningrad), Moscow, Kiev, Vladivostock, the main rivers in the west (Volga, Dnpr, Don) and the plains and steppes so useful to invaders.

Check carefully the precise syllabus advised by your board, e.g. MEG's option on *Germany 1919–45* will not set questions on military campaigns in the Second World War; while SEG's topic on *Hitler and the Third Reich* stresses the military operations that led to his defeat.

1 THE SOVIET UNION

BACKGROUND TO THE REVOLUTIONS OF 1917

Remember that:

◊ Revolutionaries were well established in Tsarist Russia, e.g. the Social Revolutionaries had split in 1903 to form the *Mensheviks* and *Bolsheviks*. Lenin's Bolsheviks were committed to the seizure of political power via small bands of professional revolutionaries.
◊ Bolsheviks were therefore a prime target for the efficient secret police (Okhrana) who forced many into exile. Lenin lived abroad for most of 1900–17.
◊ The First World War created the conditions for a successful revolution. Brusilov's offensives (1916) were a disaster and represented Russia's final military effort. Menshevik leaders overthrew Tsar Nicholas II in 1917 (the March Revolution) but persisted in fighting an unwinnable war against Germany. Thousands of Russian soldiers deserted and the Eastern Front began to collapse.
◊ It was at this stage that the Germans sent Lenin (Vladimir Ilyich Ulyanov 1870–1924) into Russia via a sealed train.

The November Revolution, 7–8 November 1917
Read the following extract:

> *Lenin returned from Finland determined to carry out a military-style coup d'état in the capital. Rallies and demonstrations were, he believed, a waste of time and time was crucial. The Germans were still happy to supply their pet anti-war revolutionary with funds but they wanted to see some results. So Lenin began the rapid training of the Red Guards as urban guerrillas. Their task was to seize all the key points in the capital at a pre-arranged signal. Lenin set up his headquarters in the Smolny Institute; Kerensky disappeared by car in search of some troops he could trust. Suddenly, the noise of gunfire announced the beginning of the revolution. Red Guards swiftly occupied the telephone exchange, the railway stations, the printing offices; they took charge of key bridges and road junctions; and moved in on the Winter Palace where a now terrified Provisional Government was in session.*

1. Name the capital of Russia in 1917.
2. Why were the Germans supporting Lenin?
3. Name six of the key points in the capital.
4. Who was Kerensky?
5. What was the Provisional Government?
6. Who were the new rulers of Russia?
7. Who was their leader?
8. Did he ever hold a free election?
9. Why did the Bolsheviks dissolve the 'Constituent Assembly'?
10. Name and date the peace treaty with Germany negotiated by Trotsky on behalf of Lenin's new 'communist government'.

The interventions
These were undertaken by the Allies (1918) in the unrealistic hope of bringing Russia back into the war. There was no hope of providing the Russian people with a free, democratic government (a secondary aim of the interventionists) and all that had been achieved by 11 November 1918 (Armistice Day) was that British, French and American troops sent to Russia were embroiled in a Civil War between the Whites and the Red Army. The Americans were the first to leave; most interventionists had quit Russia by 1920.

Examine the following extracts:

1. *I wish to be allowed to travel to Vladivostock, take ship to Europe and fight the Germans on the Western Front.*
2. *The capitalists of England, America and France are waging war against Russia in an attempt to restore the Tsar, the landowners and the capitalists. But no! This shall never be!*
3. *If we don't put our foot on the egg, we shall have to chase the chicken round the farmyard of the world.*
4. *We are constructing an army all over again, and under fire at that.*
5. *We took Kazan and advanced to the Urals, moved into the Ukraine and pushed the French out of Odessa.*

Options and topics   45

6   The Red Army soldiers were good but we held on to Vladivostock until 1922 and didn't pull out of North Sakhalin until 1925.

These extracts were spoken by the following:
- Winston Churchill
- Trotsky
- Lenin
- A member of the Czech Legion
- A Red Army soldier
- A Japanese soldier

Identify the speaker of each extract:

1 _____   4 _____

2 _____   5 _____

3 _____   6 _____

WAR COMMUNISM, 1918–20

During the Civil War between the Reds and Whites Lenin operated a harsh policy of national control called 'War Communism'. He nationalised all the means of production and required peasants and factory workers to become state employees. However, he rarely paid them in wages.

1. How did Lenin pay the workers?
2. Why were the Russian peasants displeased?
3. What did Lenin do with the deserters and unemployed?
4. What name did he give to his new secret police?
5. Why did the Russian people complain about 'little tsars' during this period?

Clearly, Lenin's new *Russian Socialist Federal Republic* (proclaimed 1919) was being run by the Communist Party and not by the people.

Extract A

We might have a two-party system, but one of the two parties would be in office and the other in prison.

Extract B

Sailors stationed at the Red Navy's base at Kronstadt mutinied against their political commissars in 1921 and demanded free elections. Trotsky invited them to surrender and when they refused he shot them down.

Extract C

There was no place for political opposition in the twentieth century's first communist state.

Extract A was spoken by a communist; Extract B refers to the 1921

Kronstadt Mutiny which made a profound impression on Lenin's later economic decisions; Extract C is a modern historian's opinion.

Do you think that it is fair to say about Lenin that he was alive to the economic suffering of his people but totally unsympathetic to their political ambitions? Would you agree that his New Economic Policy (NEP 1921–3) falls into that category? Do you think that Lenin would have survived these crisis years without the aid that came from so many private charities, especially from Britain and America? Remember that Lenin had been shot by Dora Kaplan in 1918 and had never really recovered; he was bedridden after a stroke in 1922.

Trotsky (Lev Davidovich Bronstein 1879–1940) had remarkable insight – Russia desperately needed a singleminded leader:

> *'The party organisation would first substitute itself for the party as a whole; then the Central Committee would replace the party organisation; and finally a single dictator would impose his own will upon the Central Committee.'*

Trotsky was saying that eventually a 'Communist Tsar' would emerge in Russia.

Which man do you think first deserved that title?

Stalin (Josef Djugashvili, 1879–1953)

A leadership struggle was fought out in Russia after Lenin's death in 1924. Zinoviev, Kamenev and Trotsky formed an anti-Stalin bloc. Remember that Stalin already had considerable power: Secretary of the Communist Party (1922) and now Commissar of the Workers and Peasants Inspectorate and member of the Politburo. He used this power in 1927 to expel his enemies from the Communist Party. He was then in a position to work out his three main aims:

- to reduce the excessively large rural population
- to mechanise and nationalise agriculture
- to develop and extend manufacturing industries.

Success here would enable him to achieve three important objectives:

- to increase efficiency and so gain national income
- to use new resources to improve living standards
- to develop Soviet armed forces to counter possible foreign aggression.

COLLECTIVISATION
Source 1

> *The kulaks are disrupting Soviet economic policy! We must smash the kulaks, eliminate them as a class!*

Options and topics

Source 2

Full-scale collectivisation began in 1929. Each region had to be de-kulakised and converted to collectives according to a strict timetable 1930–33. Stalin allowed two kinds of farming institutions to develop.

Source 3

Collectivisation was a terrible struggle. It was fearful. Four years it lasted.

Source 4

Livestock losses from 1928 to 1933 (in millions)

Horses		Cattle		Pigs		Sheep and goats	
1928	1933	1928	1933	1928	1933	1928	1933
33	15	70	34	26	9	146	42

	1928	1929	1930	1931	1932	1933
The grain harvest (in millions of tons)	73	72	84	70	70	68
Stalin's slice	11	16	22	23	19	23

Study the four sources:

1. What did the term 'kulak' mean in Stalin's Russia?
2. Why were kulaks the object of so much hostility?
3. Explain the term 'collectivisation'.
4. Name the two types of collective farm that developed.
5. Which type became the more common?
6. Source 3 uses Stalin's own words. How many people lost their lives during these radical changes in Soviet agriculture? (Remember that about five million kulaks disappeared across the Urals during this period; and that there were millions of deaths from malnutrition and disease during the Great Famine – coincidental with collectivisation.)
7. Why were there so many losses in livestock?
8. What is meant by the expression 'Stalin's slice' in the figures relating to grain harvests, 1928–33.

History 1: World History since 1914

INDUSTRIALISATION

Study the following sources:

Source A

> Stalin abolished NEP in 1928 and brought all the means of production under state control. He then issued production targets for each industry. Gosplan's task was to pin down every factory manager to a specific output over the next five years; and the manager's job was to persuade or force his workers to improve their productivity by extra shifts, by new manufacturing techniques or by the use of forced labour herded in from the countryside.

Source B

> Overall it was impossible to attain Stalin's targets: he demanded a 236% rise in gross output over the next five years. Even so, Soviet industry produced some striking results.

Source C

> Stalin's Five Year Plan had become the 'second revolution' in the history of the world's first communist state. Actual production figures were less important in the long run than were the attitudes that the Plan engendered. The Party line was that everyone should compete and become a 'shock worker'.

Source D

This drawing is based on a Soviet poster issued around 1950.

Note that the puny loafer has a crucifix dangling from his neck and a bottle in his left hand; and that there are spaces on the poster for workers to insert the names of any 'ill-disposed' workmates.

Source E

See map on p. 50.

1. Gosplan had been founded in 1921. What was it?
2. Is there evidence that many factory workers were totally unskilled?
3. Give two examples of Stalin's 'striking results' in the rapid industrialisation of Russia.
4. What sort of 'attitudes' was Stalin seeking to engender among his factory workers?
5. Source D identifies the lazy worker with the two main enemies confronting the atheistic state of Soviet Russia. What are these?
6. Name the canal linking the Moscow industrial region with the White Sea.
7. Why was the Irmino Coal Mine of such special importance in the history of Soviet industrialisation?
8. Name industrial regions A and B.

Options and topics

Source D

Source: J. P. Nettl, *The Soviet Achievement*. Thames & Hudson, 1969

9 Locate the biggest hydro-electric plant in Europe.
10 Name the major industry developed in Stalingrad.

STALIN AND THE TERROR

The instrument of Terror was the NKVD, Stalin's secret police officially known as the 'People's Commissariat for Internal Affairs'. It began its extraordinary catalogue of arrest and execution after the murder of Sergei Kirov (one of Stalin's most vocal supporters) on 1 December 1934. The NKVD secret police arrested 8.5 million and shot about one million. Ironically, in the midst of the Terror, Stalin issued the 1936 Constitution that guaranteed Soviet citizens their democratic

History 1: World History since 1914

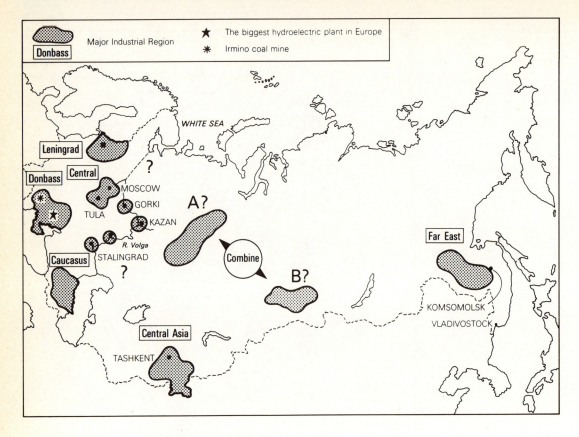

Soviet Industry, 1928–41

rights and enshrined the two principles of collective agriculture and state-controlled industry.

Why did Stalin eliminate so many people of all ranks and levels of society? Study the views of historians A and B and then read the extract from a Soviet textbook.

Historian A

> ... estimates of between one and ten million [deaths] indicate the indiscriminate ruthless nature of the purges which Stalin called 'unavoidable and, on the whole, beneficial ...'
> Richard Poulton, *A History of the Modern World*. OUP, 1981, p. 64

Historian B

> The Great Purge swallowed up so many leading engineers and technologists that industrial production slowed down in 1938. The Soviet armed forces suffered immense losses and lost more senior officers in the Great Purge than they did in the four years of fighting against Nazi Germany.

Soviet textbook, 1938

> *These enemies of the people had a definite programme, which was to restore the yoke of the capitalists and landlords in the USSR, to destroy the collective farms, to surrender the Ukraine to the Germans and the Far East to the Japanese and to promote the defeat of the USSR in the event of war. These brigands were caught and punished as they deserved.*

1. Historian A is in no doubt that Stalin was a ruthless leader. Why do you think that Stalin considered the Great Purge to be both
   (a) unavoidable and
   (b) beneficial?
2. Historian B makes the point that the Great Purge weakened both the industry and the armed forces of the Soviet Union.
   Why do you think Stalin feared leading engineers and military commanders?
3. Does the Russian textbook encourage the view that there was a conspiracy against the Soviet state?
4. Does it suggest that it was the work of a fairly small number of people?
5. Does it suggest that there might have been some sabotage incidents in Russia during the 1930s?
6. Would you regard the Russian textbook account of the terror as having a distinct bias?

THE GREAT PATRIOTIC WAR, 1941–5

In 1931 Stalin had made his famous prediction: 'We are fifty or a hundred years behind the advanced countries. We must make good this distance in ten years. Either we do so, or we go under.' In 1941 Germany began *Operation Barbarossa*, the invasion of the Soviet Union. This was nearly two years after the outbreak of the Second World War in 1939 – the year in which the Soviet Union signed the Non-Aggression Pact with Nazi Germany. Said Stalin, 'It will be asked how it was possible that the Soviet government signed a Non-Aggression Pact with so deceitful a nation, with such criminals as Hitler and Ribbentrop. We secured peace for our country for eighteen months which enabled us to make military preparations.'

Now look at these two statements:

Historian A (British)

> *This is both an untruthful and incomplete answer, for Stalin gained territory as well as time . . . And quite contrary to his claim to have secured peace, he involved Russia in the near-disastrous Winter War with Finland (1940).*

Historian B (Soviet)

> *The German proposition enabled the Soviet Union to avoid war on*

> *two fronts in unfavourable conditions and to gain time to strengthen the country's defences . . . on 23 August 1939 the non-aggression treaty was signed. The perfidious politics of the Western powers forced the Soviet Union to take this step.*
>
> Graham Lyons (ed.), *The Russian Version of the Second World War.* Leo Cooper, 1976, p. 10

1. Historian A flatly disagrees with Stalin's explanation of the Non-Aggression Pact:
   (a) Name the four areas over which Stalin gained military control in 1939–40.
   (b) Name the battle in which the Finns defeated two Russian divisions.
   (c) Name the peace that ended the Winter War in 1940.
2. Historian B supports Stalin in arguing that the Pact permitted Russia to make preparations for a German invasion. From your knowledge of the opening stages of the Great Patriotic War, do you think that this is a fair statement?
   In considering the answer to Question 2 you will have to balance:
   (a) the fact that Stalin was reluctant to mass-produce his outstanding tank, the T-34, as he wished it to be kept an absolute secret;
   (b) the fact that he kept strictly to the terms of the Non-Aggression Pact and supplied Germany with wheat, timber, iron-ore and manganese during 1939–41;
   (c) the fact that he ignored warnings of the likely German attack in 1941 and made no effort to stop Luftwaffe reconnaissance flights over western Russia;
   (d) the fact that he executed his senior air force commander just before the German invasion – and the Soviet Air Force suffered terrible casualties as a consequence;
   (e) the fact that the three main German thrusts into Russia, backed up by air superiority, rolled back the Russian defenders to Uman and Kiev where the Red Army suffered two massive defeats.

The Battle of Moscow, October–December 1941

This was one of the most important battles in the Second World War and brought the German advance to a halt.

Stalingrad and Kursk, 1942–3

These two battles represented Hitler's two major attempts, after Moscow, to win the war on the Eastern Front. Both were overwhelming Soviet victories; while for three years (1941–4) the Russians held out at Leningrad.

THE VICTORIES OF 1944–5

By the end of 1944 the Red Army had liberated all of occupied Russia. From 4 to 11 February 1945, the heads of state of the Soviet Union, USA and Britain met at Yalta to determine:
(a) the campaigns for the final defeat of Germany

(b) the structure of post-war Europe.

Meanwhile the Red Army had invaded Germany and in April captured Berlin.

Germany surrendered (two separate ceremonies in Rheims and Berlin), on 7–8 May 1945 and supreme power inside defeated Germany passed to the governments of the Allied powers.

There was to be no peace treaty with defeated Germany; the story of the 1919 Versailles diktat would not be repeated.

The defeat of Japan

Remember that throughout the war Russia and Japan remained at peace with one another. Russia declared war on Japan two days after the Americans dropped the first atomic bomb on Hiroshima. The Red Army adopted blitzkrieg tactics in the Far East and fighting with Japan went on after the official Japanese surrender (14 August 1945). Russian attacks on Sakhalin and the Kuriles, together with the occupation of North Korea, went on until 23 August 1945.

Consider these two Russian sources:

▷ By defeating Hitler's Germany, the Soviet Nation saved mankind from annihilation, or enslavement by German Fascism, and preserved world civilisation.
▷ Soviet troops broke up the Kwantung Army and defeated its units separately. The use of atomic weapons could not, and did not, have any decisive effect on the outcome of the war.

Do you agree that the Russians take the main credit for the Allied victories in the Second World War? What important events have the Russian historians neglected in the two sources quoted above?

2 NAZI GERMANY

The story of Nazi Germany conveniently breaks down into three main study sections:

▷ Weimar Germany and the rise of the Nazi Party (1919–33)
▷ Hitler's Germany: six years of peace (1933–9)
▷ Hitler's Germany: six years of war (1939–45)

Nazi Germany was a phenomenon of the twentieth century. It was a product of the many problems that had beset this great Empire, Europe's most powerful industrial state, since it was formed in 1871. Imperial institutions and imperial values still existed in post–1918 Germany despite the fact that the Kaiser had fled to Holland and that the new Germany was the 'Weimar Republic' governed by the Social Democrat party. Problems piled up thick and fast and the German people experienced the most destructive inflation ever recorded during the twenties. Increasingly, they began to look back to a past age of imperial glory and economic security – something Adolf Hitler's Nazi Party skilfully exploited.

THE GERMAN REVOLUTION 1918–19

Totally dissimilar from the Russian Revolutions of 1918: a naval revolt at Kiel spread across northern Germany, Ludendorff resigned and the Kaiser went to Holland – who should govern Germany? The Communists, dominant in Berlin where Rosa Luxemburg and Karl Liebknecht led the Spartakus-Bund revolt? The Revolutionary Socialists of Bavaria? Or the more moderate Social Democrats led by Friedrich Ebert? The Germans voted for Ebert in 1919 and he formed the first post-war government at Weimar (Berlin was seething with revolt). Ebert crushed the Communists in Berlin, survived the right-wing Kapp Putsch (1920) and sent in the para-military Freikorps to put down the Revolutionary Socialists in Bavaria.

REPARATIONS AND THE INFLATION

The 1921 London Ultimatum demanded 132 billion gold marks as Germany's reparations for the 'Great War' – to be paid off annually at six per cent interest. The German government printed paper money and exchanged this for sterling, gold and dollars on the world markets. Inevitably, the value of the paper mark collapsed. It is important to note that serious inflation had begun in Germany during 1921. These events exacerbated it, as did the following:

(*a*)   The German failure to meet the December payment of reparations.

(*b*)   The French occupation of the Ruhr in 1923.

Study these sources:

Source A

The unsuccessful Franco–Belgian attempt to run the Ruhr's mines and factories at a profit had catastrophic results for everyone. The Chancellor called on the German people to boycott the invaders and adopt a policy of passive resistance. For the first time since 1918 the people felt a spirit of unity and comradeship and to keep up their spirits Cuno printed lots of strike pay as the months dragged on. Factories stayed unmanned, shops closed down, public transport ceased. The crisis caused the collapse of living standards for almost every group of German workers. Inflation rocketed so rapidly that money became almost meaningless.

Source B

1914   1 mark was worth about £0.05 (20 marks to the pound)
1919   1 mark was worth 0.5 pence.
1920   1 mark was worth 0.25 pence.
1921   1 mark was worth about 1 US cent.
1922   1 mark was worth less than half a US cent.

At the time of the French occupation of the Ruhr it was impossible to express the value of the mark in a western currency.

Options and topics

Source C

Money really had no meaning for us as we grappled with the problems of everyday life. I saw people carrying home their wages in laundry baskets and wheelbarrows. I can remember as a little girl riding on a carousel for 2000 million marks and wondering all the time if I should have spent my money on one bread roll.

Source D

Inflation 'had the effect, which is the unique quality of economic catastrophe, of reaching down to and touching every single member of the community in a way that no political event can.'
Sir Alan Bullock, *Hitler – A Study in Tyranny*. Pelican, 1962, p. 90

1. Who was the Chancellor mentioned in Source A?
2. Why did inflation rocket so rapidly during the Ruhr crisis?
3. Did the Chancellor help inflation when he printed the strike pay?
4. Source B shows the rapid decline of the value in the mark. Name the groups of people (they were notably people on fixed incomes) who were ruined by the inflation.
5. Source C records the experience of a child during the inflation. How do you think ordinary people grappled with the problems of day-to-day living? (Think of how you would have coped without money.)
6. Source D emphasises that inflation touched everyone's lives. Show how Chancellor Stresemann solved the problem of inflation and why his methods added to the growing criticisms of the Weimar Republic.
7. There were several attempts to overthrow the Weimar government during 1923, the best known of which was that of Adolf Hitler. In what city did his Putsch take place?

ADOLF HITLER, 1889–1945

Joined the 16th Bavarian Reserve Infantry as a volunteer in 1914 and served at First Ypres 1914, Neuve Chapelle 1915 and the Somme 1916. Wounded; won Iron Cross. Fought at Arras and Third Ypres 1917 and took part in the Kaiserschlacht 1918. Awarded Iron Cross (First Class); gassed at Ypres, temporarily blinded and in hospital when war ended. Returned to Munich convinced that all the evils of the world were caused by Jews and Communists. Hitler's rank had been that of Gefreiter (Junior NCO) and his job was Company runner.

Note that the importance of the Munich Putsch 1923 was in the publicity that Hitler secured. The fact that he failed to overthrow the government was insignificant – he presented himself as a patriotic German trying to do the best for his people since the 'betrayal' of 1918. He came out of jail in 1924 and refounded the National Socialist (Nazi) Party in 1925.

Instead of working to achieve power by an armed coup, we shall have to hold our noses and enter the Reichstag against the Catholic and Marxist parties. If out-voting them takes longer than out-shooting,

at least the results will be guaranteed by their own constitution! Any lawful process is slow.
Adolf Hitler

1. What tactics did Hitler adopt after 1925?
2. Explain the meaning of 'the results will be guaranteed by their own constitution'.
3. When did the Nazi Party become the strongest Party in the Reichstag?

The Stresemann years, 1924–9

Stresemann was one of the most influential statesmen of the twenties, and Foreign Minister in all the governments up to his death in 1929.

1. Name the two US currency experts who advised Germany in this period.
2. Name the first financial plan designed to help re-establish German industry.
3. Look at this diagram. What were the dangers inherent in this system of international loans and reparation repayments?

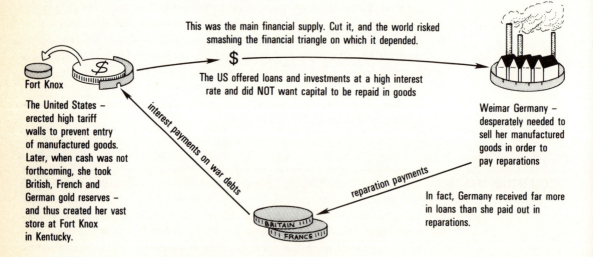

The 'triangular trade' of the twenties

4. What were the advantages to German industry when US loans flowed into the country?
5. Note that France evacuated the Ruhr in 1925 and that Stresemann negotiated the Locarno Agreements with France, Beligum, Italy and Britain. Germany was becoming a respected member of the international community.
   (a) When did she join the League of Nations?
   (b) What was so significant about Stresemann's signing the 1928 Kellogg–Briand Pact?

Options and topics

Hitler's long wait

Hitler was short of cash. His book *Mein Kampf* (*My Struggle*) – dictated when he was in prison – wasn't selling too well. He teamed up with his photographer, Heinrich Hoffman, and edited a magazine. Cash flowed in and he began to restructure the Nazi Party.

- The SA (Sturm Abteilung) would become the Party army.
- His personal bodyguard would form the nucleus of the SS (Schutz Staffeln) under the command of Heinrich Himmler (1929).
- He formed the idea of the Hitler Youth (Hitler Jugend) in 1926.
- During 1927–8 he secured funds from German industrialists. Name one.
- In 1928 he won 2.8 per cent of the national votes – and Nazis appeared in the Reichstag.
- In 1929 he staged the biggest party rally to date. Where?

The world economic crisis

Note that Germany was in financial difficulties before the 1929 Wall Street Crash. The bad winter of 1928–9 pushed unemployment up to 3 million and Germany was hard-pressed to pay the new unemployment benefits.

Yet another American plan forthcoming.

- Name it.
- How long did the Americans give Germany to pay?
- Note that the fundamental problem, Germany's shortfall in the national income, was *not* solved. She was therefore in a precarious position when the share collapse in the US ended the American boom and heralded an unprecedented economic depression in world history.
- For Germany, it meant the end of American loans and the withdrawal of American funds. Chancellor Bruning tried to meet the crisis by a series of emergency decrees as permitted under the Weimar constitution. But President Hindenburg refused to allow them and Bruning called a general election. It was this that gave Hitler his chance.

Read the following extract:

> *This election gave the Nazis the chance to publicise their own programme and thousands of SA men and Hitler Youth toured Germany in hired lorries, waving Nazi banners and shouting election slogans. Hitler ordered his political speakers to put across the party's definition of National Socialism: 'National' meant freedom from the Versailles Diktat and the end of reparations; 'Socialism' meant the right of every worker to have a job. Nazi propaganda had instant appeal among the unemployed and the school leavers who, when asked what they expected to be when they left school, answered 'Arbeitslos! – Unemployed!'*

1. Why did the Nazis appeal to the unemployed and the school leavers?
2. How many seats did the Nazis win in this 1930 election?

3   Who won the most seats?
4   How many votes did Hitler poll in the 1932 Presidential election?
5   Weimar Germany was now in chaos and neither Papen nor Schleicher (briefly, both were Chancellors) could win the support of the Reichstag. In desperation, Hindenburg turned to Hitler who became Chancellor of Germany on 30 January 1933 legally and in strict accordance with the Weimar constitution.

Hitler eliminates all political opposition

▷ He discredited the Communists
   (a)   by raiding their Berlin HQ and 'discovering' documents proving that a communist revolution was being planned.
   (b)   by exploiting the Reichstag Fire (27 February 1933) – it may have been started by the Dutch Communist Marinus van der Lubbe, a self-confessed pyromaniac.
▷ Hitler published the Decree for the Protection of the People and the State.
   (a)   Issued the day after the Reichstag Fire, it was supposed to protect the German people against communist terrorists.
   (b)   In fact, it removed from the German people their democratic rights and allowed the German State Police to arrest and execute anyone; it was used to justify police action right up to 1945.
▷ As the police began herding communist leaders into the newly opened concentration camps at Dachau and Oranienburg, the Reichstag (in which the Nazis had a small working majority) passed the Enabling Act or 'Law for Removing the Distress of People and Reich'.
1   Which of the following powers did it give Hitler for the next four years?
      The power to pass all laws.
      The power to make all foreign treaties.
      The power to control the budget of the German State (now usually referred to as the 'Reich').
      The power to change the constitution without consulting the Reichstag.
2   In April he formed the Geheimes Staats Polizei: by what name is this better known?
▷ In May Hitler abolished the Trade Unions and replaced them with his National Labour Front.
▷ Hitler announced that the Nazi Party was the sole legal political party in the 'Third Reich'.

HITLER – THE MASTER OF GERMANY

More and more people were put into concentration camps. Which of the following might have been placed there before 1936?

	YES	NO
Communist leaders	☐	☐

	YES	NO
Trade union leaders	☐	☐
Unco-operative Reichstag deputies	☐	☐
Jews who had served in the Great War	☐	☐

He had carried out a political revolution after he had come to power. However, he was unsure about the loyalty of the Brownshirts (SA or Sturm Abteilungen) and on 30 June 1934 he authorised the 'Blood Purge' or 'Night of the Long Knives'. He accused the SA Chief of Staff and his supporters of treason:

> It was clear to me that only one man could oppose the Chief of Staff. It was to me that he had pledged his loyalty and he had broken that pledge. For that reason I had to call him to account . . . I gave the orders to shoot those who were the leaders in this treason.
> Adolf Hitler, after the Night of the Long Knives

1 Who was the SA Chief of Staff?
2 Did Hitler take personal responsibility for the murders?
3 How many SA were killed?

Hitler was more cautious with the Army. He introduced a new oath of allegiance for the armed forces:

> I swear by God this sacred oath that I will render unconditional obedience to Adolf Hitler, Führer of the German Reich and People. Supreme Commander of the Armed Forces, and will be ready as a brave soldier to risk my life at any time for this oath.

1 When and why did Hitler take the title 'Führer'?
2 What does the word mean?
3 Who was now in charge of the German armed forces?
4 To what size was the German army limited by the Versailles Treaty?
5 The Army tended to support Hitler, as this source shows:

> Hitler had already gained a certain amount of favour with the Army by taking a stand against the Versailles Treaty; and by showing some real understanding of the life and needs of officers and men in the armed services. It was also in his favour that he combated communism . . .

Why was Hitler able to identify with the 'life and needs of officers and men'?

In the British House of Commons Winston Churchill warned of the growing power of Hitler and his closest supporters:

> . . . two or three men, in what may be a desperate position, have the whole of that mighty country – Germany – in their grip, have that wonderful, scientific, intelligent, docile, valiant people in their grip . . . and that there is no public opinion except what is manufactured by those new and terrible engines of broadcasting and a controlled press.

Look at the cartoon below, depicting Hitler's triumph over the SA after the Night of the Long Knives.

THEY SALUTE WITH BOTH HANDS NOW

Source: *London Evening Standard*, 3 July 1934

1. Who is the small man crouching behind Hitler?
2. What was his job?
3. Name the German General on Hitler's right.
4. Had he founded the Gestapo?
5. Whom are the troops supposed to represent (top right of cartoon)?
6. The Deputy Führer, who died aged 93 in 1987, is not shown. What was his name?
7. Who are the troops with their hands up?

THE WAR ECONOMY, 1933–9

Hitler stated in 1933:

> Within four years unemployment must be overcome . . . There are jobs to be done, marshes to be reclaimed, moorlands to be made cultivable, motor roads to be built.

He set up the Nazi Labour Service and this in turn hired millions of unemployed men, paying them only a few marks a day and enclosing them in tightly disciplined labour camps.

Said Hitler, 'it gives the men a sense of comradeship they and their elder brothers knew in the war. And above all it does away with class distinctions and differences. It unites the people.'

But Hitler did not tell the people he was specifically preparing the nation for war. His Defence Law (21 May 1935) was secret. He had, however, left the League of Nations in 1933 and begun rebuilding the armed forces in 1934. You may meet the following German expressions in your reading. What do they mean?

Wehrmacht? _____
Luftwaffe? _____
Kriegsmarine? _____

Condition of the German people

Wage increases common 1934–37; plenty of overtime; diet mainly meat, fish, coffee and dairy products; plenty of alcohol and cigarettes (consumption rocketed among women); better housing conditions – so much better than the days of the slump when there were six million unemployed in conditions of poverty. The people were very enthusiastic about holidays provided by the state:

▷ *Kraft durch Freude* (Strength through Joy) – Labour Front holidays in Europe (e.g. Norway, Madeira).
▷ Hitler encouraged big business to subsidise holidays – Harz Mountains, 28 marks; Italy, 155 marks; Lake Constance, 65 marks. This was when weekly wage was 27 marks. Holidays such as these beyond the dreams of British workers in the thirties.

The people tended to accept the systematic destruction of the Weimar state; and approved of the defiance of the hated Versailles Diktat. There was public tolerance and goodwill – and the Nazis took advantage of this to shape people's attitudes through propaganda and education, emphasis on the family and the creation of young people's peer groups.

Source A

We start our work when the child is three. As soon as it begins to think, a little flag is put into its hand. Then comes school, the Hitler Youth, the Storm Troop . . . We never let a single soul go.
(Robert Ley, Head of the Labour Front, 1933–45)

Source B

Girls joined the Young Maidens and then the League of German Girls, to be prepared for the day when they would become mothers. Boys joined the German Young People and then at fourteen transferred into the Hitler Youth. Members of the Hitler Youth had to salute women wearing the 'Honour Cross of the German Mother', one of the numerous decorations devised by Hitler for the German people. Baldur von Schirach, Party Youth Leader from 1933 to 1940, had no difficulty in recruiting young Germans.

Source C

I want my young people strong and beautiful. I want youth that are athletic.
(Adolf Hitler)

Source D

Again and again in Germany, even in Catholic Bavaria and the Black Forest, I found cases of children whose Roman Catholic parents tried to keep them in the few struggling Church societies that still existed for children. In every case the children wanted to join the Hitler Jugend . . . To be outside Hitler's organisation was the worst form of punishment. I have seen groups of boys in their teens gaping almost with idolatry at one of their fellows who had been singled out for a salute from Baldur von Schirach; and I soon learnt not to answer the children's stock query: 'Have you seen the Führer?' by answering 'Yes, and I have spoken with him.' The resultant worship was too distressing. Their attitude of mind was totally uncritical.
Stephen Roberts, *The House that Hitler Built*, Methuen & Co., 1938, p. 10

Source E

Hitler radically changed teacher training so that their products could lead the nation's youth towards a 'real national consciousness'. This meant that all children had to understand the notion of 'racial purity' and the need to maintain 'the racial blood unadulterated' after they left school. Teachers were there to mould young Germans into active and politically reliable German citizens – in other words, good Nazis.

Source F

Hitler's dictatorship differed in one fundamental point from all its predecessors in history. His was the first dictatorship in the present period of modern technical development, a dictatorship which made complete use of all technical means in a perfect manner for the domination of its own country.
Albert Speer, Hitler's Minister for Armaments and War Production

1. In Source A Robert Ley specifies the age when a child became part of the Nazi system of propaganda and control. What age was that?
2. In B, why did members of the Hitler Youth (Hitler Jugend) have to salute certain German women?
3. Who was Baldur von Schirach?
4. Note Hitler's priorities in Source C. Do you think he was in favour of the Boy Scouts and religious education?
5. Does Source D state that Catholic children wanted to join the Hitler Jugend?
6. Why were they so keen?
7. Who displayed totally uncritical attitudes of mind?

Options and topics 63

8 In Source E, what did Hitler mean when he spoke about 'racial purity' and the need to maintain the 'racial blood unadulterated'?

9 In Source F, what were the technical means used by Hitler to dominate his own country?

10 To which of the above sources do you think this picture is most relevant?

PERSECUTION OF THE JEWS

Note that anti-Jewish prejudice had been a recurring feature of social life since the fourth century. On 1 April it became the official policy of the Nazi state. Hitler ordered the nation to boycott all Jewish shops. Simultaneously all Jewish professionals – especially doctors, lawyers and dentists – lost their licences to practise. A spate of laws followed, defining a Jew as one who had a Jewish parent or grandparent or as one who practised the Jewish religion. These 'non-Aryans' were barred from many jobs.

Read the following extract:

> During 1935 Hitler announced two new laws. The Nuremberg Laws created an apartheid for 'Aryans' and Jews, 'for the protection of German blood and honour'. No Jew was allowed to marry a 'citizen of the state'. In this way German, and later, Austrian Jews were set apart and humiliated at every opportunity. Grinning SS men baited Jews in Vienna, forcing them to wash the public roadways. Jews had to endure a red J stamped on their passports. Only in 1936 did the persecution relax slightly but it was soon to reach a new climax on Crystal Night 9–10 December 1938.

1. Do you agree that a kind of apartheid was created by Hitler?
2. How did Hitler define a Jew?
3. This poster was typical of many displayed outside German towns. It was taken down for a brief period in 1936. What event in Germany caused a reduction in the persecution of the Jews?
4. What was the cause of Crystal Night in 1938?
5. Describe briefly the nature of Crystal Night and the suffering of the Jews on that occasion.

One of Germany's aims before 1939 was to encourage Jews to emigrate in large numbers. By 1942, however, Germany had occupied most of Europe and had penetrated deeply into the Soviet Union. What was to be done with the millions of Jews now under Nazi control? On 20 January 1942 top Nazis attended a conference at Wannsee, just outside Berlin. The Final Solution that emerged from the Wannsee Conference was that all Jews should be deported to extermination centres in the east.

Read the following extract:

> *Heydrich assured the Conference that the Allgemeinen-SS (the regular SS as distinct from the Waffen-SS who fought side by side with the Wehrmacht) would take charge of the extermination programme which would be located in special camps in Poland: Chelmno, Auschwitz, Belzec, Maidanek, Sobibor and Treblinka. Some Jews would be placed in armament factories prior to extermination but the vast majority of victims would go to the special gas chambers, currently being developed by German technical experts, as soon as they detrained from the cattle-trucks. The present arrangements at Chelmno, where Jews were systematically being exterminated inside trucks converted into mobile gas chambers, would be 'improved'.*

1 Who was Heydrich and what was his fate?
2 Name the conference where it was decided to proceed with the Final Solution.
3 Where were the extermination camps located?
4 Is there evidence that Jews were being systematically exterminated before the Final Solution?
5 Most Jews had to accept their fate. Thousands, however, formed a resistance movement inside the Warsaw ghetto.
   (a) How long did the resistance last?
   (b) What was the 'ghetto'?
   (c) How did SS Gruppenführer Stroop put down the resistance?
   (d) To which camp were most of the survivors sent?

REARMAMENT AND TERRITORIAL EXPANSION TO 1939

Rearmament had begun secretly in 1934, when Hitler authorised the construction of new U-boats. The new Luftwaffe began forming its first combat squadrons in 1935, some of which saw service above the towns and cities of Republican Spain during the Spanish Civil War (1936–9). By 1935 the Wehrmacht was forming its first tank units with the new Krupps' 5.4 ton tank, the Panzer Kw I.

Three German infantry battalions marched across the Rhineland bridges in 1936 in Hitler's spectacular reoccupation of the Rhineland. The previous year, the people of the Saar had voted to return to German rule. In 1938 Hitler was even more daring: he summoned the Austrian Chancellor Schuschnigg to Berchtesgaden and demanded an 'anschluss' between Germany and Austria. Hitler then appeared in Vienna as the liberator of Austria, now part of the German Reich.

Later that year he laid claim to the Sudetenland region of Czechoslovakia, where substantial numbers of Germans lived. Eventually, the western democracies agreed to let Hitler have the Sudetenland.

Read Hitler's views of these events:

The Rhineland and Austria

> *Don't think for one moment that anybody on earth is going to thwart my decision. Italy? I see eye to eye with Mussolini. England? England won't lift a finger for Austria. France? She could have stopped us in the Rhineland and then we would have had to retreat. But now it is too late for France.*

The Sudetenland

> *My opponents are little worms. I saw them at Munich.*

1. Did France and Britain ever intend to stop Hitler from reoccupying the Rhineland?
(In your answer consider that the British Foreign Office regarded the Rhineland as German's property. The British were anxious to ensure that Hitler did not resort to force; while the thirteen French divisions facing the Rhineland had orders not to oppose the Germans.)
2. What was this policy of constantly placating Hitler called?
3. Who was Mussolini?
4. Was Hitler contemptuous of the British and French?
5. What was Stalin's attitude to this steady expansion of the German state and the systematic dismantling of the Versailles Treaty?
(Note that Stalin had urged the western democracies to use force to prevent the expansion of Nazi rule in Europe.)

On 15 March 1939 German troops occupied the Czech territories of Bohemia and Moravia; one week later Hitler arrived in Memel (Lithuania) and proclaimed the city as part of the Third Reich.

This is Article 1 of the Anglo–Polish Agreement, 25 August 1939:

> *Should one of the contracting parties (Britain and Poland) become engaged in hostilities with a European power in consequence of aggression by the latter against that Contracting Party, the other Contracting Party will at once give the Contracting Party engaged in hostilities all the support and assistance in its power.*

This was Britain's belated answer to Hitler's policy of lebensraum (living space).

1. Why do you think Britain, who had sacrificed Austria, Czechoslovakia and Memel in the hope of permanent peace, should decide to fight for Poland?
2. Poland was a very long way from Britain, quite inaccessible by air and sea. What help could Britain give Poland in the event of German attack?
3. Below are some of the terms of the Versailles Treaty. Hitler had said in 1939 that he had endeavoured to destroy 'sheet by sheet, that

Options and topics

treaty which in its 448 articles contains the vilest oppression which a people have ever been expected to put up with'.

Which of these had he destroyed?

		YES	NO
(a)	Germany may not fortify the left bank of the Rhine.	☐	☐
(b)	Germany may not create an anschluss with Austria.	☐	☐
(c)	Germany may not raise an army of more than 100,000 men.	☐	☐
(d)	Poland's independence is guaranteed by Germany.	☐	☐
(e)	Germany gives the Saar coalfields to France.	☐	☐
(f)	Danzig will be a free city under the control of the League of Nations.	☐	☐
(g)	Germany will not construct any U-boats.	☐	☐
(h)	Germany will not create a military air force.	☐	☐
(i)	Germany will have no colonial possessions.	☐	☐

Several boards require you to know details of the Second World War and its effects upon Germany (e.g. MEG). Details of German gains, the gradual conversion to a war economy, the bombing and main military events are in Chapter 6, The Second World War.

CHAPTER THREE

PEACE-KEEPING 1919–39: THE LEAGUE AND THE INTERNATIONAL TREATY SYSTEMS

CONTENTS

- The League of Nations — 71
- International treaty systems — 75

The League and the treaty systems

1 THE LEAGUE OF NATIONS

In 1899 and 1907 international conferences at the Hague had tried and failed to outlaw war. In January 1918 Woodrow Wilson, Democratic President of the United States, presented to Congress his ideas for a humane and lasting world peace.

WOODROW WILSON'S FOURTEEN POINTS

1. No more secret diplomacy.
2. Absolute freedom of the sea for all nations.
3. No more economic barriers to hinder world trade.
4. A world-wide reduction in armaments.
5. All colonial problems to be settled fairly.
6. Evacuate all Russian territory and leave the people to settle their own affairs.
7. Belgium must be reconstructed – to be symbolic of the wish to help small nations.
8. All French territory to be restored.
9. Italy's frontiers to be settled.
10. Independence for the 'suppressed nationalities' of the Austro–Hungarian Empire.
11. All foreign troops to leave the Balkans.
12. 'Suppressed peoples' of the Ottoman Empire to seek their own independence.
13. A new nation state of Poland to be created.
14. A GENERAL ASSOCIATION OF NATIONS MUST BE FORMED . . . – this was the plea for a League of Nations to be formed after hostilities ceased.

These Fourteen Points made an immense impact – in leaflet and poster form, translated into many foreign languages, the first and last Points making an especially deep impression. When the President arrived in Paris (14 December 1918) delirious crowds called him 'Wilson le juste'. At the Paris Peace Conference, Woodrow Wilson insisted that everyone should approve the creation of a League of Nations and that this idea should be built into the first five peace treaties.

1. Name the first five peace treaties signed in palaces close to Paris.
2. All had to subscribe to the 'Covenant' of the League.
Explain the meaning of the word 'covenant'.

Look at the photograph overleaf of three victors at the Paris Peace Conference in 1919. President Woodrow Wilson is on the right.

Source: BBC Broadcasts to Schools, *Modern History*. Autumn 1962

1. Name the French leader in the centre.
2. Name the British leader on the left.

THE COVENANT OF THE LEAGUE

It had two basic aims:

◊ to persuade every country in the world to disarm to the lowest level consistent with national safety.
◊ to settle all disputes openly and without resort to war.

All members of the League of Nations (there were forty-two in 1920) agreed to uphold the Covenant's twenty-six articles – they needed very little amendment during the history of the League 1920–46. Its composition was based on an *Assembly*, a *Council* and a *Secretariat*, with an *International Court of Justice* based at The Hague. The Council, composed of the 'great powers' and selected smaller states, recom-

The League and the treaty systems

mended any *sanction* needed to carry out a League decision. Sanctions could take three forms:

- MORAL: to be settled by diplomacy, arbitration or by a judgement at the International Court of Justice.
- ECONOMIC: whereby the League would bring pressure on an offending nation by forbidding trade and foreign travel.
- MILITARY – never invoked as the League never had a military force of its own.

Weaknesses of the League

Lack of military forces was fundamental. Member states would not surrender any of their sovereign powers and hand over control of their armed forces. Collective military action proved impossible. Member states who broke the Covenant could resign – no significant action ever taken against them. Even more frustrating was that some major powers were not members.

Indicate below the states that were *not* members of the League in 1920:

	Non-member	Member
The United Kingdom	☐	☐
The United States of America	☐	☐
The Soviet Union	☐	☐
Germany	☐	☐

1. Did the US ever join the League?
2. On what grounds did the Senate Foreign Relations Committee reject the Covenant?
3. Why did it reject the Treaty of Versailles?
4. How did the US make peace with Germany?
5. Why was Germany excluded from the League?
6. The following statement helped to persuade the League not to send aid to Russia during the 1922 famine:

    > 'the Soviet government . . . could greatly mitigate its ravages if they diverted for that end of the money they were now spending on . . . a huge Red Army, purchasing armaments . . . and organising propaganda against civilised states.'

    Who said this?
7. Name the great Norwegian explorer who rescued thousands of prisoners in Russia 1920–22 and simultaneously organised famine relief there.

Disarmament

Financial difficulties had forced most countries to cut back their armed forces. There was popular support for total disarmament but no country dared take this risk, e.g. France still feared the resurgence of Germany. The famous 1922 Washington Naval Treaty was the one example of mutually agreed balanced reductions in armed forces: the major powers agreed to reduce their warship construction programmes. The ratio between Britain, the US and Japan would be 5:5:3; and between 1922 and 1932 there would be a 'naval holiday' in which no new capital ships would be built and no cruiser would exceed 10,000 tons.

The League of Nations at work
Study this map.

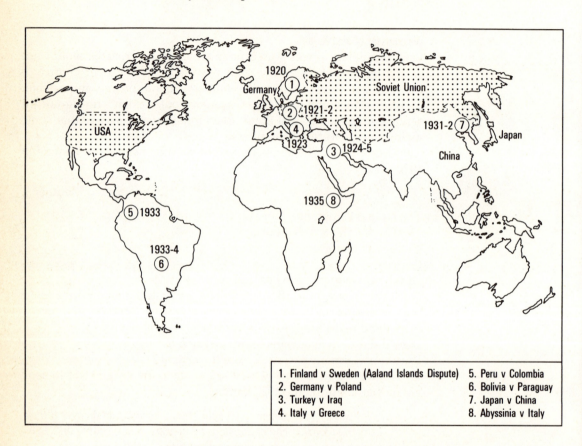

1. Finland v Sweden (Aaland Islands Dispute)
2. Germany v Poland
3. Turkey v Iraq
4. Italy v Greece
5. Peru v Colombia
6. Bolivia v Paraguay
7. Japan v China
8. Abyssinia v Italy

1 Put **1** in the circle relating to the Aaland Islands dispute.
2 Put **2** in the circle relating to the dispute over Upper Silesia. How did the League of Nations become involved in this and what was its decision?
3 Put **8** in the circle relating to the Abyssinian crisis 1935–6. Note that the League imposed economic sanctions on Italy but did not extend them to oil.

(*a*)   'If the League had extended economic sanctions to oil, I would have had to withdraw from Abyssinia within a week.' Who said this?

(*b*)   How did Britain and France show, in the 1935 Hoare-Laval Pact, that they had no intention of supporting a League decision over Abyssinia?

4 Would it be true to say that 'sanctions failed' with regard to the Abyssinian crisis?
5 In 1936 an even more serious crisis developed – the Spanish Civil War, when General Francisco Franco invaded Spain from military bases in Spanish Morocco.
   (*a*)   Name the two European dictators who sent aid to Franco.
   (*b*)   Which side did the Soviet Union support?
   (*c*)   Name the policy adopted by the League of Nations with regard to Spain.

2 INTERNATIONAL TREATY SYSTEMS

Because it was obvious that the League of Nations could not guarantee world peace, separate alliances and agreements were common between the great powers during the 1920s and 1930s. One of the first was the Russo–German Treaty of Rapallo (1922). Under this treaty, German pilots secretly trained at the Soviet base of Lipetsk; while the Russians secretly produced military equipment for the small German army, contrary to the terms of the Versailles Treaty.

The Locarno Treaties (1925) attempted to bring about stability in Europe. By these, Germany, France and Belgium recognised the permanence of their frontiers. Filled with the 'spirit of Locarno', Stresemann went along with Kellogg (US) and Briand (France) to sign the Kellogg–Briand Pact (1928) – a pact renouncing war. Not all signatories kept to their word, e.g. Japan attacked China within three years.

The World Disarmament Conference (1932–3) assembled in Geneva to consider arms reductions, strongly opposed by France who was also hostile to any suggestion that Germany might be allowed to rearm. The Conference achieved nothing of permanent value but it is important as a sign of the 'parting of the ways' in world history.

▷ Germany left the League in 1933 and was not involved in League diplomacy thereafter.
▷ Japan also left the League (having conquered Manchuria and renamed it Manchukuo) and the League had no later influence over Japan, e.g. during the Sino–Japanese 'Incident' (1937) when Japan invaded China.

The Stresa Front saw a brief alliance between Italy, Britain and France who drew together when Hitler announced the re-introduction of conscription (the diplomats met at Stresa in northern Italy); but when Britain unilaterally signed the Anglo–German naval agreement (1935 – allowing the Germans to build U-boats!) the Stresa Front dissolved. Thereafter, the treaties between the dictators, the aggressive nation states, had more significance than did those that pretended to defend democracy, e.g.

- Rome–Berlin Axis (Italy and Germany).
- 1936: Germany–Japan Anti-Comintern Pact (anti-Communist International designed in 1919 to foster communist revolutions abroad).
- 1937: Mussolini signed the Anti-Comintern Pact and promptly left the League of Nations.
- 1939: Pact of Steel – Italy and Germany.

Perhaps the most cynical international agreement of all was the Secret Protocol between Germany and Russia (23 August 1939). The following three extracts show how Hitler and Stalin proposed to divide up eastern Europe.

THE SECRET PROTOCOL

1. *In the event of a territorial and political rearrangement in the areas belonging to the Baltic states (Finland, Estonia, Latvia, Lithuania) the northern boundary of Lithuania shall represent the boundaries of the spheres of influence of Germany and the Soviet Union . . .*

2. *In the event of a territorial and political rearrangement of the areas belonging to the Polish state, the spheres of influence of Germany and the Soviet Union shall be bounded approximately by the line of the rivers Narew, Vistula and San. The question of whether the interests of both parties make desirable the maintenance of an independent state and how such a state should be bounded can only be definitely determined in the course of future political developments. In any event, both governments will resolve this question by means of a friendly agreement.*

3. *With regard to south-eastern Europe, attention is called by the Soviet side to its interest in Bessarabia. The German side declares its complete political disinterestedness in these areas.*

Signed: Von Ribbentrop; Molotov

Now look at the map on page 77 carefully.
1. Mark with a coloured felt pen the northern boundary of Lithuania.
2. Identify the city in Poland marked W.
3. Identify the region marked B.
4. Shade in those territories actually acquired by Stalin
   (a) as a result of the secret protocol (shade in red).
   (b) as a result of war (shade in black).
5. These newly acquired territories appear as a solid barrier against Nazi expansion. Were they of any use in 1941?
6. Who was von Ribbentrop?
7. Who was Molotov?

THE FUTILITY OF THE LEAGUE

Read the following extract:

Faced with the Sudeten crisis, its biggest international crisis to date, the League did absolutely nothing. No one ever referred the Czech

The League and the treaty systems

problem to the League; so it never appeared on its agenda. Then in the following year, when the Polish crisis was in full swing, the League was discussing a request by the Finns and Swedes to be allowed to build gun emplacements on the Aaland Islands, scene of the first dispute tackled by the League in 1920! And although the League kept Carl Burckhardt as its High Commissioner in Danzig up to the end of August 1939 it never used him as a mediator. Its last working meeting had elements of farce. The Second World War had begun and the Soviet Union had launched its 'Winter War' against Finland. The League summoned Russia to attend a meeting of the Assembly and explain this act of aggression. But the Russians refused to come to neutral Switzerland and so seven members of the Council (including Britain and France) solemnly expelled Russia from the League (14 December 1939).

1   Give the date of the Sudeten crisis.
2   Where was this settled?
3   Who was Carl Burckhardt?
4   Why was Danzig of special importance to the League?
5   Name the city in neutral Switzerland to which the Russians refused to come.

Consider these two views of the League. In the first, Stalin is confiding to Walter Duranty who worked for the *New York Times* in Moscow:

> *The League may be something of a check to retard the outbreak of military actions or to hinder them. If historical events should follow*

> such a course, then it is not impossible that we should support the League of Nations despite its colossal defects.

The second was spoken by Litvinov, Russia's representative at the League, just before Munich 1938:

> The League was created as a reaction to world war . . . its object was to make that the last war, and to replace the system of military alliances by the collective organisation of assistance to the victim of aggression. In this sphere the League has done nothing.

1. List briefly the 'colossal defects' to which Stalin referred.
2. What was Litvinov's main criticism of the League?
3. Can you give an example where the Soviet Union came to the assistance of the victim of aggression during the thirties? (Remember the Spanish Civil War.)

The League was formally abolished in April 1946, after the Second World War. Was the League a complete failure? Did it deliberately neglect its responsibilities? There is no doubt that over Manchuria (the Japanese invasion of 1931) and Abyssinia (the Italian invasion of 1935), the inactivity of the League was almost criminal; and it certainly neglected its responsibilities during the Spanish Civil War (1936–9), especially after the interventions of Hitler and Mussolini. But it was not a total failure. Whilst all the international crises and diplomatic exchanges were going on, several League agencies carried out sterling work in many parts of the world. Four examples illustrate the valuable work of the League:

- The International Labour Organisation persuaded many governments to introduce old-age pensions, sickness benefit and a satisfactory minimum working wage.
- The League's Health Organisation tried to combat epidemics and helped to reduce the typhus breakout in Russia during the twenties.
- The special League commission set up to administer the Saar supervised the famous plebiscite (1934–5) and persuaded some nations to send a nominal peace-keeping force to the region.
- The Permanent Mandates Commission supervised the colonies of the former German and Turkish Empires and required the nations to whom these were awarded to regard them as a 'sacred trust of civilisation'. There were three types of mandate:

    > 'A' mandate: a country soon to become independent.
    > 'B' mandate: a country with no immediate prospect of independence.
    > 'C' mandate: sparsely populated and exceptionally 'backward'.

Study the two maps opposite.

The League and the treaty systems

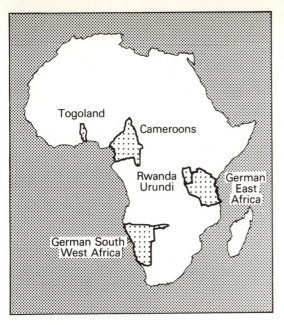

Former German colonies in Africa

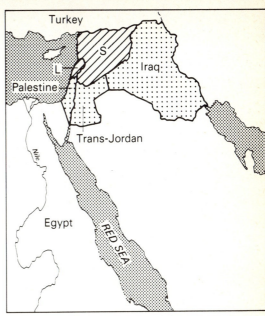

Former Turkish colonies in the Middle East

1 Who shared Togoland and the Cameroons?
2 Who secured German East Africa?
3 By what name was it then known?
4 Who gained Rwanda Urundi?
5 Which country gained the mandate to German South West Africa?
6 Britain received three mandates in the Middle East. In which one had she decided to establish a 'National Home for the Jews'?
7 Name the two French mandates in the Middle East, marked L and S?
8 In the Pacific, it was policy to award mandates to the countries that had originally conquered the colonies from the Germans.
   (a) Name the three Pacific island groups secured by Japan.
   (b) Name Australia's mandate.
   (c) Name New Zealand's mandate.

CHAPTER FOUR

AGGRESSIVE NATIONALISM: JAPAN AND ITALY

CONTENTS

▶ **Japan** 83

▶ **Italy** 89
The birth of Fascism 90

Aggressive nationalism: Japan and Italy

1 JAPAN

It is sometimes said that Japan is the world's perfect nation state. The Japanese are one people, united by a common language and a long cultural heritage, possessing extraordinary drive, energy, talent and dedication.

Japanese attitudes in 1919

The Japanese had a justifiable sense of superiority in the immediate post-war world.

- Their armed forces had not been defeated since 1895.
- They now had an extensive colonial empire, having secured the mandate for the Carolines, Marianas and Marshalls in the Pacific.
- Their agriculture and industry had made a profit out of the 1914–18 war.

Strengths and weaknesses

- The Zaibatsu – the big, private enterprise firms – had begun to provide housing and welfare services; but not everyone worked for the Zaibatsu.
- Most people worked on the land or in small workshops – with no unemployment insurance protection and no access to hospitals.
- Theirs was an overcrowded society – accommodation was always in short supply; the birth rate was rocketing.
- Some social reforms carried out in the twenties, e.g.
    (a)   Trade unions legalised 1923.
    (b)   Adult male suffrage 1925.
    (c)   Shorter working day for women and children – ten hours! (1925).
    (d)   State education for most children by 1930.

Persistent inflation

This undermined all attempts to secure steady social reform in Japan and eventually caused widespread violence. By 1923 this was serious and in 1925 the Japanese government eventually passed a repressive Peace Preservation Law:

- All left-wing political organisations illegal.

- Exceptional powers granted to the Japanese police forces.
- Japanese press under heavy censorship.

Effect of the World Trade Depression

By 1929 Japan was a developing industrial nation with a set of unique problems:

- The population explosion meant one million new mouths to be fed every year.
- Every year half a million new workers were coming on the labour market.
- The value of the Japanese yen had fallen dramatically on the world money markets.

Japan was thus not well equipped to deal with the unprecedented trade depression that began in 1929 – 'the economic blizzard'. She was totally dependent on imported oil, iron ore and aluminium. Suddenly, she could find no buyers for her staple exports – manufactured goods and raw silk.

- Unemployment hit millions of Japanese, many of whom had recently left the farmlands and fishing villages in search of work in Japan's newly established factories and shipyards.
- The Japanese people couldn't emigrate – Canada, Australia and the US didn't want to mop up surplus populations as everyone was in an ever-worsening economic condition.

Remember: the 'economic blizzard' was universal – at least thirty million people were unemployed in the world's principal industrial nations (with the notable exception of the Soviet Union). Poverty and malnutrition stunted the lives of urban as well as rural workers all over the world – but reaction to the situation varied everywhere. As in Germany, there were special reasons for the growth of militaristic ambitions in both Japan and Italy.

Japan rationalised her position she argued for the 'Third Door' – territorial expansion. Already 250,000 Japanese were living in China, mainly in Manchuria. Possession of Manchuria, with its oil, coal, iron and bauxite reserves and vast potential for settlement (it was about the size of Germany and France combined) seemed the immediate answer to Japan's prayers.

The historian Christopher Thorne has noted that by 1931 'the overwhelming majority of Japanese politicians, soldiers and public saw Manchuria as a vital interest ... a powerful asset for those conducting the country's foreign relations.'

Remember that Japan was the first member of the League of Nations to carry out a serious breach of the Covenant, the deliberate invasion of Manchuria. It was totally unexpected and completely contrary to the accepted pattern of international relations.

Some evidence of this can be gauged by Britain's Lord Cecil

Aggressive nationalism: Japan and Italy

speaking to the League of Nations a week before the Japanese attacked:

> *I do not think there is the slightest prospect of any war. I know . . . how rash it is to prophesy as to the future of international affairs; but, nevertheless, I do not believe that there is anyone in this room who will contradict me when I say there has scarcely ever been a period in the world's history when war seemed less likely than it does at the present.*
> (10 September 1931)

18 September 1931: the Japanese attack on Manchuria

◊ The Japanese had an army, known as the Kwantung Army, based on the former Liaotung Peninsula leased from China.
◊ Some Japanese staff officers exploded a small bomb on the Japanese-run South Manchurian Railway.
◊ The Kwantung Army blamed 'Chinese saboteurs' and attacked a Chinese base outside Mukden.
◊ Three months later the League of Nations appointed Lord Lytton to head a Commission to investigate the war in Manchuria. By the time he reported, Japan had captured Manchuria and declared it the new province of Manchukuo.
◊ The League refused to recognise this and wanted Japan to surrender Manchuria. Japan's response was to withdraw from the League. Why did the Japanese do this?
(a)   They felt insulted over Manchuria, just as they had felt insulted over the Washington Naval Treaties (1922).
(b)   They intended to occupy more of China.
(c)   They knew that they had 'committed blatant aggression and got away with it.' (G. Scott, *The Rise and Fall of the League of Nations*. Hutchinson, 1973, p. 241)

1 Place a tick against the term used for Japanese currency:
☐ Mark
☐ Dollar
☐ Escudo
☐ Yen
☐ Peseta

2 Place a tick against the term used for the huge Japanese private firms responsible for pushing forward the national economy:
☐ Combines
☐ Collectives
☐ Zaibatsu
☐ Multinationals
☐ Corporations

3 Place a tick against the *one* factor that was *not* a major Japanese problem in 1930:
☐ Unemployment
☐ Decline of silk farming

☐ Decline in manufactured exports
☐ Overpopulation
☐ Immigration

4 Place a tick against the railway that was the scene of the bomb incident in 1931:
☐ Trans-Siberian Railway
☐ North China Railway
☐ South Manchurian Railway
☐ Chinese Eastern Railway
☐ Kwantung Railway

5 Place a tick against the name of the Japanese army located in what was formerly the Liaotung Peninsula, leased by Japan from China:
☐ Red Army
☐ Kwantung Army
☐ Nineteenth Route Army
☐ Manchukuo Army
☐ Manchurian Army

THE SINO–JAPANESE INCIDENT, 1937

The following words have been taken out of the extract describing the 1937 Sino–Japanese Incident, an event that led to the renewal of war between China and Japan.

Russia   Peking   Marco Polo
communists   guerrilla   Japanese
Sino–Soviet Non-Aggression Pact

Insert these words into the extract so that the passage makes good historical sense. Note that the term 'Sino-' means 'Chinese'.

On the night of 7-8 July 1931 Chinese soldiers fired on _____ troops carrying out manoeuvres close to the _____ Bridge near _____. This was the incident that led to a Japanese attack by air, land and sea designed to capture Peking, the whole of the North China Plain and to penetrate the valley of the Yangtse-kiang as far as possible. Chiang Kai-shek immediately sought military aid from _____ (who always feared Japanese expansion) and signed a _____ in August 1937; and confirmed the existence of a Second United Front with the communists the following month. The _____, who usually adopted _____ tactics, fought a pitched battle against the Japanese at Pinghsinkuan – and won.

Now read the following extract carefully:

Neither the Japanese nor the Chinese admitted that they were actually at war with one another. Japan did not want to arouse the hostility of the imperial powers who maintained substantial numbers of warships, troops and aeroplanes in the Far East; while China knew that if she admitted to the existence of a war then, because it was the policy of the United States at that time not to send arms to warring

Aggressive nationalism: Japan and Italy

nations, she would lose all of her American aid. But there was little risk that China would lose the sympathy of the western nations. Japanese aircraft bombed and sank the US gunboat *Panay* and damaged HMS *Ladybird* and three Standard Oil tankers during 1937. It was obvious to the Japanese that Chiang Kai-shek, who had moved his capital to Chungking, could hold out as long as Russian aid funnelled through Lanchow and British and American aid came in through the southern ports such as Swatow and Canton.

1. Why did Japan play down the idea that she was actually at war with China in 1937?
2. Why did China decide it was to her advantage not to admit to the existence of a war with Japan?
3. Why were (*a*) Russia (*b*) Britain (*c*) United States sympathetic towards China rather than towards Japan?
4. Who was Chiang Kai-shek?
5. Name the leader of the Chinese Communists.

Map shows: 1. Extent of Japanese expansion until 1937. 2. Sources of foreign aid to Nationalist China. 3. Main ports still in Nationalist hands. 4. Location of Chinese Communist party guerrillas

HOW DID JAPAN TRY TO RESOLVE THE PROBLEM OF CHINESE RESISTANCE?

◊ She decided to concentrate her air attacks on the key communication routes leading to Chungking.
◊ Secondly, she decided to make a series of seaborne landings on the Chinese coast to capture the key ports. For this, Japan designed special assault ships, capable of carrying specialist stores and small assault landing craft. Japan was undoubtedly the most advanced nation in the skills of amphibious warfare.
◊ Thirdly, Japan made the disastrous decision to challenge the Soviet Union in Outer Mongolia and to deter Stalin from sending aid to China under the newly signed Non-aggression Treaty (1937). In 1938 they attacked in strength along the Outer Mongolian border in a vicious war that lasted throughout 1938–9.

Look at the following extracts. Identify the speaker and insert the correct extract code letter in the box:

Extract A

Soviet–Mongolian aircraft are bombing our positions and their artillery never stop shelling us. After each raid or artillery bombardment the enemy infantry charges into the attack. The last one killed all of our officers and I became company commander.

Extract B

The fighting was most bitter in the south, no matter what they say about the battles around Nomonhan and Khalkin Gol. We lost nearly all our tanks in attack after attack on the Japanese hill positions.

Extract C

I am pleased to see you back in Moscow, my dear General Zhukov. How did our troops fight? They did well? Excellent. And our tanks – the bystro-khodnii (fast moving) BT-7s? They catch fire easily, you say?

Extract D

We first spotted the Japanese assault ship two years ago when we were on the Sandwich *based at Tangku. It was carrying marines and they were practising launching their assault craft from the stern of the* Shinshu Maru.

Josef Stalin ☐
A Red Army soldier ☐
A Japanese sergeant ☐
A British sailor in the Royal Navy ☐
A Japanese fighter pilot ☐
A British civilian in Shanghai ☐

Despite the Japanese setback in the Russo–Japanese War 1938–9, she

Aggressive nationalism: Japan and Italy

had secured her other objectives. Japanese marines and infantry had captured all the main Chinese ports, penetrated the valley of the Yangtse-kiang and were blockading the entire Chinese coastline. The Japanese were now locked into a deadly war of attrition in which the Chinese nationalists were willing to 'trade space for time', extend the Japanese lines of communication and thus make them more liable to disruption by guerrilla attacks. Stalemate had arrived in China.

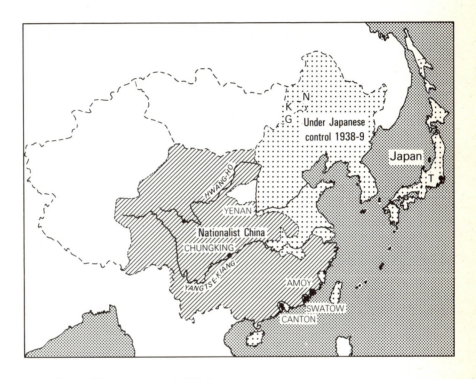

Extent of Japanese control, 1938–9

1. Shade in pencil the three provinces – Tanna-Tuva, Outer Mongolia and Sinkiang over which the Soviet Union exercised control.
2. Mark the battles of Nomonhan (N) and Khalkin Gol (K G).
3. Name the off-shore island from which Japan launched the attacks on Canton, Swatow and Amoy.
4. Name the Japanese capital at T.
5. Insert the name *Soviet Union* in the correct part of the map.

2 ITALY

In 1919 Italy was a major European power, an Allied nation with a consistent if brief tradition of constitutional government. But Versailles and the other peace treaties did no justice to a people who had lost 460,000 killed and a million wounded since joining the Allied cause in 1916. Italians were contemptuous of their political leaders (notably Orlando at Versailles) who had failed:

- to secure any part of the Ottoman Empire, as originally promised in the secret 1916 Sykes–Picot deal;
- to win the coast of Dalmatia and in particular the port of Fiume;
- to secure Albania, briefly occupied by Italian troops in 1918;
- to control the wartime inflation – 500 per cent!
- to cure the squalor in southern Italy;
- to improve conditions for peasants on the big Lombardy Plain estates;
- to find jobs for returning ex-servicemen;
- to end the rash of strikes in Milan and Turin.

Gabriele D'Annunzio

He took matters into his own hands and marched into Fiume with his Arditi (blackshirted commando fighters). He set up his headquarters there for a year and became a centre of pilgrimage for all those who wanted to learn more about propaganda, national security, trade-union reform, oratory techniques and party management. He made a great impression on the new Fascist Party.

THE BIRTH OF FASCISM

Benito Mussolini, former socialist, newspaper editor, teacher and ex-serviceman, founded the Italian Fascist Party (Fascio Italiano di Combattimento) in Milan on 23 March 1919. He was anti-socialist and specialised in breaking up political meetings and beating up opponents. His followers wore black shirts and adopted the ancient Roman sign of authority, fasces, as their symbol. He had a political rival in the person of Antonio Gramsci, a young Sardinian radical, who encouraged workers to occupy the factories in a Lenin-style revolution.

1921 was a key year:

- Mussolini's blackshirts were now expert in breaking up the socialist movement, e.g. in Bologna.
- They were winning support from employers increasingly frightened of communist pressure.
- Gramsci formed the Italian Communist Party in January.
- Mussolini's Fascists won thirty-five seats in the 1921 elections.

The March on Rome, 1922

This became one of the myths in the story of how the Fascist Party came to power in Italy.

Remember that the Fascists had significant political power both inside and outside parliament at a time of increasing violence and unemployment in the industrial heartland of Italy. He ensured a great deal of political support by announcing that:

Aggressive nationalism: Japan and Italy

▷ he supported King Victor Emmanuel.
▷ Italy should remain a monarchy.

He then concentrated his main forces at Perugia for a 'march on Rome'.

Now read this extract:

> *At first the government wanted to use troops to disperse the Fascists but the King overruled this suggestion and invited Mussolini to come to Rome, form a new government and become Prime Minister. So, despite the later myths, Mussolini never had to march on Rome. Fêted by thousands of Fascists, he caught the 20.30 Milan–Rome express and travelled to Rome by train, with the job of Prime Minister in his pocket. But although Mussolini and many of his Fascists didn't have to march on Rome, thousands of ordinary Italians were determined to make the effort. One mounted a machine-gun on his Fiat sports car and drove to the capital; others commandeered plough horses and rode in wearing fancy dress; most came on foot, highly conscious that, for a moment, they were creating history.*

1. Name the King of Italy.
2. What was the symbol of Mussolini's party?
3. Who was Gramsci?
4. Do you agree that the writer of the following extract was fairly typical of most conservative Italians in the immediate post-war years?

> *... Without Mussolini, three-quarters of the youth of Italy returning from the trenches would have become Bolsheviks. Mussolini deviated the course of events; he gave to fighting youth that programme of radical negation of the present, and even more, beyond the revolutionary event, a positive mirage; government by youth, Italy of Vittorio Veneto in power, the Fascist State.*
>
> (This was written by Air Marshal Balbo in 1932; the Battle of Vittorio Veneto refers to the successful advance on the Italian front in 1918.)

5. What does the writer mean by the expression: 'Mussolini deviated the course of events'?
6. What do you think a programme of 'radical negation of the present' means?
7. Does the expression 'a positive mirage' seem like a contradiction in terms?
8. Does Fascism appear to be more concerned with destruction than construction?

Mussolini was now Prime Minister of a Fascist-led coalition government. His work, between 1922 and 1929, falls into two distinct parts:

▷ The Fascist attack upon democracy 1922–5.
▷ The Fascist Revolution 1925–9.

The Fascist attack on democracy, 1922–5

Mussolini's new electoral law, the strongest party at the next election would automatically have two-thirds of the seats in parliament, was applied in 1924. Fascist militiamen were at the polling stations armed with clubs and revolvers – Mussolini won half of the votes! He then eliminated the opposition leaders:

- Murder of socialist leader, Giacomo Matteotti, June 1924.
- Gramsci, the communist leader, jailed for twenty years.

In 1925, Mussolini took responsibility for all the murder and violence:

> *I alone assume moral, political and historical responsibility for all that has taken place . . . Italy wants peace and quiet, work and calm. I will give these things with love if possible and with force if necessary.*

THE FASCIST REVOLUTION, 1925–9

The year 1924 had marked the beginning of Mussolini's dictatorship. He now began his 'revolution from above', imposing his ideas on the Italian people by force.

- The 'Fascist Grand Council' issued lists of parliamentary candidates. Against the names of a ready-made government the Italian voter could only record 'yes' or 'no'.
- Having eliminated a parliamentary opposition, Mussolini now eliminated parliament. In 1929 he replaced parliament with a National Council of Corportions (five years later he replaced the Trade Unions with twenty-two corporations).
- Strikes and lockouts became illegal; all industrial disputes had to be settled by arbitration.
- All Cabinet ministers were now responsible to Mussolini.
- All members of the armed forces owned their allegiance to him.
- Mussolini now called himelf Il Duce (The Leader) and boasted that his new 'Corporative State' would solve all of Italy's social and economic problems.

Fascist propaganda

Mussolini used with great skill all the resources of modern technology to ram home that his personal power was really a reflection of the new-found power of the Italian people. Radio, newsreel films, newspaper articles, posters and leaflets were all used to proclaim:

> *Fascism is a Militia designed to realise the greatness of the Italian people.*

The function of the Militia was to rally the people in support of Il Duce's policies and to whip up a sense of pride in the armed forces and the colonial empire. About 200,000 members of the militia

Aggressive nationalism: Japan and Italy

resorted to every propaganda trick they knew. Children were a special target.

◊ 'Children, more than anybody else, must know how to obey, to acquire the duty of commanding; more than the rest, they must know how to dare . . .'

◊ School textbooks glorified Il Duce and the 'Revolution of 1922' when, it was claimed, the Blackshirts marched on Rome to put everything in order.

◊ Mussolini's Youth Organisation was the Balilla – drawing many recruits from the Boy Scouts.

◊ Fascist University Students drew its recruits from Catholic undergraduates.

Eventually, Fascism was presented as a culture, or way of life, in its own right:

> Fascism, in short, is not only a lawgiver and a founder of institutions, but an educator and promoter of spiritual life. It does not merely aim at remoulding the forms of life but also their content, man, his character and his faith . . . It enters into the mind and rules with undisputed sway.

Mussolini's words were claptrap, an insult to every thinking person.

Why do you think there was very little resistance to them?

Look at this cartoon, part of Mussolini's propaganda machine. What do you think it is trying to put across to Italian children when they see it in their school textbook?

Translations:
Benito Mussolini deeply loves children.

Italian children deeply love Il Duce.

Long live the Leader!

Let us greet the Leader!

He is ours!

BENITO MUSSOLINI
ama molto i bambini.
I bimbi d'Italia amano
molto il Duce.

VIVA IL DUCE!

Saluto al Duce:

A noi!

Source: Herman Finer, *Mussolini's Italy*. Grosset and Dunlap, New York, 1965

AN AGGRESSIVE FOREIGN POLICY, 1923–9

One of the many problems that faced the League of nations was the precise definition of the Albanian frontier. The Italian General Tallini was marking this out when he was murdered. Mussolini suspected the Greeks – and sent them an ultimatum and a bill for fifty million lire.

The Corfu Incident, 1923

- Mussolini's marines landed on Corfu after a preliminary bombardment.
- The Greeks paid up.

This hardly brought credit to a prominent member of the League of Nations especially as, in the middle of the Incident, Mussolini began negotiations with Yugoslavia over the future of Fiume, currently a 'Free State' under League protection. Yugoslavia let the Italian dictator have Fiume and the port of Zara – provided he surrendered all claim to the coast of Dalmatia.

Significance

- His foreign policy was acclaimed in Italy – he had bombarded Corfu and secured Fiume and Zara.
- His success encouraged him to make pacts with Albania and Hungary (1926–7).
- These actions all seemed anti-League in so far that they were both aggressive and seemed to be encouraging unilateral revision of the treaties made after the Great War.

The Lateran Agreements with the Pope, 1929

Mussolini clearly understood the importance of winning the friendship of the Catholic Church. Italy was a Catholic country and the Head of the Church lived in Rome. The Lateran Agreements negotiated by Mussolini in 1929 consisted of

(a)   a Treaty and
(b)   a Concordat.

The 1929 Treaty created the Holy See in the City of the Vatican, an independent micro-state inside the Italian capital. The 1929 Concordat confirmed Catholicism as the state religion – religious education now compulsory in secondary schools as well as in primary schools.

Significance

- In general, the Catholic Church supported Mussolini's dictatorship – though there were later disagreements, e.g. over the role of the Fascist Youth Organisation and Mussolini's treatment of the Jews.
- Within seven years Mussolini had established his Fascist dictatorship

Aggressive nationalism: Japan and Italy

and secured the blessing of the Papacy – seen as the biggest setback for European democracy during the twenties.

Were there any positive achievements?

- New roads, railway electrification, hydro-electric plants and public works schemes.
- 1925 – so-called 'Battle of the Grain' (to make Italy independent of wheat imports (never achieved despite increases in grain production).
- Pontine Marshes drained by ex-servicemen's associations.

Comment

Did it need a Fascist revolution to carry out such projects? Far more significant was the fact that Mussolini was preparing for war:

> 'War is to man as maternity is to woman!'

- Emphasis on new armaments industry.
- New Italian navy.
- Research into mustard gas that could be sprayed from aircraft.

MUSSOLINI'S WAR POLICY

From 1932 onwards he prepared for a war against Ethiopia:

- to avenge the Italian defeat at Adowa (1896).
- to link his two existing colonies in Somaliland and Eritrea.
- to secure raw materials – he thought there were oil and copper reserves in Ethiopia (Abyssinia).
- to provide new lands for ten million Italians.
- to recruit two million Ethiopians into a new Italian 'African Army'.

(Note that just before he invaded Ethiopia in 1935 he formed the Stresa Front with Britain and France.)

Study the map on page 96.
1. Shade in the war gains (Tyrol-Trentino and Istria).
2. Mark Fiume at F.
3. Show by means of arrows the direction of Italy's interests in Dalmatia and Albania.
4. Mark Yugoslavia (Y) and Greece (G) and name the island of Corfu bombarded in 1923.
5. Mark Turin (T) and Milan (M) and shade in the Lombardy Plain.
6. From which city did Mussolini catch the train for his 'March on Rome' in 1922?
7. Locate the Vatican City.
8. Mark Sicily and name the Mediterranean Sea.
9. Draw an arrow to show the direction Italian troops would have to sail in order to reach Ethiopia.

History 1: World History since 1914

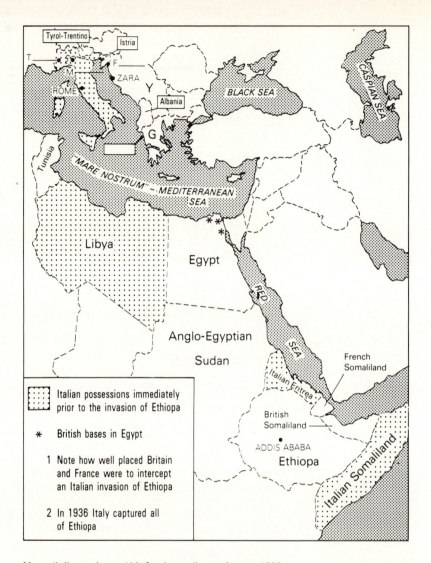

Mussolini's empire and his foreign policy projects to 1935

10 Through which canal would they pass?
    Read the following sources:

    A   On 2 October 1935 Mussolini broadcast to the Italian people that
        Ethiopian invaders had attacked Eritrea at Wal Wal and that war
        had begun. Aircraft of the Regia Aeronautica were already winging
        their way to bomb Adowa.

    B   Strange containers burst open almost as soon as they hit the ground
        or water, releasing pools of colourless liquid. I was completely
        stunned. I didn't know how to fight this terrible rain that burned and
        killed.*

*Ras Imru, quoted by T. M. Coffey in *Lion by the Tail*, Hamish Hamilton, 1974.

Aggressive nationalism: Japan and Italy

†From Carlo Levi's *Christ Stopped at Eboli*, describing the reaction of the peasants in Gagliano to the war in Ethiopia.

C   3 October, which marked the official opening of the war, was a miserable sort of day. Twenty or twenty-five peasants, roped in by the Carabinieri and the Fascist scouts, stood woodenly in the square to listen to the historical pronouncements that came over the radio.
Don Luigi, the Fascist schoolmaster, had ordered flags displayed over the town hall, the school and the houses of the well-to-do . . . the bell-ringer rang out the usual funeral strains and the war so light-heartedly set in motion in Rome was greeted in Gagliano with stony indifference.†

Source A
1. Do you think that Mussolini that contrived the war in Ethiopia?
2. What do you think the words 'Regia Aeronauticas' mean?
3. What was the political importance of the first target to be attacked by Italian aircraft?

Source B
1. What was in the 'strange containers'?
2. From where had the 'terrible rain' come?
3. Who do you think authorised the use of this terrible weapon?

Source C
1. Why had the peasants come to the square in Gagliano to listen to the radio and Don Luigi?
2. Don Luigi had decorated the most important political centres of Gagliano. What were they?
3. What evidence is there that the peasants thought that the war had been started without proper care and consideration?

The Hoare-Laval Pact
Read this extract:

> Then came an extraordinary event. Samuel Hoare, the British Foreign Secretary, was off on holiday to Switzerland and on the way he visited Paris a few days before the oil sanctions were going to be imposed. He had some talks with his French opposite number, Pierre Laval, in which the pair agreed on an iniquitous plan, known as the Hoare-Laval Pact. Simply, if Mussolini would simply stop fighting immediately he could have most of Abyssinia. He had already captured half of it!

1. Was the Hoare–Laval Plan ever carried out?
2. What then is its political significance?
3. Who was the ruler of Ethiopia (Abyssinia)?
4. What was his fate?
5. When did Mussolini complete his conquest of Abyssinia?

Mussolini's later foreign policy

▷ He sent troops and his latest aircraft to help Franco during the Spanish Civil War 1936–9.

◊ He worked closely with Hitler in Spain, describing the link between the two dictators as the 'Rome–Berlin Axis' around which all Europe's affairs must revolve.
◊ He declare the Mediterranean 'Mare Nostrum' – 'Our Sea'.
◊ He signed the Anti-Comintern Pact with Japan and Germany (1937).
◊ He left the League of Nations at the end of 1937.
◊ He backed Hitler at the Munich Conference on the future of Czechoslovakia (1938).
◊ April 1939 saw the Italian expedition to Albania – King Zog forced from the throne and the country turned into a military base.
◊ In May 1939 he signed the Pact of Steel with Hitler.

Hitler and Mussolini

1 This photograph depicts the first meeting between Mussolini and Hitler. When was this?
2 What ideas did these two men have in common?
3 Hitler always felt he was in debt to Mussolini over a crucial incident in 1936. What was this?

CHAPTER FIVE

THE UNITED STATES TO 1941

CONTENTS

- **The United States and the First World War** — 101

- **Post-war boom and post-war prejudice** — 103
  The boom   103
  The prejudice   105

- **The Wall Street Crash, 1929** — 106

- **Franklin D. Roosevelt and the New Deal** — 109

- **The United States, 1939–41** — 115

1 THE UNITED STATES AND THE FIRST WORLD WAR

In 1914 President Woodrow Wilson regarded it as his duty to keep America out of Europe's 'Great War'. He therefore advised the American people to 'remain neutral in fact as well as in name . . . impartial in thought as well as in action'.

Remember:

- The Americans had no treaty system binding them to any European power.
- They had little time for Europe's problems – it was because of these problems in Russia, Germany, Austria and Italy that they had left their homelands in the first place to become immigrants.
- There was a long tradition of resentment against British warships interfering with US shipping during times of European warfare.
- Among some Americans, however, there was a general belief that somehow the well-being of the United States was tied up with an eventual British victory.

How did German–American relations worsen?
Largely because of activities of the German U-boats during 1915 and 1917.

- The German declaration of a 'war zone' around Britain enraged Wilson, especially when the U-20 sank the *Lusitania* with the loss of 1198 people, 128 of them Americans. While Wilson protested, a U-boat sank another ship with Americans on board. The Germans apologised.
- 'I order the unrestricted submarine campaign to begin on 1 February 1917 with the utmost energy.' With these words the German Kaiser almost guaranteed that America would enter the war on the side of the Allies. However, he was unrepentant: 'If Wilson wants war let him make it and then let him have it.'
- Wilson's decision to enter the war was very largely the result of skilful intelligence work by the British. Mexican bandits had caused a great deal of trouble north of the Rio Grande and on 8 March 1916 their leader Villa had attacked the American town of Columbus. General Pershing was in Mexico in 1917 trying to find Villa. In the midst of this, British naval intelligence intercepted the famous Zimmerman

Telegram that indicated German support for a Mexican invasion of Texas. Part of the telegram read:

44858	gemeinsam	. . . make
5905	krieg	. . . war
17166	fahren	. . . together

British intelligence passed this to Wilson who revealed it to Congress – America, he said, 'must exert all its power and employ all its resources to bring the government of the German Empire to terms and end the war.'

On 6 April 1917 Congress declared war on Germany.

The American contribution to victory

- *On land:* America had an army that was essentially infantry – no tanks, very little artillery, no air force operating outside the US. Numbers reaching France 1918 still small – but played an important part in the battles at Cantigny (May), Château-Thierry (June), St Mihiel (September) and, the greatest American attack, on the Argonne in September and October 1918. By 11 November 1918, the AEF (American Expeditionary Force) had made a major contribution to the Allied attacks that defeated Germany.
- *In the air:* American volunteers had already flown with the Escadrille Lafayette. Using British and French machines, the Americans finally assembled forty-five Squadrons and attacked German targets behind the lines.
- *At sea:* invaluable aid to the British as convoy escorts in the Atlantic – no US soldier died going 'over there'. In 1918 the US Navy laid a huge barrage of mines between the Shetlands and Norway – an anti-U-boat screen.

Wilson the Peacemaker

President Wilson was an idealist, something most Americans could not stomach after the First World War. The USA had never been one of the Allies; instead she had adopted the status of an 'Associated Power'. Moreover, the 1918 Congressional elections had returned Republican majorities to the Senate and the House of Representatives. Consequently, Wilson was the only member of the 'Big Four' at the Paris Peace Conference and the Versailles Treaty who did not speak for his people.

Rejection of the Covenant and the Peace Treaty

Wilson exhausted himself in Europe where he tried to sew up the Covenant of the League with the Versailles Peace Treaty so tightly that not even the US Senate could unravel it.

- 28 June 1919: Germans accepted the Versailles Treaty
- 8 July 1919: Wilson took the draft treaty to the Senate – which rejected the entire treaty (eventually the US and Germany signed the 1921

The United States to 1941

Treaty of Berlin that omitted all reference to the League and the Covenant).
◊ Too ill to contest the next Presidential election (1920), Wilson tried to turn the election campaign into a referendum on the League.
◊ Harding, the Republican candidate, offered 'return to normalcy' and he became President.

US aid to Russia, 1921–3

Once Wilson saw that the counter-revolutionaries in Russia were totally incapable of providing the Russian people with a democratic government, he removed all US troops from Russia. Other Americans began sending humanitarian aid:

◊ Lenin accepted offers of help from the American Relief Administration.
◊ The first shipments of food reached Russia 1921.
◊ Seedcorn and hospital equipment sent – US teams inoculated millions of Russians against the epidemics sweeping the country.

It is interesting to note that while Americans were sending help to the Soviet Union, a wave of anti-Bolshevik feeling flared in the United States. In fact, the period after 1918 is marked by intense US prejudice towards all foreigners, Jews and blacks. It was during the 1920s that the Ku Klux Klan flourished.

2 POST-WAR BOOM AND POST-WAR PREJUDICE

THE BOOM

The arrival of millions of 'demobbed' soldiers in an industrial system trying to gear itself to a civilian rather than a military market tended to dislocate the economy.

◊ Brief period of unemployment.
◊ Widespread industrial action.
◊ The new President, Warren G. Harding, urged businessmen to invest in consumer industries. He died in 1923, but his message had gone home – investment had begun.

Harding was succeeded by his Vice-President, Calvin Coolidge (1923–9), and during his administration the USA enjoyed unparalleled prosperity.

◊ There were over 11,000 dollar millionaires by 1926.
◊ America owned about forty per cent of the world's wealth.
◊ America became the biggest consumer society in the world.

Why?

◊ New production methods.

◊ Zero inflation.
◊ Full employment.
◊ 10 per cent drop in price of manufactured goods 1924–9.

All this meant that all sorts of new and exciting products came within the range of American families. The motor car helped to create dozens of new industries and literally millions of new jobs. Road-building doubled from 1920 to 1929 and garages, filling-stations, eating-houses mushroomed around the new highways. The electrical industry turned out spark plugs, generators and starter motors; while the oil industry flourished as did the paint, steel and aluminium producers.

Manufacturers had stimulated demand as never before by bringing a universally desired product within the range of most people's pockets – the motor car.

An electronic revolution enabled the American people to enjoy the products of Hollywood (films) and the new broadcasting stations (radio). Advertising quickly appeared on radio (by 1929 the three big companies were ATT – American Telephone and Telegraph – General Electric and Westinghouse).

Characteristics of 'the American way of life' discernible:
(a)   Mass production of telephones.
(b)   Refrigerators common – 755,000 'ice boxes' sold in 1929.
(c)   Gramophones for the new mass-produced records.

One area of decline – agriculture
Farmers did not share in the prosperity as food prices had slumped on the world markets. Many farmers could not meet their mortgage payments and had to surrender their farms. Thirteen million acres of farmland fell into disuse – and because farmers lacked purchasing power agriculture remained in a depressed state into the thirties.

Tick the boxes you believe are correct:
1   The following US Presidents were Republicans:
    ☐ Woodrow Wilson
    ☐ Warren G. Harding
    ☐ Calvin Coolidge
    ☐ Herbert Hoover
2   The following were battles at which Americans distinguished themselves during the First World War:
    ☐ Château Thierry
    ☐ St Mihiel
    ☐ The Argonne
    ☐ The Bulge
3   The following are important American electronic companies:
    ☐ General Electric

The United States to 1941

        ☐ Plessey
        ☐ ATT
        ☐ Westinghouse

4 American farmers could not share in the general prosperity because:
        ☐ Food prices had slumped on the world markets
        ☐ There was an export ban on US foodstuffs
        ☐ There was a shortage of good farmland
        ☐ Immigrants took over farmlands and charged low prices

Prohibition

Read this, the Eighteenth Amendment to the US Constitution:

1919   After one year from the ratification of this article, the manufacture, sale, or transportation of intoxicating liquors within, the importation thereof into, or the exportation thereof from the United States and all territory subject to the jurisdiction thereof, is hereby prohibited.

This Amendment to the US Constitution ushered in the period known as 'Prohibition'. All public inns and taverns had to close – and the shortage of liquor encouraged the rise of the 'gangster'.

1 Why did Congress agree to the Eighteenth Amendment?
2 Do you agree that Prohibition was a 'degrading farce' for the American people?
3 Name two countries, north and south of the United States, from which smugglers brought in illicit liquor.
4 Who was a 'bootlegger'?
5 What was a 'speakeasy'?
6 Name the boss of Chicago's underworld.
7 What was the St Valentine's Massacre (1929)?

THE PREJUDICE

The Red Scare 1919–20 concerned the activities of the Wobblies (The International Workers of the World, founded by W. D. Haywood in 1905) and the Union of Russian Workers. There were strikes, parcel bombs and even a gun battle – involving extremists. But Americans were ready to generalise and there was a rapid growth of hostility towards Anarchists, Communists – and recent immigrants from South–East Europe who might be both!

Sacco–Vanzetti case, in which two Italian immigrants were accused of murder and anarchism, was one example. Found guilty on flimsy evidence in 1921, they were electrocuted in 1927.

America wanted to preserve its WASP image (White Anglo-Saxon Protestant) and discriminated against coloured and SE European immigrants via two acts (1921, 1924) that created the 'National Origins' system of immigration (it lasted until 1965). These acts set a quota for each country; they totally discriminated against the Japanese.

American blacks suffered from a long-standing racist division in the United States. Congress had passed the Thirteenth Amendment (31 January 1865) abolishing slavery. However, it was one thing to abolish slavery and quite another for a white man to reconcile his beliefs in Christianity and democracy with the deep-rooted fear that, if he treated blacks as equals, he would jeopardise the 'purity' of his race. Various states enacted codes of law to limit the rights of black Americans – the so-called 'Jim Crow' laws. In doing this, they contradicted the words of the US constitution especially:

(a)   *Second Amendment 1791:* the right of the people to keep and bear arms.

(b)   *Fourteenth Amendment 1868:* no state might make a law that reduced the privileges of a citizen.

(c)   *Fifteenth Amendment 1870:* the right to vote cannot be removed on grounds of colour, race or previous condition of servitude.

The following extract shows how difficult it was to implement these laws in the Deep South.

> *People who denied the blacks any form of integration would certainly stop their voting in local elections. Anyone who protested against the way blacks were treated invited the attention of the Ku Klux Klan formed in 1865. The Klan's self-appointed task was to discipline former slaves and their white sympathisers by threats, house-burnings, tarring and feathering. All too frequently, they burned black murder suspects at the stake or lynched them from the nearest tree. So, outwardly, the blacks had to come to terms with segregation and exclusion – if only to have a quiet life. Said one black minister, 'I don't have much trouble travelling in the South on account of my colour for the simple reason that I am not in the habit of pushing myself where I am not wanted . . .' But Black Codes and Jim Crow laws never crushed the blacks' demands for civil rights, 'to be treated like men, like anybody else, regardless of colour'.*

1 Why do you think the whites in the Deep South wanted to stop the blacks from voting?
2 What might happen to you if you supported a black man's demands for civil rights?
3 Had the Ku Klux Klan any right to discipline former slaves?
4 What might happen to a black murder suspect?
5 How did most blacks manage to have 'a quiet life'?

The Ku Klux Klan was refounded in 1915 and worked against the blacks who had moved north to find work in the factories. By 1923 there were supposed to be five million supporters of the Klan.

3 THE WALL STREET CRASH, 1929

After winning the 1928 Presidential election, Herbert Hoover took office in 1929 as the third Republican President in a row. He claimed that 'the business of this country ... is on a sound and prosperous basis'. But this was totally misleading, for investors were speculating on the Wall Street Stock Exchange as they had never done before. During the spring of 1928 the value of shares reached their highest point; then during the summer they began to rise again. The temptation to buy was irresistible. There were enormous dangers in this as the following extract shows:

> People borrowed money from brokers to finance share purchases. This meant they were now 'margin buyers', paying only part of the cost and borrowing the rest at five per cent or six per cent. Brokers' loans to investors doubled to about eight million dollars during 1929 and even banks were using their depositors' money to buy shares. But the actual value of these investments had never been tested, as these two examples show. Share values in RCA (Radio Corporation of America) zoomed by 400 per cent! But RCA had never paid a dime to any of its shareholders so who knew what it was worth? Similarly, people invested in investment trusts and their 'off-shoot' companies formed to attract investors' money. But these companies had no real wealth – they owned no factories, air lines, ranches or oil wells. All they offered was a share certificate.

1. What does the expression 'margin buyer' mean?
2. Would you regard this as a safe financial situation to be in?
3. Were banks taking risks during this share-buying boom?
4. Why was it unwise to invest in RCA?
5. What might happen if lots of people wanted to sell their shares in an investment company at the same time?

In fact, during September 1929 a group of stock-exchange traders decided it was the right moment to take their profits by cashing in large blocks of shares. Worried brokers immediately called in the cash they had lent to the margin buyers. These naturally dumped their shares to raise the money. 'Black Thursday' was on 24 October when investors unloaded thirteen million shares. By 29 October almost every shareholder had lost the value of his or her investment. This was the infamous **Wall Street Crash.** It ended the American boom and heralded an unprecedented world economic depression.

Unemployment

Unemployment jumped from around two million in 1929 to an estimated fifteen million in 1933 (they were not officially counted at the time). America had no national unemployment insurance, no national system of public relief.

◊ Factories, offices, shops began to close down.
◊ The new unemployed had no means of paying off hire-purchase debts and mortgages.
◊ Some people in the cities faced with starvation.

Read this extract:

They had to beg, seek public charity and build their own emergency accommodation. The most desperate built shanties in settlements called 'Hoovervilles'; from a shack made of packing cases and corrugated iron, a family would search the junkyards for a derelict car that might still have some old seats or an undrained oil sump. Others refused to become scavengers. They sold apples on the sidewalks or stood in breadlines organised by city charities. If they met a wartime buddy they might ask him for the price of a cup of coffee: 'Brother, can you spare a dime?' This was the title of a song written by Yip Harburg at the end of 1929 and later recorded by Bing Crosby.

Try to find the words to this song and then write an account of the plight of the people in America's great depression. Write your account in two parts:

(*a*)　　How your family invested its savings in shares during 1928 and then lost the lot in the 1929 Crash.

(*b*)　　How you and your family survived in a Hooverville and how your father, a First World War veteran, decided to join the BEF

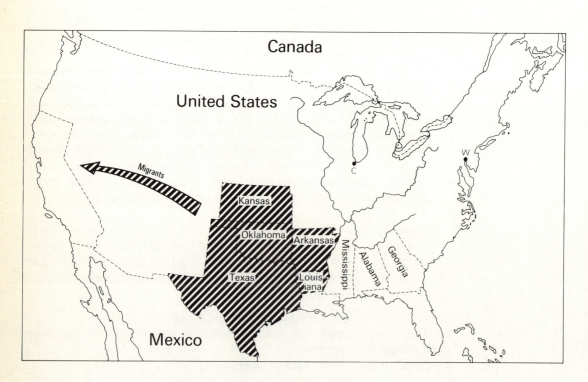

America in the first years of the Depression

The United States to 1941

(Bonus Expeditionary Force) in a camp at Washington DC and the conflict with the city police that followed.

In desperation, some city dwellers migrated to the countryside – but conditions were just as bad there.

- Unwise farming methods had led to erosion, especially in the Tennessee Valley.
- Persistent drought added to the problem and eventually created a giant dust bowl.
- Homesteaders moved out in search of the 'Promised Land' – usually California.
- Simultaneously, blacks were leaving the Deep South in search of jobs in the northern cities; while jobless whites wandered aimlessly through the countryside – the 'free riders' hitching a lift on freight trains.

1. Name the city C.
2. Mark the US capital at W.
3. Mark the Tennessee River.
4. What was the name given to migrants from Arkansas?
5. What was the name given to migrants from Oklahoma?
6. The states suffering from drought are marked with crosshatching; in pencil, shade in the states suffering from erosion.
Name the state to which the migrants are going.

By Christmas 1932 about twelve million Americans were jobless – twenty per cent of the US workforce. Many others were on short time – about fifty per cent of the American people felt seriously deprived. Yet there was remarkably little violence.

- Congress repealed Prohibition in 1933.
- Gangsters tended to fight among themselves or turned to bank raids.
- Kidnapping was rife – most celebrated of the many tragic cases was the Lindbergh affair (1932).

4 FRANKLIN D. ROOSEVELT AND THE NEW DEAL

When Franklin D. Roosevelt, Democrat Governor of New York, was nominated at the Party Congress in Chicago (1932) he made one of the most famous political promises in recent history:

I pledge you, I pledge myself, to a new deal for the American people.

The new deal, said Roosevelt would include:
(a)   state unemployed relief;
(b)   old age pensions;
(c)   a huge expansion in public works.

'This country needs bold, persistent experimentation. It is

commonsense to take a method and try it. If it fails, admit it frankly and try another. But above all, try something!'

Roosevelt won the election and was inaugurated in 1933. His words gave the people hope:

'So first of all let me assert my firm belief that the only thing we have to fear is fear itself . . . This Nation asks for action and action now . . . I unhesitatingly accept the leadership of this great army of our people . . . We do not distrust the future of essential democracy.'

This speech began the 'Hundred Days' during which Roosevelt gave his people the New Deal that would rescue millions from degradation, despair, unemployment and poverty.

Adolf Hitler  Franklin D. Roosevelt

Both men took office in 1933; both were to die in 1945.

Roosevelt was one of the greatest benefactors in the history of the world; Hitler brought to that world more misery than any man before.

The Roosevelt magic

Roosevelt went on radio to broadcast his memorable 'Fireside Chats' to the American people. He urged them not to withdraw their deposits from the banks. He would guarantee them through a new Federal Deposit Insurance Corporation. It worked:

Emergency Banking Act guaranteed deposits up to 10,000 dollars.

Home Owner Loan Act offered government loans to enable people to pay off their mortgages and then repay the government at low rates of interest.

Roosevelt secured the full co-operation of Congress to carry out crucial laws:

National Industrial Recovery Act, 1933 set up the NRA (National Recovery Administration). Its task was to draw up codes of sound business practice:
e.g.   better working conditions, pay increases through free collective bargaining, guaranteed minimum working wages.
Most businesses co-operated and displayed the NRA symbol (the Blue Eagle) and the NRA motto 'We do our part'.

The Agricultural Adjustment Act, 1933 (The Triple A) This set out to reduce farm production and restore farm prices to pre-1917 levels. The Triple A encouraged farmers
(a)   to kill off surplus stock;
(b)   to destroy surplus crops;
(c)   to let fields fall fallow.
Result: farm prices rose and American agriculture prospered.

Public Works Programmes were designed to cope with the immediate problem of the unemployed. Roosevelt decided to spend 500 million dollars through the Federal Emergency Relief Act. His adviser, Harry Hopkins, persuaded him to allocate a billion dollars to the WPA (Works Progress Administration) which led to eight million jobs over the next ten years.

Civilian Conservation Corps – America's superb state parks and beautiful forests owe much to the highly disciplined, low paid young people who formed the backbone of the CCC.

Tennessee Valley Authority (TVA) of 1933 radically changed the huge, depressed Tennessee Valley. The hydro-electric power schemes provided the cheapest energy in the whole United States.

OPPOSITION TO THE NEW DEAL

There was considerable opposition:

- Senator Huey Long (better known as the Louisiana Kingfish) denounced the New Deal as a means of making bankers and financiers even richer. He led the 'Share-Our-Wealth' movement; an assassin shot him in 1935.
- Father Charles E. Coughlin – the 'Radio Priest'. His broadcasts beamed out of Station WJR in Detroit and accused Roosevelt of being a communist.
- Dr Francis Townshend highlighted the fact that America still did not look after its old people. He planned his famous but impracticable 'Revolving Pensions' scheme.

- May 1935: Supreme Court declared the National Industrial Recovery Act and the NRA to be illegal. Roosevelt's reaction was to plan his 'Second New Deal' (sometimes called the 'Second Hundred Days').

The 'Second New Deal'

- The Wagner Act (National Labour Relations Act) guaranteed workers to bargain with their employers through trade unions.
- The Wealth Tax increased taxes on people with incomes over $50,000.
- Rural Electrification Administration lent money to farmers' co-operatives.
- Social Security Act (August 1935) set up old-age insurance though these pensions (payable at 65) depended on the previous earning power of the pensioner.

The following two extracts show different points of view about the New Deal and also say something about the bias of the authors.

Extract A

The view of a Republican Senator, 1934.

> The Administration's programme abandons the principles of democracy in favour of a system that partakes of the fascism of Italy, the communism of Russia, the ancient feudal system of England that was discarded 400 years ago and the planned economy of Diocletian that resulted in such disaster to the Roman people. It is not a progressive programme. It is reactionary.

Extract B

The view of an historian writing over twenty years ago

> When Congress adjourned on 16 June, precisely one hundred days after the special session opened, it had written into the laws of the land the most extraordinary series of reforms in the nation's history. It had committed the country to an unprecedented programme of government-industry co-operation; promised to distribute stupendous sums to millions of staple farmers; accepted responsibility for the millions of unemployed . . . pledged billions of dollars to save homes and farms from foreclosure; undertaken huge public works spending; guaranteed the small bank deposits of the country . . .*

*Extracts A and B are taken from Michael Bassett, *The American Deal*. Heinemann Educational Books.

1. In Extract A, why do you think the speaker believes that Roosevelt has abandoned the principles of democracy? (Remember in your answer the deep-seated hostility to all kinds of Federal power that existed in the US.)
2. Why did the speaker believe the New Deal to be 'reactionary'?
3. Would you consider Extract A to be a biased account of the New Deal? Why?
4. In Extract B, why does the historian comment on the 'unprecedented programme of government-industry co-operation'?

5   Does the historian convey the idea that the New Deal is 'a good thing'? Is this a form of bias?
    Examine the two following extracts and consider whether they
    (a)   contradict one another or
    (b)   support one another.

†Op. cit. p 23.

Extract A†

Black Americans, however, made only minor gains from many New Deal reforms. Most relief schemes were segregated although some Government agencies, especially the Department of the Interior, worked hard to eliminate discrimination. In rural areas, and especially in the South, the New Deal did little to alter the Negro's position of inferiority. In the cities the blacks formed the major part of those unemployed.

Extract B

No group was more grateful for Federal intervention than the American blacks. Some managed to improve their standard of living. Nearly three million now lived in the North and a few of them formed a Negro middle and upper class of business and professional leaders. In the North, black racial pride was constantly boosted by the famous 'glamour personalities': Jesse Owens, the winner of four Gold Medals in the 1936 Berlin Olympics; the brilliant footballer, singer and movie star, Paul Robeson; the renowned contralto, Marian Anderson; and the world heavyweight champion, Joe Louis. And the arrival of the motor car was beginning to chip away some of the features of racial prejudice and discrimination in the South. Petrol stations could hardly provide separate pump facilities for whites and blacks; and white drivers could hardly insist on the right of way on national highways! But 10 million blacks still lived in a segregated South and suffered deliberate suppression by whites. The law, as it stood, made American blacks of an inferior status. So Roosevelt's policies appealed to them and they voted Democrat, as did most other Americans, in the 1936 Presidential election.

THE END OF THE NEW DEAL

There were widespread strikes during 1937 for a forty-hour week and higher wages. Violence returned – ten strikers died at the Republic Steel Plant, Chicago (June 1937). 1937 was a 'turbulent year' and caused widespread alarm.

Did Roosevelt misinterpret what was happening? It appeared that he did. Most American industries were making a profit and so he decided to cut back Federal aid. This led to the 'Roosevelt recession' – two million people lost jobs, share values declined. Industry cut back production and by 1938 the economy was in the doldrums again. Roosevelt then boosted the economy with a big Triple A public works spending package.

Observations on the New Deal

◊ Clearly, it had not given back to America its pre-1929 prosperity.
◊ Nor had it solved the problem of unemployment.
◊ It would be orders generated by the Second World War that brought prosperity and full employment to the United States, not the economic policies of President Roosevelt.
◊ However, it would be wrong to undervalue the enormous contribution made by the President and his New Deal to American history:
(a) the New Deal Agencies gave the US time to rebuild its factories and farms in time to become the 'arsenal of democracy' in the Second World War;
(b) there was remarkably little violence – the New Deal had been supported by the mass of the people;
(c) the New Deal had elevated new institutions – notably the trade unions and the new social security and industrial codes – into a position where they became a part of 'the American way of life'.

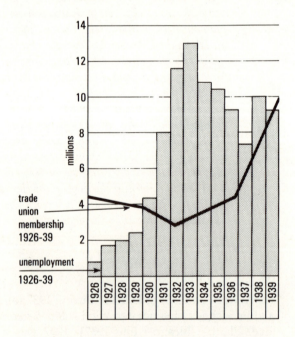

Unemployment and trade union membership, 1926–39

Note this graph showing unemployment and trade union membership 1926–39.

What does it show about the power of the American trade union movement during and after the Second New Deal?

Why do you think there was such a marked decline in trade union membership during the period 1929–32?

Law and order

It is interesting that the period of the New Deal coincided with a deliberate attempt by the Federal government to reduce the organised crime that persisted even though the 1933 Twenty-First Amendment to the US Constitution had ended Prohibition.

Read the following extract:

> As gangsters began to specialise in inter-state bank robberies, newspapers reporting these events elevated criminals such as Baby Face Nelson and Pretty Boy Floyd into virtual folk-heroes.
>
> In 1934 Congress defined specific Federal offences, notably inter-state racketeering, kidnapping and the shipment of stolen goods across a state line. This meant that a gangster was no longer safe if he fled from one state to another. If he did this after a crime he would now be pursued by Government agents (G-men) from the Federal Bureau of Investigation. Between 1934 and 1936 the G-men, using the fast cars and sub machine-guns so beloved by their gangster opponents, managed to eliminate most of America's 'public enemies'. Their hunt for John Dillinger was the most spectacular. He had twice escaped from jail: from Lima in 1933 and Indiana in 1934. G-men tracked him from Warsaw, Illinois, to Chicago – where they killed him in 1934. By 1936–7 the age of the gangster, as typified by men such as Al Capone and John Dillinger, was over.

1. Explain the expression 'inter-state'.
2. What did the media do in reporting the details of gangster activities?
3. What were the three Federal offences mentioned in this extract?
4. What was a G-man?
5. What do the initials FBI represent?
6. What was the colloquial expression for the sub machine-gun?
7. When did the gangster age end?

5 THE UNITED STATES, 1939–41

Most Americans had a very hazy view of Europe's problems since the beginning of the depression. Generally, public opinion was opposed to any involvement in European problems.

The few Americans who joined the Abraham Lincoln Brigade and fought against Franco in the Spanish Civil War were the exception.

Most people went along with the Neutrality Laws:

1935 Neutrality Act: required the President to declare an arms embargo on any nation involved in war.

1937 Neutrality Act: forbade Americans to engage in direct trade with a belligerent power.

The Second World War began on 1 September 1939 and after Britain and France declared war on Germany they put in lots of orders for war materials to American firms.

American industry faced two major difficulties:

- It lacked the resources to produce war materials quickly.
- How could it get round the 1935 arms embargo rule?

Roosevelt was very alive to the menace of Adolf Hitler and on 4 November 1939 he said that he would allow all belligerents to collect their military orders on a 'cash and carry' basis. It was easy for Britain and France, with Canada's long frontier with the US, to collect their weapons; but quite impossible for Nazi Germany to do the same.

Then came the dramatic news of France's surrender. Isolated Britain would take anything the Americans could send. This led to the famous exchange: fifty American First World War destroyers for British-owned bases in the Atlantic. Roosevelt made no bones about the fact that Britain's survival was vital for the future of the security of the Western Hemisphere – so America must become the **arsenal of democracy**.

Lend-Lease Act, 1941
This permitted the President to send to Britain and her allies any weapon that 'would promote the defence of the United States'. The Federal government now invested billions of dollars in Lend-Lease and in re-equipping the US armed forces.

Effects

- Industrial workers benefited when new shipyards, new bomber and tank factories sprang up in many American states.
- Farmers gained from the huge demands made by Britain for dried milk and dried eggs, canned fish and frozen pork.

American farmers remembered the depression and were suspicious. But they were soon told that 'every farm was a 'battle station in the defence of the United States against a Hitler victory!' and that they were part of a 'Food for Freedom' campaign.

Remember that, up to 7 December 1941, America was neutral.

American aid to China and Russia
Most American aid to China arrived via the Burma Road. Even then the trucks were subject to Japanese air attack. Chiang Kai-shek then signed up 250 Americans to form the American Volunteer Group – better known as the 'Flying Tigers' though they did not see action until the end of 1941.

US aid to Russia tended to arrive via the Pacific, the Persian Gulf and the dangerous Arctic convoy route.

Read this view of US aid to China and Russia (by Edward Stettinius):

The United States to 1941

Do we fear Communism in Russia? Why should we? We have been working out our own experiment for more than 160 years. Let us continue to do so, and let the Soviet Union work out its own experiment in its own way. We have nothing to fear from Russia. We have everything to gain by a close, effective and friendly collaboration . . . Do we fear a reborn China? Of course not. China has been the world's most peaceful great nation for more than 2000 years. The new China emerging in this war has become a moral leader for all.

1. Was there a growing spirit of co-operation between Russia and America between 1938 and 1941?
2. Do you think that Roosevelt was an admirer of Stalin as the ruler of a great power?
3. Do you think that Stettinius had a good grasp of Chinese history?

Now complete the following exercises by ticking the boxes next to the answers you believe to be correct:

1. Franklin D. Roosevelt promised in 1932 that his New Deal would include:
   - ☐ State unemployed relief
   - ☐ Old-age pensions
   - ☐ Public Works programmes
   - ☐ Rearmament

2. The symbol shown overleaf belonged to:
   - ☐ The Triple A
   - ☐ The CCC
   - ☐ The NRA
   - ☐ The WPA

3. One of the great electrification programmes was carried out by:
   - ☐ The Tennessee Valley Authority
   - ☐ The National Recovery Act
   - ☐ The Social Security Act
   - ☐ The Wagner Act

4. Opposition to Roosevelt's New Deal came from:
   - ☐ Senator Huey Long
   - ☐ Harry Hopkins
   - ☐ The Supreme Court
   - ☐ Father Charles Coughlin

5. The Civilian Conservation Corps (CCC):
   - ☐ Planted half the trees that have ever been planted in the history of the USA
   - ☐ Fought forest fires
   - ☐ Restocked lakes and rivers with fish
   - ☐ Built new bomber factories

6. The G-men were led by:
   - ☐ President Roosevelt
   - ☐ Harry Hopkins
   - ☐ Edgar J. Hoover
   - ☐ John Dillinger

The Blue Eagle symbol

7 The two main American Neutrality Acts were dated:
- ☐ 1935; 1937
- ☐ 1936; 1938
- ☐ 1938; 1939
- ☐ 1939; 1940

8 Lend-Lease meant that Britain and her allies could have American war materials and foodstuffs:
- ☐ In exchange for bases in Britain
- ☐ On a cash and carry basis
- ☐ If payment were made within six months
- ☐ Without payment

THE SECOND WORLD WAR, 1939–45

CONTENTS

- Origins of the Second World War — 121
- From the Polish campaign to the blitz on Britain — 126
  The Polish campaign 126
- The invasion of Russia — 131
- Japan's Pacific blitzkrieg, 1941–2 — 132
- Hitler's defeats, 1942–3 — 135
- The bombing of Germany — 138
- The war at sea — 142
  The Battle of the Atlantic 142
- The defeat of Germany, 1944–5 — 145
- The defeat of Japan, 1943–5 — 148
  The China-Burma-India front 148

The Second World War, 1939–45

1 ORIGINS OF THE SECOND WORLD WAR

Historians can readily find the roots of war in the Versailles Treaty of 1919, a treaty that reduced the German nation state to the level of a second-class country. The German people felt immense hatred for this treaty and Adolf Hitler skilfully used this hatred as a means of leading the reinvigorated 'Third Reich' into the conflict that became the Second World War.

HITLER'S CHARACTER

Hitler was an unpredictable leader who had every intention of achieving the aims set out in *Mein Kampf* and in his foreign policy speeches. Determined to resolve Germany's problems by the use of force, he constantly obscured his real intentions through propaganda, threats, worthless promises and the use of terror. He was dangerously different from any other leader in history in that he believed in a 'master race'. This 'master race' of 'pure Aryans' would create the 'thousand-year Reich'. It would dominate the world by virtue of its 'inalienable right' to enslave 'inferior races'.
Note carefully: the fact that Hitler's misunderstanding of human biology and human affairs was based on the false teachings of
(a)   pseudo-scientists and
(b)   geo-politicians
should not obscure another and much more important fact that the major responsibility for the outbreak of war in 1939 was his and his alone.

HITLER'S PLANS FOR WAR

Hitler spelt out his longing for lebensraum, the new living space in which the German people could live, in his speech at the 1936 Nuremberg rally:

> *If the Urals, with their immeasurable wealth of raw materials, Siberia with its rich forests and the Ukraine with its limitless cornfields, lay within Germany, this country under National Socialist leadership would swim in plenty. We would produce so that every single German had more than enough to live on . . .*

1   To which country was Hitler referring?

2   What did Hitler covet in
    (a)   the Urals
    (b)   Siberia
    (c)   the Ukraine?
3   How would the ordinary German benefit?
4   Why did Hitler make this speech in Nuremberg, rather than in Berlin?
5   What single word is normally used in place of the expression 'National Socialism'?

Hitler understood that before he unleashed his armed forces against the Soviet Union he would have to destroy both Czechoslovakia and Poland. He also understood that Britain and France would react to his planned aggression; therefore it was vital to have a plan to bring the western democracies to heel. On 5 November 1937 Hitler called a meeting in Berlin to decide on how to allocate resources between the three armed services: the Wehrmacht, the Kriegsmarine and the Luftwaffe. This meeting has become very famous in history for several reasons:

◊   Colonel Hossbach took some notes on part of the proceedings.
◊   These notes (or a copy of a document that purported to be these notes) were produced by the Americans after the war to 'prove' that Hitler had always intended to use military force.
◊   However, the importance of the so-called Hossbach Memorandum is that it underlines Hitler's intention to change from a defensive to an aggressive foreign policy.

Note that Hitler did not 'plan' the Second World War. He had vivid memories of the long war of attrition that had weakened Germany 1914–18. He foresaw a series of short wars (later known as the 'blitzkrieg' or 'lightning war'), not a general war. Remember that Hitler maintained a relatively small army (fifty-six divisions compared with the Czech army's thirty-five divisions) and enough reserves of petrol and ammunition for a war of six to eight weeks' duration.

The most important aspects of the 'Hossbach Memorandum' are listed below:

◊   *The aim of German policy is to make secure and to preserve the racial community and to enlarge it. It is therefore a question of Lebensraum – living space. Germany's future is therefore conditional on the solving of the need for space.*

◊   *Germany's problem could only be resolved by means of force and this was never without attendant risk . . . The equipment of the armed forces was nearly completed; any further delay might lead to obsolescence; while secrecy about these new weapons could not be preserved forever.*

◊   *If the Führer is still living, it was his unalterable resolve to solve Germany's problem of space by 1943–5 at latest. There could be some necessity for action before 1943;*
    e.g.   if internal strife in France should develop into a domestic crisis that completely absorbed the attention of the French

> army. This would mean that it couldn't be used against us and that we could take action against the Czechs . . .

Clearly, Hitler was engaging in a lot of guesswork.

1. Of the two western democracies, which did he consider to be the most unstable?
2. Why was Hitler especially worried about the new equipment coming into service in the Wehrmacht, Kriegesmarine and Luftwaffe?
3. Which country did Hitler expect to attack first?
4. Was the French army ever 'completely absorbed' by a domestic crisis between 1937 and 1939?
5. Why do you think the German military leadership readily accepted that Germany's future was 'conditional on the solving of the need for space'?

THE CRISIS OVER CZECHOSLOVAKIA

After his bloodless occupation of Austria (the Anschluss) in 1938, Hitler wanted to make the Czech Sudetenland, with its 3.25 million German-speaking population, part of the Third Reich. He had his own political chief in the Sudetenland – Konrad Henlein – based there to whip up enthusiasm for unification with Germany. He was very successful, as the words of the British military attaché showed:

> 'Nazism has gone to their heads . . . Nothing short of incorporation in the German Reich will satisfy them.

Note the three important stages in the Czech crisis of 1938:

- The Berchtesgaden meeting (16 September 1938) between Hitler and the British Prime Minister Chamberlain.
- The Godesberg meeting, when Hitler told Chamberlain he would take the Sudetenland by force if necessary.
- The Munich Conference, at which Chamberlain and Daladier (the French Prime Minister) gave Hitler the Sudetenland in order to preserve peace.

At Berchtesgaden, Hitler promised not to unleash the Wehrmacht against Czechoslovakia until Chamberlain had worked out a deal with Dr Beneš, Prime Minister of Czechoslovakia. Chamberlain forced Beneš to agree to hand over to Hitler those parts of the Sudetenland where a German-speaking majority existed.

On 22 September Chamberlain flew to Godesberg to tell Hitler of his success – but the Führer refused to accept the deal! Hitler handed Chamberlain the Godesberg Memorandum – German troops must occupy the whole of the Sudetenland by 1 October or there would be war! But Hitler knew he could get everything he wanted without going to war – he contacted Chamberlain to persuade the Czechs to hand over the whole of Sudetenland.

At the Munich Conference (29–30 September) Chamberlain and

Daladier agreed to the Godesberg Memorandum – Hitler could have the whole of the Sudetenland. Said Beneš:

> *If you have sacrificed my nation to preserve the peace of the world, I will be the first to applaud you. But if not, gentlemen, God help your souls.*

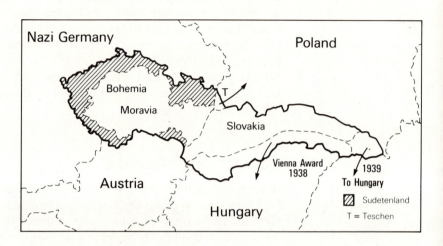

The Sudetenland territories

Indicate below the two countries that were excluded from any participation in the decision-making at Munich.
- ☐ Czechoslovakia
- ☐ France
- ☐ Great Britain
- ☐ Soviet Union
- ☐ Italy

Hitler's behaviour after Munich

*In his *Origins of the Second World War*. Penguin, 1964, page 239.

As A. J. P. Taylor has pointed out,* 'Hitler was a rational, though no doubt wicked, statesman.' He bided his time before making any other territorial demands in Europe.

So there were 'six months of peace' though in fact
(a)   a war raged between China and Japan;
(b)   Hitler was still exploiting the Spanish Civil War by testing out a new version of the Ju-87 Stuka dive-bomber.

In November 1938 Hitler authorised Ribbentrop to make the Vienna Award. Now look at the map above and indicate below the countries who secured parts of Czechoslovakia:
(a)   Teschen went to _____.
(b)   Parts of Slovakia and Ruthenia went to _____.

Note how Hitler was apparently winning friends in eastern Europe.

Finally, in March 1939, Hitler annexed Bohemia and Moravia. He allowed 'Slovakia' to exist as a semi-independent state and gave the rest of Ruthenia to Hungary.

Then he occupied Memel in Lithuania and simultaneously offered Poland a 25-year non-aggression pact if the Poles would hand over Danzig and provide a rail link with East Prussia. When the Poles refused, this led to a revolution in the foreign policies of the western democracies.

The future of Danzig and the 'Polish Corridor' (the rail link) became the crucial issue for Europe and, ultimately, the world.

(a)   31 March 1939 Chamberlain guaranteed Poland's independence.

(b)   23 August 1939 Germany and Russia signed their Non-Aggression Pact (see page 76).

(c)   25 August 1939 A Nazi Gauleiter claimed to be 'Head of State' in Danzig.

(d)   25 August 1939 Britain signed an Agreement of Mutual Assistance with Poland – she would come at once to Poland's aid if Poland were attacked.

So now there was a very real risk of war in Central Europe – nevertheless, Hitler took that risk on the assumption that Britain would be unable to intervene in a war so far away as the plains of Poland. He therefore ordered the German armed services to invade Poland at 0445 hours on Friday, 1 September 1939.

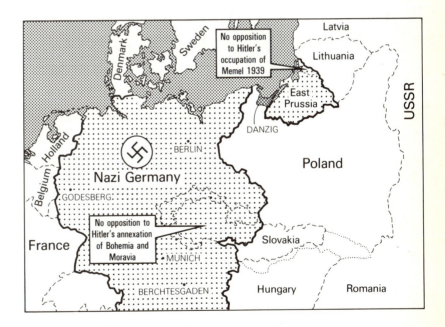

The aftermath of Munich: Hitler's gains 1938–9 (up to the invasion of Poland, 1 September 1939)

2 FROM THE POLISH CAMPAIGN TO THE BLITZ ON BRITAIN

THE POLISH CAMPAIGN

Hitler's invasion did not take the Poles entirely by surprise. They had ordered their destroyers to take refuge in Britain and had their fighter aircraft ready for action. But they were no match for the fast-moving Panzer divisions, supported by 800 Stukas and medium bombers. The Poles were already desperate when Britain and France declared war on Germany (3 September 1939).

Read the following extract:

> Polish hopes that Britain and France would come to their aid with an offensive in the west were soon dashed. There was virtually no military activity in the zone between the Maginot Line and its German counterpart, the Siegfried Line. Then, without warning, Soviet armies invaded Poland on 17 September. German aircraft – over one thousand bombers were involved – attacked Warsaw on 24 September and three days later the capital surrendered. On 6 October, the last Polish troops stopped fighting and Hitler and Stalin then partitioned Poland as agreed in their secret protocol two months earlier. In the words of the Führer, 'Poland has ceased to exist.'

1 Name the country that had built the Maginot Line.
2 Why had neither Britain nor France launched a single offensive against the German defences?
3 Name the capital of Poland.
4 Why did this city surrender so quickly?
5 About 100,000 Polish servicemen managed to escape. Through which countries did they make their bid for freedom?

The 'phoney war', 1939–40

All but one of the following statements are true. Which is false?

		TRUE	FALSE
1	There were no casualties when the British Expeditionary Force and 9,500 RAF ground crew sailed to France.	☐	☐
2	No British soldier was killed in action on the Western Front until December 1939.	☐	☐
3	U-boats sank the British carrier *Courageous* and the battleship *Royal Oak*.	☐	☐
4	The German surface raider *Graf Spee* scuttled herself after the Battle of the River Plate.	☐	☐
5	British bombers attacked the German fleet and the Luftwaffe attacked the Firth of Forth in reprisal.	☐	☐
6	Britain called this period 'the twilight war'; the Germans dubbed it the 'Sitzkrieg'; while		

		TRUE	FALSE
	an American Senator said it was a 'phoney war'.	☐	☐
7	Prime Minister Chamberlain said in January 1940 that he expected the war to end within a few weeks.	☐	☐

THE GERMAN BLITZKRIEG IN THE WEST, 1940

Hitler had in fact planned a combined invasion of Denmark and Norway and this began on 9 April 1940. There was no fighting in Denmark but British and Norwegian forces resisted the German attacks on the main ports of Narvik, Trondheim, Stavanger, Kristiansand and Oslo.

Then, on 10 May 1940, Hitler attacked the Low Countries and France. Rotterdam and Brussels capitulated after German air attacks while British and French forces fell back in the face of 'the giant phalanx of armour' crossing the Meuse en route to the Channel ports. A Panzer division, aided by Stukas, forced the surrender of Calais.

Then came the order: 'Dunkirk is to be left to the Luftwaffe.'

1 Who issued this order?
2 Why do you think he did this?
3 Do you agree with the opinions expressed by General Blumentritt who was Chief of Operations (Army Group B) at the time?

Document 1

> *The halting of the tank squadrons in the near vicinity of Dunkirk had several reasons. Hitler thought a lot of his Panzers and had seen in Poland, during the fighting inside Warsaw, that there will always be heavy losses in tank battles inside cities. Also, he didn't like the terrain in Flanders – damp, criss-crossed by watercourses with lots of hedges. He had fought in that country himself. Another reason was that he was worried about the number of unserviceable tanks we had each day, even though repairs could be carried out in twenty-four hours. Goering was another factor. He wanted the Luftwaffe to share in the glory – and Hitler jumped at the idea because this would save his tanks for future operations designed to take German troops as far south as the Spanish frontier. So it was up to the Luftwaffe to carry the blow against the English.*
> (General G. Blumentritt, in a letter to the author)

Document 2

See illustration on p. 128.

Document 3

> *The officer says, come on you two, fall in behind. So we do. It was all Grenadiers. But there were German planes overhead and all that so*

Document 2. The evacuation from Dunkirk

Source: Imperial War Museum.

> we thought it best to drop and let them march on. About 1 p.m. we got to the old stone jetty at Dunkirk. We saw a sailor putting men aboard the old *Ben-my-Chree*, *the Isle of Man paddle-steamer. Four bombs fell alongside her, in the sea. Charlie says, 'I'm not getting in her, that's too dangerous.' The boat starts to move so we jump aboard anyway. When we got to Folkstone we got an orange, a twopenny bar of Cadbury's chocolate and a cup of tea . . .*
> (Quoted by Nicholas Harman, *Dunkirk – the necessary myth*. Hodder & Stoughton, 1980, pages 199–200).

Over 330,000 British and Allied troops managed to escape from Dunkirk – some after spending a week on the sand dunes of Dunkirk which was under German air attack until 31 May 1940.

1. In Document 1, what evidence is there that Hitler was influenced by his own experience in the First World War when it came to making crucial military decisions?
2. What evidence is there that Hitler was anxious to keep as many tanks as possible in good mechanical condition?
3. In Document 2, what evidence is there that the main problem during the evacuation was getting the soldiers to the waiting ships?
4. The painting shows great palls of smoke hanging over the scene. What was the cause of these?
5. In Document 3 what evidence is there that many groups of soldiers had lost their officers and had to fend for themselves?
6. Was a British naval vessel waiting at the stone jetty to rescue them?
7. What evidence is there that the troops were without much food and drink on the beaches?

After Dunkirk, Mussolini declared war on Britain and France (10 June 1940) and four days later the Germans entered Paris. Prime

Minister Reynaud fell from power in France and Marshal Pétain formed a new government. Pétain asked for an armistice and Hitler agreed to it on 25 June 1940. Hitler's motives were:

(*a*) to allow the French to keep some dignity by retaining the unoccupied zone of 'Vichy France';

(*b*) to let the French keep control of their navy and colonial empire – and thus keep them from going over to the undefeated British.

Hitler's next plan was the invasion of Britain. Read his directive for this plan – Führer Directive No. 16.

On preparations for a landing operation against England

> *Since England, in spite for her hopeless military situation, shows no signs of being ready to come to an understanding, I have decided to prepare a landing operation against her . . . The aim of this operation will be to eliminate the English homeland as a base for the prosecution of war against Germany and, if necessary, to occupy England immediately.*
>
> 1. *There will be a surprise crossing from about Ramsgate to the Isle of Wight.*
>
> 2. *The English Air Force must be so reduced that it is unable to deliver any significant attack against the crossing . . .*
>
> 3. *The invasion will carry the code-name 'Seelöwe' – Sea-lion.*

Operation Sea-lion involved wiping out RAF Fighter Command and this started on 10 July 1940 – the beginning of the Battle of Britain.

1 What was the main objective of Operation Sea-lion?
2 Had Hitler expected to undertake this operation?
3 Now read the following account of the Battle of Britain:

> *At first, the Luftwaffe concentrated on coastal convoys, dropping magnetic mines and bombing a few inland targets. In August the German raiders attacked the radar towers and fighter airfields. Then came Eagle Day (13 August 1940) when the Luftwaffe made 1485 sorties against Britain. Every day after this the fighting increased in intensity and spread far beyond the main battle area of the southeast. During August and September a war of attrition went on day and night until the Germans changed their tactics. Hitler was furious that his timetable for 'Sea-lion' wasn't going to plan and decided to bomb London – a target previously forbidden to the Luftwaffe. Nearly a thousand German aircraft came over the coast in wave after wave, all heading for London. The British government thought the invasion had begun. The attack reached its height on 15 September – when the RAF shot down sixty German aircraft for the loss of twenty-six fighters and thirteen pilots. Hitler had failed to destroy Fighter Command and was forced to postpone Sea-lion.*

1 What was a magnetic mine?

2   What were the first objectives of the German raiders?
3   Why was Hitler's decision to bomb London so important?
4   Would you agree that the Battle of Britain, a victory for the fighter pilots and the British people, was really a victory of survival?
5   Had the Luftwaffe been defeated?
6   At the time, the British people saw both Dunkirk and the Battle of Britain as major victories. What effect did these experiences have on morale? Do you think they helped the British to survive the blitz of 1940–41?

The blitz on Britain, 1940–41

British searchlights, anti-aircraft guns and barrage balloons did not deter the German night bombers during 1940. Britain did not have the technical skill to 'bend' the German navigation beams; nor did she have the specialist nightfighters capable of locating and destroying the German raiders until the famous Bristol Beaufighter was delivered in substantial numbers. Most big cities and many small towns and isolated villages suffered from this constant bombardment from the air and undoubtedly the attacks would have increased had not Hitler decided to carry out his dearest wish – the invasion of Russia. As early as 18 December 1940 he had issued Führer Directive No. 21:

Operation Barbarossa

> *The German armed forces must be prepared, even before the conclusion of the war against England, to crush the Soviet Union in a rapid campaign . . . The Air Force will have to make available for this Eastern campaign supporting forces of such strength that the Army will be able to bring land operations to a speedy conclusion . . .*

Originally forty-four German bomb groups had conducted the blitz against Britain; by 10 May 1941 only four were left to carry out the raids – the rest of the bomb groups had slipped away to the east, to prepare for Barbarossa.

The expansion of German military power

In Europe: Hitler persuaded Hungary, Bulgaria and Romania to become his allies. He occupied Yugoslavia and sent help to Mussolini who was being defeated by the Greeks. When the British, who had come to the help of Greece, evacuated their forces to Crete, Hitler launched an airborne invasion of the island (May 1941).

In Africa and the Middle East: by February 1941 the British and Italian armies faced one another along the Gulf of Sirte. The arrival of Rommel, the 'Desert Fox', changed the situation. His Afrika Korps bypassed Tobruk and pushed the British into Egypt (Rommel captured Tobruk in 1942). However, Hitler was unable to reinforce Mussolini's armies in Ethiopia (Abyssinia) where British Imperial troops

The Second World War, 1939–45

defeated the Italians and Emperor Haile Selassie returned in triumph to his capital (1941).

3 THE INVASION OF RUSSIA

The conflict begun by Hitler between Nazi Germany and Communist Russia lasted four years (1941–5) and led directly to the deaths of at least thirty millon people. Stalin called it 'a war of engines', a clash between mechanised armies on a gigantic scale. Occasionally, the fighting did take this form, notably at the great Battle of Kursk (1943) but as often as not it was the infantry units that bore the brunt of the fighting. It is also interesting to note that Stalin appealed not to Marxist-Leninist thought as the road to victory but to the Russian people's sense of patriotism. Soviet historians in fact refer to the conflict as the 'Great Patriotic War'.

The opening stages of the invasion

There were three major penetrations of Russia:

- The assault on Leningrad.
- The advance on Moscow.
- The southern prong, aiming first for Kiev and then the city of Stalingrad on the River Volga.

Read the following extract:

> Operation Barbarossa began on 22 June 1941 and as usual the blitzkrieg tactics were completely successful. The Panzers swarmed all over Western Russia and by September they had captured Kiev and were besieging Leningrad. Moscow itself was not many kilometres to the east and an exultant Führer claimed that 'the enemy in the East has been struck down'. But the Führer had failed to provide his troops with winter clothing and November saw the onset of a bitter Russian winter. Many a German tank stalled for lack of anti-freeze and many a German soldier died from frostbite. Nevertheless, the Wehrmacht pushed on to Moscow and in December its patrols claimed to have seen the spires of Moscow. But the Soviet commander, Zhukov, was simply 'trading space for time'. Each time he pulled back the German panzers encountered stronger defences and evenutally Hitler agreed to pull back his tanks and go on the defensive. He had lost the Battle of Moscow.

1. What was the codename for the invasion of Russia?
2. Did the Germans manage to capture any of their main objectives?
3. Were the Germans prepared for a winter war?
4. Name the Soviet commander defending Moscow.
5. What does the expression 'trading space for time' mean in military terms?

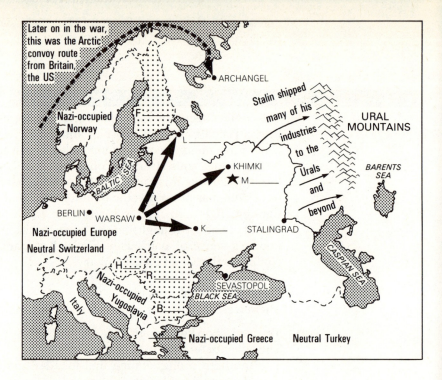

Barbarossa: The German invasion of Russia

1. On the map, mark Leningrad, Moscow and Kiev.
2. Name Germany's allies (shaded).
3. Why do you think Finland attacked Russia?
4. Mark Sevastopol (surrendered July 1942).
5. Did Leningrad ever surrender?

4 JAPAN'S PACIFIC BLITZKRIEG, 1941–2

It is important to remember that the war in the Pacific was fought out quite independently of the wars raging in Russia, North Africa and (from 1943 onwards) in western Europe. After the Japanese attack on the US Fleet at Pearl Harbor (7 December 1941), Hitler could send his new ally very little in the way of war material, though he did pass on technical data concerning U-boat and aircraft production later in the war. The Soviet Union did not participate at all and remained neutral in the Pacific conflict until after the atomic attack on Hiroshima.

PEARL HARBOR

Note that the Japanese had lost nearly all their oil imports in July 1941. This resulted from Japanese pressure on the French to give

The Second World War, 1939–45

them bases in Indo-China. Britain, the USA and the Dutch East Indies stopped all trade with Japan as a reprisal.

The Japanese therefore determined to take over the entire East Indies and to neutralise the British and US fleets in the Pacific. This was the motive behind the daring and remarkably successful attack on Pearl Harbor. The Japanese Admiral Yamamoto had drawn up the master plan:

> 'In the first six months to a year of war with the US and England I will run wild; and I will show you an uninterrupted succession of victories.'

Admiral Nagumo was in charge of the attack on Pearl Harbor.

> Yamamoto's plan hinged on Nagumo's ability to take a fleet of aircraft carriers across the North Pacific Ocean and then, 200 miles (320 km) north of Hawaii, fly off squadrons of dive-bombers and torpedo-bombers to attack the American ships at anchor in Pearl Harbor. Nagumo's task force left Japan on 25 November 1941 and US radio operators monitoring its signals lost all track of it. Everyone assumed that the Japanese were in their home ports. Certainly, the Americans were unprepared for attack and on Saturday/Sunday 6-7 December they gave most of their sailors leave passes to go ashore in Hawaii. At 0615 hours the Japanese took off from their carriers. An hour later two radio operators on Oahu saw some large blips on their screens at a range of 220 km. They reported these but their HQ said they were Flying Fortresses coming in from the United States. The first Japanese strike came at 0750 hours. By 1000 hours the Japanese aircrews had put the US Pacific Fleet's battleships out of action.

1. Name the Japanese Admiral in charge of the air attack on Pearl Harbor.
2. What evidence is there that the Americans had no hint of an impending attack by Japan?
3. Were the Japanese attackers spotted by radar?
4. Why were the radar reports ignored?
5. Certain ships (they were called *Enterprise, Yorktown, Lexington, Saratoga* and *Hornet*) were not at Pearl Harbor. What sort of warships were they?
6. President Roosevelt called December 7 'a day of _____'.

Declarations of war
8 December 1941   Britain and the US declared war on Japan.
11 December 1941   Germany and Italy declared war on the US.

Japanese successes
Christmas Day 1941   Hong Kong surrendered
31 January 1942   Malaya surrendered
15 February 1942   Singapore surrendered

Meanwhile, the Japanese had sunk two British battleships, *Repulse* and *Prince of Wales*, and had captured Wake Island, Guam and the Philippines and even had a foothold in the Aleutians. In February 1942 Japanese aircraft attacked Darwin in Northern Australia. There was an urgent need for the Americans to build up a task force to end this Japanese domination of the Pacific.

Coral Sea and Midway – two important battles

At Coral Sea (May 1942) no Japanese or American ships actually made visual contact with one another. The battle was fought by naval aircraft. Coral Sea was a setback for the Japanese; Midway (June 1942) was a major disaster. Here Japan lost her best carriers and her best aircrew but – unlike America – was hardpressed to replace them. Japan now had to fall back on a war of attrition and combat American technological superiority with sheer human courage. On 20 November 1943 the US Second Marine Division landed on Tarawa atoll. Read this extract:

> First they negotiated the coral reefs under heavy Japanese fire and then tried to attack the enemy defence positions. This was to become a typical problem in atoll warfare but rarely did the Marines have to overcome the resistance they encountered at Tarawa. After losing over 1,000 killed and 2,000 wounded the Marines counted their own prisoners: out of 4,836 Japanese and Korean defenders, 146 survived. And there were thousands of atolls! Naturally, the Americans were reluctant after their experiences at Tarawa to assault every atoll in turn. They therefore decided on a policy of 'atoll-hopping' designed to isolate large Japanese garrisons. Pacific islands suitable for air bases became the prime target and by 1944 the Americans had the skill and the equipment to put their new style of warfare into effect.

1 What is an atoll?
2 Why were the coral reefs so difficult to negotiate?
3 Why were there Korean defenders on Tarawa?
4 What was 'atoll-hopping'?
5 The Japanese aircraft shown below was one of the most feared throughout the Pacific War. By what name was it most commonly known?

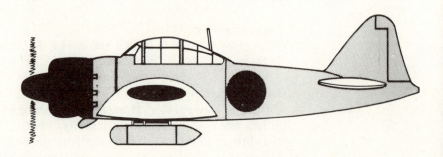

The Second World War, 1939–45

5 HITLER'S DEFEATS, 1942–3

Hitler had fresh plans for 1942. He would link up two giant thrusts across southern Russia and North Africa. In Russia, his armies were to capture the Volga industrial complex; in Africa, Rommel was to break through into Syria and Iran. Hitler's prize would be the oilfields of the Caucasus and Middle East. The key to the plan was the capture of the city of Stalingrad.

Read the following three documents carefully:

Document A

Instead of isolating Stalingrad and advancing onwards to further the original Hitler plan, von Paulus determined to take on the Red Army in some of the most devastating street fighting in the whole of history. He threw away all the advantages of fast-moving Panzers backed up by experienced ground attack aircraft in exchange for a war in the rubble, a war dominated by the hand-grenade, sub-machine-gun and assault rifle. This static fighting enabled the Russians to bring up their deadly Katyusha rockets and heavy artillery. Von Paulus retaliated by throwing in heavily armoured assault guns. Encircled by the Red Army, von Paulus surrendered on 2 February 1943. Hitler had lost 330,000 men. Almost every German family (and many in Italy and Romania) was affected. But the defeat at Stalingrad did not reduce the offensive spirit of the Wehrmacht. Hitler had decided to smash the huge Soviet salient jutting out from Kursk: 'The victory at Kursk must be like a beacon fire to the world!'

Document B

Surrender is forbidden. VI Army will hold their positions to the last man and to the last round and by their heroic endurance will make an unforgettable contribution towards the establishment of a defensive front and the salvation of the western world.

Document C

The battle at Stalingrad was the greatest military and political event of the Second World War. This victory turned out to be the beginning of a fundamental change in the course of the war to the advantage of the USSR and the whole of the anti-Fascist coalition. From the banks of the Volga the Red Army began its advance which culminated in the unconditional surrender of Hitler's Germany.

(Extracted from Graham Lyons (ed.) *The Russian Version of the Second World War*. Leo Cooper, 1976, page 54).

1. The sources of these documents were Adolf Hitler, a Soviet school textbook and a British historian. Identify the source of each document in the boxes provided.

Document A [   ]
Document B [   ]
Document C [   ]

2   In Document A:
    (a)   Who was von Paulus?
    (b)   What was a Katyusha rocket?
    (c)   When did the German troops at Stalingrad surrender?
    (d)   What evidence is there that the German people and their allies suffered heavily in this battle?
    (e)   Did the defeat at Stalingrad reduce the offensive spirit of the German army?
3   In Document B:
    (a)   By what number was the German army at Stalingrad known?
    (b)   Did Hitler make any attempt to save his men after they were encircled?
4   In Document C:
    (a)   Do you agree with the statement in the first sentence of this document?
    (b)   Was Stalingrad the first major defeat suffered by Hitler?
    (c)   Did the Germans manage to halt the Russian advance after Stalingrad?

The Battle of Kursk, 1943
Codenamed 'Operation Citadel', the Battle of Kursk saw Hitler employ his latest technical equipment and finest troops. His new Panther and Tiger tanks, supplemented by the secret Ferdinand (a Tiger chassis mounting an 88 mm gun) had the support of specially armoured aeroplanes designed to wipe out the latest versions of the Soviet T-34 tank. However, the defences built by the Russians outside Kursk were unparalleled on the Eastern Front; while the Red Army had 6.4 million men – far more than the Wehrmacht. Additionally, there was a security leak in German headquarters: ten German officers passed Hitler's secrets to Rudolf Rossler living in Switzerland. This was the so-called 'Lucy Ring' that fed all this data directly to Stalin. The Russian leader therefore knew in detail all of Hitler's plans. The turning point came on 12 July 1943 when the Germans lost 340 tanks and over 10,000 men. Kursk had lasted fifteen days and was probably the biggest tank battle in history.

Hitler's third and last major offensive on the Eastern front had failed.

Look at these two drawings opposite carefully. They show the main types of tank that clashed at Kursk. At the time they were the most advanced types of tank design in the world and neither Britain nor the USA had anything to match them. Identify tank A and tank B.

Tank A

Tank B

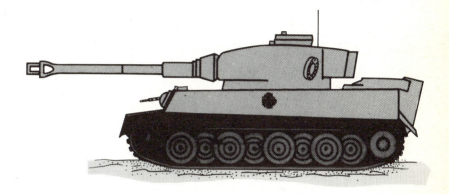

Tank B was astonishing in terms of size and firepower. Try to visit the Royal Armoured Corps Museum at Bovington, Dorset, where you will be amazed at the size of the German tank.

The German defeats in North Africa: El Alamein to Cape Bon 1942–3

Twice, during July–August 1942, Rommel tried to smash his way past El Alamein towards the Suez Canal and the Middle East oilfields. General Auchinleck stopped him at the First Battle of El Alamein and when Rommel switched his forces to the south a new British commander, General Montgomery, stopped him at the Battle of Alam Halfa.

The great Battle of El Alamein began on 23 October 1942 and after a fortnight of fierce fighting the Afrika Korps began its long retreat, chased by the Eighth Army's armoured divisions. On 7 November 1942 an Anglo-American force landed in Morocco and Algeria. This was Operation Torch. It was designed to catch Rommel's Afrika Korps in the rear and force its surrender. Over 200,000 Axis soldiers surrendered at Cape Bon (Tunisia) in May 1943.

So, as the result of three major defeats in 1943, at Stalingrad, Kursk and in the Desert War, the German Army had lost over one million men.

138 History 1: World History since 1914

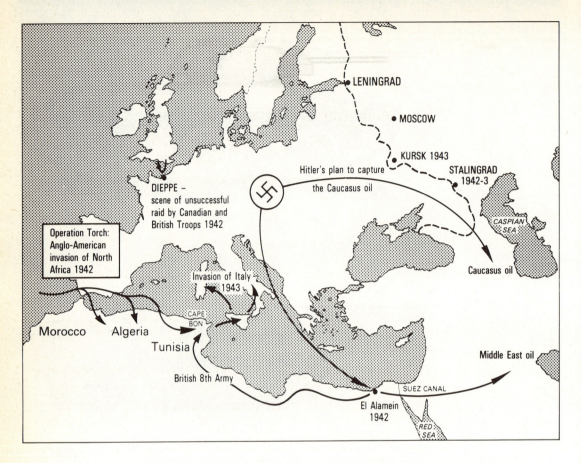

Operation Torch: the Anglo-American invasion of North Africa, 1942

6 THE BOMBING OF GERMANY

In January 1943 Roosevelt and Churchill met at the Casablanca Conference and agreed to fight on until both Germany and Japan surrendered. Both recognised that a 'Second Front' in Europe could not begin in 1943. They also agreed that an unrelenting policy of air warfare was the only major offensive they could undertake. Continuous attacks on German ports, oil refineries, rail and canal systems, shipping – plus area bombing designed to destroy workers' houses as well as factories and thus break the morale of the German people – would be the best way of reducing Germany's power and of helping the Soviet Union.

At *Casablanca*, Roosevelt also agreed that air attacks on Germany should have priority over those on Japan.

Once Churchill lifted restrictions on bombing German civilians (he did this after the German raid on Rotterdam, page 127), the RAF began attacking area targets. The first night raid on Germany was 15 May 1940. However, the RAF had to use the early types of twin-engined bombers (e.g. Whitley, Hampden and Wellington). More modern aircraft (e.g. the four-engined Halifax and Lancaster) came into service during 1942 when the following men took up their appointments:

Air Marshal Harris: RAF Bomber Command leader.

General Eaker: commanding the US 8th Army Air Force based in Britain.

Albert Speer: Minister for Armaments and War Production in Nazi Germany (Hitler's personal appointment).

The great air battles began in 1943. Read the following account:

1943 saw both attackers and defenders take a fearful punishment as a war of attrition in the air began. The RAF carried out the 'Battle of the Ruhr' during March to July; 617 squadron attacked the German dams 16-17 May; Hamburg suffered the horrors of a firestorm; Peenemunde research station came under fierce bombardment; and throughout, the RAF and the Luftwaffe waged the great 'Battle of Berlin'. The Americans trusted to massed formations protected by hundreds of air gunners armed with .50 calibre machine-guns. Twice they attacked the ball-bearing plants at Schweinfurt. In the August raid they lost sixty aircraft; in the October attack, which lasted a week, they lost 148 bombers. The RAF's night raids had to face radar-equipped night fighters, armed with cannon of the 'slanting music' variety mounted to fire upwards into the unprotected bellies of the British bombers. The Eighth Air Force had to face massed attacks from heavily armoured fighters, or from rockets fired by German aircraft flying just outside the range of the bombers' machine-guns.

1 What name is commonly given to 617 Squadron?
2 For what was Peenemunde famous?
3 What did the Germans manufacture at Schweinfurt?
4 Why were British bombers so susceptible to attacks from underneath the fuselage?
5 What did the Germans hope to achieve when they fired rockets into the massed formations of American bombers?

THE EFFECT OF THE BOMBING ON THE GERMAN ECONOMY

The devastation caused by the bombing was immense. Yet air attacks are often ineffective against factories – the building may be destroyed but it was often easy to salvage the vital machine tools. During the first two years of war, the production of consumer goods in Germany actually increased. After the Polish campaign, Hitler ordered the demobilisation of some of his troops. Not until 1942 was the German economy at all stretched. In fact, one German general complained that the people couldn't expect to defeat England with 'radio sets, vacuum cleaners and brand new cooking stoves'! By 1942 Hitler's main problem was not air raids but the shortage of labour. The

Russian campaign forced him to call up 7.5 million men. He drafted in 3.8 million workers from Occupied Europe and used the inmates of the scores of concentration camps, plus the Jews who worked in the SS arms production workshops attached to the extermination centres. Extraordinarily, Hitler did not make up his shortfall by recruiting women. Their numbers in industry fell during 1939–43. Most German housewives enjoyed a life of leisure, creating an air of normality in a nation on the verge of destruction from the air.

Once the Anglo-American strategic bomber offensive got into top gear (1943–4) the Germans began converting their economy to the demands of war.

Note carefully:

- The bombing did not bring about the collapse of the German war machine; nor did it destroy the morale of the German people.
- Speer was so successful in reorganising the German economy that his production of war materials dramatically increased 1943–4:

Tank Production

January 1943	760 per month
December 1943	1,229 per month
July 1944	1,669 per month

Aircraft Production

1942	15,288
1943	25,094
1944	39,275

- But once oil production came under attack in 1944 it did not really matter how many aircraft or tanks the Germans produced if they hadn't the petrol to make them work.
- However, American long-range fighters such as the Mustang destroyed most of the Luftwaffe when it came up to attack the huge American bomber formations. Consequently, the Luftwaffe was unable to oppose the Allied landings in Normandy (D-Day, 6 June 1944) and the Allied soldiers enjoyed the fruits of total air superiority. It is hard to see how this could have been achieved without the bombing raids on Germany – there was no other way to wipe out the enemy fighters.
- Bombing also forced the Germans to tie up vast numbers of anti-aircraft guns in the West, guns that would have been invaluable on the Eastern Front. Moreover, these guns, the searchlights and the radar systems, absorbed about one million men to operate them, including schoolboys who served on many gun sites during 1944–5.

What was it like under the bombs?

These are the words of a fifteen-year-old apprentice who worked in the Schweinfurt ball-bearing factory:

> *We youngsters knew nothing about bombs. We didn't know what a bomb sounded like and we certainly didn't know what it all meant. I was frightened but not so much as in later raids when I knew more about it. After the bombing finished, I ran home. I wanted to know what happened to my mother . . . I ran flat out all the way. At the station the trains were all burning . . . The bomb craters were already filling with ground water. Opposite the station there was a large wooden Red Cross hut where passengers could rest and eat. It had received a direct hit and I saw my first dead people. I looked away; I daren't look at them. There were arms and legs blown off – it was all terrible . . .*

(Quoted by Martin Middlebrook, *The Schweinfurt-Regensburg Mission.* Allen Lane, 1983, page 239).

What was it like to take part in these raids?

These were the impressions of Flt. Lt. D. F. Gillam, 100 Squadron RAF, during the night raid on Nuremberg on 30 March 1944 – a mission which proved to be the most costly of the entire war for RAF Bomber Command.

> *I watched a Lancaster flying about 2,000 feet below and about two miles off to my starboard. It had a great dirty contrail out of the back. I watched, fascinated, as a twin-engined German type overtook him, approaching under the contrail. I could see everything perfectly clearly, but couldn't help. The German got underneath the Lancaster and fired straight into his belly with an upward-firing gun. The bomber took no evasive action at all. There was an explosion and it blew clean in half. There were no parachutes. My stomach turned over and we tried to get even higher. By then I was feeling very cheesed off with the powers-that-be for sending us out on a night like this.*

(Quoted by Martin Middlebrook, *The Nuremberg Raid.* Allen Lane, 1980, pages 140–41).

A note on Dresden

The RAF was the most powerful air force in Europe by 1945 with immense destructive power. On 13–14 February 1945 it attacked the ancient city of Dresden, the largest German city still largely untouched by war. It was destroyed in an air raid that has caused more controversy than perhaps any other apart from the atomic attacks on Hiroshima and Nagasaki.

Consider the following statements:

1. Dresden was not a major military centre but was an important communications area into which refugees and soldiers had fled – for the advancing Russians were not very far away.
2. Dresden suffered hideously from the bombing which caused a fire-

storm similar to that which developed at Hamburg. 35,000 people lost their lives.
3 The raid cannot be condemned on the grounds that the war was nearly over. No one knew that at the time. German bombers were still raiding Britain. V-2 rockets were still falling on Britain.
4 The attack on Dresden, together with similar attacks on other German cities in 1945 (the main thrust of Air Marshal Harris's raids was still against the cities), was symbolic of the powerful RAF's determination to win the war as quickly as possible and to force the enemy to surrender.

Remember: the RAF had lost far more aircrew in combat 1939-45 (55,573) than the British Empire had lost officers during the First World War (38,834).

Now look at the evidence on pages 140–41 and then prepare an essay answer to this question:

> What part did the Anglo-American strategic bomber offensive play in the ultimate defeat of Nazi Germany?

All but one of the aircraft pictured opposite were engaged in the air war over Germany. Indicate the aircraft that did *not* take part.

7 THE WAR AT SEA

THE BATTLE OF THE ATLANTIC

The battle began on 3 September 1939 when a U-boat torpedoed the SS *Athenia* off the Irish coast; it ended on VE-Day, 8 May 1945, when Admiral Doenitz (Hitler's successor) surrendered at Rheims.

It was a battle on which everything else depended as all the convoys, whether they were carrying precious aviation spirit from the USA or refrigerated meat from New Zealand, had to enter the perilous waters known as the Western Approaches of the North Atlantic. Convoys from North America ran the greatest risk, exposed to:
(a)   U-boats, frequently organised into 'wolf-packs'.
(b)   Long-range German reconnaissance bombers.
(c)   Surface raiders.
(d)   Magnetic mines.

The most dangerous surface raider was the German battleship *Bismarck*. It appeared off Iceland with the heavy cruiser *Prinz Eugen*. After losing the *Hood*, the Royal Navy, aided by Fleet Air Arm aircraft, sank the *Bismarck* (May 1941).

Sea battles
There were few decisive naval battles in the war against Nazi Germany and its European allies.

◊ In March 1941 the Royal Navy defeated the Italian Navy at the Battle of Cape Matapan off Crete.
◊ New style radar (centimetric radar) fitted to frigates and corvettes

The Second World War, 1939–45

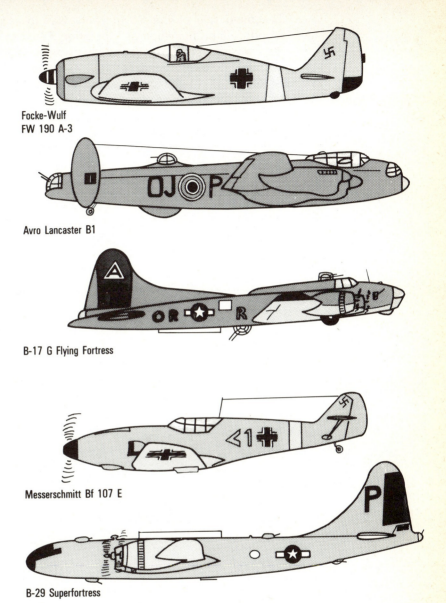

Focke-Wulf FW 190 A-3

Avro Lancaster B1

B-17 G Flying Fortress

Messerschmitt Bf 107 E

B-29 Superfortress

could locate a surfaced U-boat in any conditions; small escort carriers sailed with convoys; new depth charge bombs (Squid and Hedgehog) sank numerous U-boats – all these combined in the Battle of Convoy ONS-5, regarded as the turning point in the Battle of the Atlantic.

◊ The German battleship *Tirpitz* was a constant threat to Allied convoys sailing to Russia. Many attempts were made to sink her 1941–4 (dive-bombing attacks, midget submarines, the Norwegian resistance, the Russian Air Force – all tried and failed). Eventually RAF Lancasters flying from a Russian base sank the *Tirpitz* in 1944.

The main role of the Royal Navy was to escort convoys, protect seaborne landings such as Operation Torch in North Africa (1942), the invasion of Italy (1943) and the invasion of Normandy (1944); and, of course, to cover the early withdrawals such as Dunkirk in 1940 and Crete (1941). In the process, the Royal Navy suffered very heavy losses as the following statistics show:

British and Empire Naval losses, 1939–45

	1939	1940	1941	1942	1943	1944	1945
Battleships		1		2			
Battlecruisers			2				
Aircraft carriers		1	1	1	2		
Escort carriers				1	1	1	
Cruisers		3	10	13	2	4	
Destroyers	3	37	23	49	17	18	2
Minelayers			1		2		
Submarines	1	24	11	20	14	6	1
Corvettes		2	8	11	5	8	4
Frigates		4			1	9	1
Minesweepers			4	9	8	9	5
Sloops		3	3	6	1	2	1
Armoured Merchant Cruisers	1	9	4	1			

1. How many aircraft carriers were lost during the Second World War?
2. What type of vessel suffered the most losses?
3. Why do you think so many destroyers were lost in:
   (a)   1940 and
   (b)   1942?
4. One of the battlecruisers lost in 1941 was sunk by the *Bismarck*. What was its name?

The Second World War, 1939–45

5 Many of the Royal Navy's frigates and corvettes were supplied under American Lend-Lease. How many vessels of these two types were lost during the Second World War?

It is worth noting that when the war ended the Royal Navy was relatively small when compared with the massive strength built up by the United States. Britain had no hope of ever again being a major naval power as far as size of fleets was concerned.

8 THE DEFEAT OF GERMANY, 1944–5

D-Day, 6 June 1644: the Allied invasion of Europe. In February 1944 General Eisenhower was appointed Supreme Commander. He was given the task of opening a Second Front in Europe.

Document 1

You will enter the continent of Europe and, in conjunction with the other United Nations, undertake operations aimed at the heart of Germany and the destruction of her armed forces. The date for entering the Continent is May 1944. After adequate Channel ports have been secured, exploitation will be directed towards securing an area that will facilitate both ground and air operations against the enemy.
(Instructions to the Supreme Commander)

Document 2

Eisenhower knew he had to use all the Allies' technological ingenuity to effect a landing on the Channel coast of Europe. He decided not to attack a port. He would assault the Normandy beaches and bring in his own prefabricated Mulberry harbours with him. PLUTO (Pipe Line Under The Ocean) would provide fuel from Britain. He would take the defenders by surprise, using paratroopers and glider regiments; then, under the cover of naval and air bombardment, he would assault five beaches with landing craft backed up by Duplex-Drive 'swimming' tanks.
(British historian)

Document 3

In the short time left before the great offensive starts, we must succeed in bringing all defences to such a standard that they will hold up against the strongest attacks. Never in history was there a defence of such extent with such an obstacle as the sea. The enemy must be annihilated before he reaches our main battlefield. We must stop him in the water, not only delaying him but destroying all his equipment while it is still afloat.
(Marshal Erwin Rommel, commanding the German defences)

Document 4

A Sherman Flail Tank – called 'The Crab'.

Document 5

> In June 1944 when it had become obvious that the Soviet Union was capable of defeating Hitler's Germany with her forces alone, England and the USA opened the Second Front. On 6 June the Allied forces landed in Normandy. The Anglo-American forces met with practically no opposition from the Hitlerites and advanced into the heart of France.
>
> (Soviet school textbook quoted by Graham Lyons in The Russian version of the Second World War, Leo Cooper 1976, page 69).

1. In Document 1, what evidence is there that it was impossible to keep to the timetable for the invasion of Europe?
2. Was Eisenhower able to secure the Channel ports before beginning his main advance?
3. In Document 2, explain why Eisenhower was unwilling to attack a Channel port.
4. What were the Mulberry harbours?
5. What was PLUTO?
6. In Document 3, explain how Rommel intended to defeat the invading Allies.
7. What evidence is there that he believed the Atlantic Wall defences were the strongest ever built?
8. Document 4 depicts a 'flail' tank. What was its role?
9. Eisenhower described such weapons as 'novel mechanical contrivances'. What was the popular name given to flail tanks, DD tanks and Crocodile flame-throwers?
10. Does the content of Document 5 show signs of bias against the Allied invasion of Western Europe?
11. Select one sentence from this document and give reasons why a British or American historian might wish to disagree with it.
12. Can you think of reasons why the Soviet Union believed, as it often

The Second World War, 1939–45

stated, that the Soviet-German front remained the most important one in the Second World War?

Once the Allies had broken German resistance in France at the Battle of the Falaise Gap (August 1944), the path was open for the 'Great Swan' – the name given to the rapid advance of Allied armour through North-West Europe. You should note that the Germans were far from finished:

- Their 'reprisal weapons' – the V-1 'doodle-bugs' and V-2 rockets began hitting southern England and the port of Antwerp.
- German panzer units annihilated the British and Polish paratroopers who dropped on Arnhem in September 1944 – the ill-fated Operation Market Garden that tried to secure the bridges across the rivers Weser and Rhine.
- In December Hitler launched Operation Christrose – his last counter-attack in the West. His troops advanced through the Ardennes in the famous Battle of the Bulge. The pitched battle that followed was on the same scale as Stalingrad, involving over one million men.

Read the following account:

> *Von Rundstedt, the German commander, freely admitted that the battle was a gamble. In January 1945 it was obvious that the Germans had lost and the defeated Wehrmacht fell back towards the Rhine, leaving in the snow of the Ardennes 100,000 dead, captured or wounded comrades as well as their latest tanks and precious reserves of fighter-bombers. They were all irreplaceable. The Americans lost as many tanks and aircraft – and suffered 81,000 casualties. But they could bring up infantry replacements within a few hours and brand-new Shermans within a week. America's greatest asset in the Second World War, apart from the valour and competence of her fighting men, was her ability to produce war material more quickly and in greater quantities than could any other nation in the world.*

1. What had happened to Rommel, the German commander?
2. 'The pitched battle fought during December 1944-January 1945 was the biggest ever fought by US troops.' True or false?
3. Very few British troops participated. Who said that the battle was 'an ever-famous victory'?
4. Why was America able to replace her losses so quickly?
5. What was a 'Sherman'?

German resistance to Hitler

During the period June 1944–July 1944 German officers previously totally loyal to Adolf Hitler now began to question his leadership. Many assumed that it was he and he alone who was causing the life-blood of Germany to drain away. They hoped for some kind of settlement with the West so that they would then have a chance of fighting for survival against the Russians in the East.

The military were not the only resisters – though they were the most powerful:
(*a*)   The Kreisau Circle, mainly German intellectuals, planned to overthrow Hitler but did nothing to implement their ideas.
(*b*)   The White Rose student group did distribute leaflets hostile to Hitler – their leaders were executed.

In 1944 the military conspiracy developed Plan Valkyrie: to kill Hitler, take over power in Germany and try to emerge from the war with minimum territorial losses.

The leaders were:

General Beck
Field Marshal Witzleben } both were retired.

They recruited von Tresckow (Eastern Front) and von Stulpnagel (Western Front). Colonel von Stauffenberg was selected as the assassin and on 20 July 1944 he placed the brief-case bomb in the Führer's Rastenburg headquarters. The bomb exploded but Hitler was only wounded.

Beck committed suicide; Stauffenberg was executed and Witzleben was put on trial before the so-called 'People's Court'. He was hanged, together with twelve generals and thirty-four colonels.

The defeat of Germany, 1945

Throughout February and March 1945 the Western Allies and the Soviets made massive inroads into Hitler's Third Reich. After the crossing of the Rhine – preceded by a huge airborne operation – the British General Montgomery wanted to press on to Berlin. But Eisenhower opposed this as it was in the area promised to Russia as a post-war occupation zone. Russian armies therefore encircled Berlin while other Soviet units pushed on to link up with American units who had been sitting on the Elbe, waiting.

30 April 1945 Hitler committed suicide.
7 May 1945 German surrender at Rheims (to the Anglo-Americans).
8 May 1945 German surrender in Berlin (to the Russians).

9 THE DEFEAT OF JAPAN, 1943–5

THE CHINA-BURMA-INDIA FRONT

Since 1942 the Japanese had cut the Burma Road along which the US had supplied China. This forced the US to fly in supplies over the 'Hump', the towering mountain ranges east of the Brahmaputra River. Chiang Kai-shek was supposed to use these against the Japanese but in fact he kept his best troops in Northern China to bottle up the troops fighting for Mao Tse-tung. Eventually a new road (the Ledo Road) was opened in 1944, the year when US B-29 bombers began operating from Chengtu. Whilst these spectacular communication systems were being developed, little help was forthcoming for

The Second World War, 1939–45

the British Fourteenth Army and their American forces who were bogged down in Burma, one of the most difficult and unrewarding campaigns of the Second World War.

Atoll-hopping

In 1944 the Americans began bypassing Japanese forces in the Pacific and headed for the Marshall Islands. The fighting was so intense on Kwajalein atoll that one US serviceman remarked that 'the entire island looked like it had been picked up to 20,000 feet and then dropped!' Then the Americans fought the Battle of the Philippine Sea (June 1944), sometimes called the 'Great Marianas Turkey Shoot' because so many Japanese aircraft were shot down.

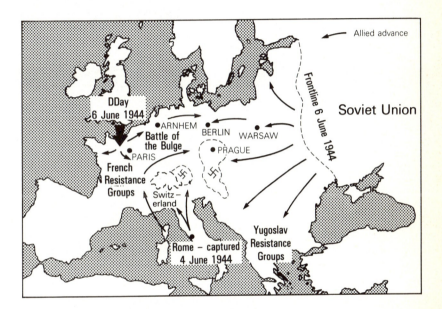

The defeat of Germany, 1944–5.

The Americans then went on to capture the Marianas, attracted by the big air bases on Saipan, Tinian and Guam – the last Japanese soldier on Guam didn't surrender until 1960! Now the US forces were ready to return to the Philippines and on 20 October 1944 the Americans landed on Leyte from the biggest invasion fleet ever assembled in the Pacific. The Japanese attacked this huge fleet in the Battle of Leyte Gulf – the turning point of the Pacific War.

- After this battle the Japanese had no fleet large enough to challenge the Americans.
- Thousands of Japanese soldiers and a great deal of war material were trapped on distant Pacific islands.
- Their air force could now only sacrifice itself in kamikaze (suicide) missions against the enemy.

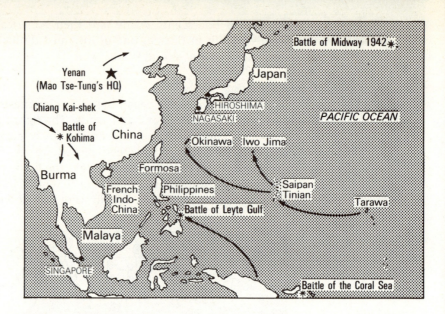

The defeat of Japan, 1943–5.

The attacks on Iwo Jima and Okinawa
Read this account:

> The fight for Iwo Jima was the most violent confrontation in the Pacific War. Over 23,000 Japanese soldiers defended the island, a mere eight square miles in area. Before the attack went in US aeroplanes strafed the island for seventy-two days; the US Navy hammered the beaches for three days. Then for the next thirty-six days the Americans tried to winkle the enemy out of his maze of underground strongpoints and bunkers, all linked by elaborate tunnel systems. Only 1,083 Japanese surrendered; 6,821 Americans died. To take Okinawa, much closer to Japan, was a daunting prospect. It would need a bigger force and for this assault the Americans assembled nearly half a million men. Their main landings took place in April 1945 and almost immediately the kamikazes came crashing down on the destroyers on picket duty and then on the wooden-decked carriers. More American sailors died at Okinawa than at any other naval battle; nearly 8,000 troops were killed. Japanese casualties included 100,000 dead combat troops and about 10,000 civilians. It did not bode well for an amphibious invasion of Japan, planned for November 1945.

1. Why were the Japanese so difficult to defeat on Iwo Jima?
2. Where else, in recent Far East history, have American troops had to contend with an enemy using underground strongpoints and elaborate tunnel systems?
3. What percentage of the American troops died at Okinawa?
4. What is significant about the Japanese losses at Okinawa?

The Second World War, 1939–45

5   Why were the aircraft carriers in the US Pacific Fleet especially vulnerable to kamikazes?

The air war against Japan

Japanese cities were especially vulnerable to fire and fire raids against major Japanese industrial targets became the standard mission for the American crews flying the huge B-29 Superfortress bombers (see page 143). The most terrible raid of all – the most terrible in all history, including Dresden, Hiroshima and Nagasaki – took place on 9–10 March 1945. Post-war Japanese casualty lists showed that 83,783 people died in the holocaust that engulfed Tokyo: 'This staggering raid, bringing destruction on an unprecedented scale, rocked the Japanese nation.'*

*Roger Freeman, *The US Strategic Bomber*. Macdonald, 1975, page 102

The nuclear attacks on Japan, August 1945

Read the following account explaining why President Truman (President Roosevelt had died on 12 April 1945) authorised the use of atomic weapons:

> *It is possible that constant air assault might have brought about a Japanese surrender. However, many Allied leaders, including President Truman, did not think this likely. They had the experience of the strategic bomber offensive against Germany to bear in mind – that had not forced the people to surrender. Truman approved plans for two amphibious assaults on Japan: Operation Olympic, scheduled for November 1945, and Operation Coronet, to take place early in 1946. He anticipated at least half a million American casualties because he knew that over 2 million Japanese soldiers, a substantial part of the civilian population, 5,000 kamikaze pilots and the crews of 3,000 suicide ships had already steeled themselves for a fight to the finish. His threat, issued at the Potsdam Conference, that America had a weapon of 'unusually destructive force' merely brought the response that Japan would 'ignore' this information. For all sorts of reasons, Truman decided against demonstrating the new weapon in an uninhabited part of Japan. He therefore decided to hit a Japanese city with Little Boy, the first of the two atomic bombs being prepared on Tinian. On 6 August 1945 this fell on Hiroshima and killed 70,000 people. Two days later, Stalin declared war on Japan. On 9 August 1945 another B-29 dropped Fat Man on Nagasaki, killing 36,000 people. Still the Japanese government refused to surrender, so the 'conventional' air war went on. Then, on 13 August 1945, the biggest number of B-29s ever put up in one day (809) bombed targets all over Japan. That was the day that the Japanese discovered that the US Eighth Air Force, together with RAF Lancasters, were coming from Europe to join in the destruction. They decided to surrender.*
>
> *On 15 August 1945 Emperor Hirohito's pre-recorded voice beamed out to the Japanese people:*

'We have resolved to pave the way for all the generations to come by enduring the unendurable and suffering the insufferable.'

On this day the Western Allies celebrated VJ-Day.
On 23 August Stalin announced his victory over Japan.
On 2 September 1945 Japan signed the unconditional surrender.

1. Name the two amphibious assaults planned for 1945–6.
2. Why did Truman expect the American invasion troops to suffer such high casualties?
3. In which country was the Potsdam Conference held?
4. What reasons do you think Truman had in mind for not 'demonstrating' the atomic bomb to Japan?
5. Where was Tinian?
6. Give the codenames for the two atomic bombs.
7. Why was 13 August 1945 especially significant in the air war against Japan?
8. Name the Japanese Emperor.

CHAPTER SEVEN

THE UNITED NATIONS, INTERNATIONAL ALLIANCES AND ARMS LIMITATIONS TO 1986

CONTENTS

- The collapse of wartime unity — 155
- The United Nations Organisation (UNO) — 156
- The Berlin blockade (1948–9) and its results — 160
- The war in Korea, 1950–53 — 163
- International crises after Korea — 166
- Peaceful co-existence, 1963–79 — 170
- The superpowers after 1979 — 175
- COMECON and the EEC — 176

The UN, alliances and arms talks

1 THE COLLAPSE OF WARTIME UNITY

In 1944 both the US and the Soviet Union accepted the recommendations of the European Advisory Commission regarding the precise occupation zones they would have in post-war Germany.

Significance:

◊ The Red Army, then bearing the brunt of the fighting against Germany, would be allowed to occupy Europe as far as the Elbe.

◊ Anglo-American armies probably could have captured Berlin – in April 1945 they and the Red Army were roughly equidistant from Berlin. General Omar Bradley said later:

> *At the time we could probably have pushed on to Berlin had we been willing to take the casualties Berlin would have cost us. Zhukov had not yet crossed the Oder and Berlin now lay almost midway between our forces.**

*General Omar Bradley, A Soldier's Story. Holt, Rinehart & Winston, Inc., 1952.

◊ However, Eisenhower honoured the 1944 agreement. His Ninth Army soldiers had to wait on the Elbe and their reconnaissance units had to withdraw from the right-hand bank of the river.

◊ It is therefore important to recognise that:
(a) the Soviet Union, the USA, Britain and France occupied pre-arranged zones in Germany at the end of the war;
(b) this was irrespective of the fighting qualities and achievements of individual armies.

From this territorial arrangement came the threat of an 'Iron Curtain' being drawn by the Russians across Europe.

◊ President Truman abruptly ended all Lend-Lease arrangements with Stalin.

◊ Stalin interpreted this as a move to block Russia's post-war recovery.

◊ Stalin reasoned that it was vital to take over political control of all his occupied territories.

◊ Churchill had anticipated this and had spoken about the dangers of an Iron Curtain as early as May 1945.

◊ But the Americans weren't worried: they thought that all post-war problems could be handled by the new United Nations Organisation.

◊ So Churchill appealed directly to Stalin:

> *There is not much comfort in looking on to a future where you and the countries you dominate, plus the communist parties in many*

> *other states, are all drawn up on one side, and those who rally to the English-speaking nations are on the other. It is quite obvious that a quarrel would tear the world to pieces, and that all of us leading men on either side who had anything to do with that would be shamed before history.*

But Stalin didn't reply and Churchill (now out of office) went to Fulton (USA) to make his famous Iron Curtain speech:

> *An Iron Curtain has descended across the continent. Behind that line lie all the capitals of the ancient states of Central and Eastern Europe . . . this is certainly not the liberated Europe we fought to build up.* (1946)

This won a reaction from Stalin:

> *'It is a call to war with the Soviet Union.'*

Many westerners condemned Churchill as 'an old war horse who couldn't get the scent of battle out of his nostrils.'

However, the Americans listened hard. President Truman had watched the UN hold its first meetings and it didn't seem to him that:
(a)   its structure and
(b)   its powers
were the best guarantee for the preservation of world peace.

Consider the above statements and the quotations from men such as Bradley, Churchill and Stalin. Then prepare a short essay explaining in your own words why the spirit of wartime unity seemed to collapse so suddenly during 1945–6.

2 THE UNITED NATIONS ORGANISATION (UNO)

Its origins

In 1941 Churchill and Roosevelt met on board a British battleship off Newfoundland. They issued the Atlantic Charter:

- General disarmament vital.
- A 'wider and permanent system of security' needed.
- This needed a United Nations Organisation committed to the defence of the 'Four Freedoms':

> Freedom from want
> Freedom from fear
> Freedom of speech
> Freedom of religious belief

UNRRA

This was the United Nations Relief and Rehabilitation Administration. It began working in Italy during 1943 to help newly liberated peoples. Soon the Russians suspected that American UNRRA workers were really CIA agents in disguise! Such was the measure of distrust the new organisation would have to overcome.

Foundation of the UN
1944 saw discussions at Dumbarton Oaks; at Yalta (February 1945) the great powers agreed to keep a veto for themselves on a new Security Council. On 26 June 1945 representatives of fifty nations signed the Charter of the United Nations. The UN came into existence on 24 October 1945 with its headquarters in a skyscraper towering over Turtle Bay in New York.

The Charter

> We, the peoples of the United Nations, determined to save succeeding generations from the scourge of war, which twice in our lifetime has brought untold sorrow to mankind, and to reaffirm faith in fundamental human rights, in the dignity and worth of the human person, in the equal rights of men and women and of nations large and small, and to establish conditions under which justice and respect for the obligations arising from treaties and other sources of international law can be maintained . . . have resolved to combine our efforts to accomplish these aims.

The principal organs of the UN
A General Assembly, a Security Council, an Economic and Social Council, an International Court of Justice and a Secretariat were set up. These formally replaced the organs of the League of Nations, abolished in April 1946.

General Assembly: delegates discussed crucial world issues aided by a host of statisticians, translators and technicians who worked for the Secretariat under the control of the first Secretary-General, Trygve Lie (1945–53).

The Economic and Social Council dealt with health and nutritional problems and passed on its recommendations to the General Assembly.

The International Court of Justice stayed at The Hague.

The Security Council with its five permanent members (at that time the USSR, the US, Britain, France and Nationalist China) was the most revolutionary part of the new structure. It dealt with any world problem that threatened peace. Each of these nations could veto a decision; representatives of ten other nations served on the Security Council.

Specialised agencies
These had the task of dealing with human problems in certain specialist fields:

FAO (Food and Agricultural Organisation) had the task of boosting food production and coping with the disease and locust plagues that destroyed so many cattle and crops each year.

WHO (World Health Organisation) joined in 1948 with UNICEF (UN International Children's Emergency Fund) workers in the fight against diseases such as malaria, yaws, trachoma (blindness) and trypanosmiasis (sleeping sickness).

ILO (International Labour Organisation) – the sole surviving League of Nations agency – examined working conditions all over the world.

UNESCO (UN Economic, Scientific and Cultural Organisation) concerned itself increasingly with propaganda – the dissemination and control of information.

For the first five years of its existence the UN had no armed force at its beck and call – no way of dealing directly with a series of dangerous crises that developed in Europe and the Far East.

The first of these:
(a) Russia's deliberate break with the West
(b) the creation of a system of Soviet satellites in Eastern Europe
(c) the Communist take-over in Czechoslovakia
(d) the currency crisis in Germany
(e) the Soviet blockade of Berlin

were all characteristic of the new 'Cold War' and were played out quite independently of the UN.

Multiple-choice questions

1 The expression 'Iron Curtain' is usually attributed to
- [ ] Winston Churchill
- [ ] Joseph Stalin
- [ ] Harry S. Truman
- [ ] Clement Attlee

2 In 1941 Churchill and Roosevelt met on board a battleship and issued the
- [ ] United Nations Charter
- [ ] The People's Charter
- [ ] The Atlantic Charter
- [ ] The Freedom Charter

3 The Four Freedoms include
- [ ] Freedom of Speech
- [ ] Freedom from Taxation
- [ ] Freedom from Trade Union Membership
- [ ] Freedom from Passport Control

4 All countries of the world may be represented in
- [ ] The Secretariat
- [ ] The Security Council
- [ ] The General Assembly

The UN, alliances and arms talks

5 The first Secretary-General was
- [ ] U Thant
- [ ] Dag Hammarskjöld
- [ ] Kurt Waldheim
- [ ] Trygve Lie

6 The surviving agency from the League of Nations was
- [ ] WHO
- [ ] UNESCO
- [ ] ILO
- [ ] FAO

7 The five permanent members at the first meeting of the Security Council were
- [ ] Britain, USA, USSR, France and Germany
- [ ] Britain, USA, USSR, France and Communist China
- [ ] Britain, USA, USSR, France and Italy
- [ ] Britain, USA, USSR, France and Nationalist China

The Truman doctrine 1947

During 1945–7 Prime Minister Attlee of Britain tried to guarantee the stability of Greece and Turkey, two countries that guarded the eastern end of the Mediterranean against possible Soviet expansion. When he couldn't afford to continue aid, Attlee asked Truman to help out. Truman agreed and made his famous speech to Congress now called the Truman doctrine:

> *I believe that it must be the policy of the United States to support free peoples who are resisting attempted subjugation by armed minorities or by outside pressures . . . I believe that our help should be primarily through economic and financial aid which is essential to economic stability and orderly political progress.*

President Truman then defined his view of the difference between the 'free world' and the 'communist world':

> *Our way of life is based on the will of the majority and is distinguished by free institutions, representative government, free elections. The second way of life is based upon the will of the minority forcibly imposed upon the majority. It relies upon terror and oppression.*

The Truman doctrine was followed by George Marshall's European Recovery Programme – generally called the Marshall Plan. Any nation willing to participate in the rehabilitation of war-torn Europe could have dollar aid – including Russia and her satellites. Stalin refused the offer. He believed this was America's way of winning world domination. He therefore called a meeting in Warsaw (1947) to set up the COMINFORM (Communist Information Bureau). Its job was to spread news of the hostility of Eastern Europe towards new-style US Capitalism.

Stalin's victories, 1948–9

- Czechoslovakia 1948: here the Czech people asked for Marshall Aid, though Foreign Minister Masaryk had no intention of falling under US control. Stalin was furious. He sent in agents to take over the mass media; by February 1948 the communists had control and a fortnight later Jan Masaryk was found dead under a window of the Foreign Office in Prague.
- Yugoslavia: when Marshal Tito said he did not intend to toe the communist line Stalin expelled him from the Cominform (1948).
- Stalin then executed Kotsov (Bulgaria) and Rajk (Hungary). He arrested Gomulka (Poland) and then announced his answer to Marshall Aid: COMECON (The 1949 Council for Mutual Economic Assistance).

Significance

The US saw Cominform and Comecon as twin threats to the free people of the USA and Western Europe. Somehow, they would have to counter this threat. So the 'Cold War' was in full swing and would take a dangerous turn in the changes taking place in the four zones of occupied Germany.

Stalin's attitude

He refused to help the recovery of Germany – after all, the Germans had killed twenty million Russians. Millions of Germans had fled from his zone to the West – but Stalin denied any responsibility. So the West had to cope with millions of refugees, a housing crisis, black market and inflation. On 1 January 1947 the British and Americans formed their two zones into Bizonia and tried to beat inflation with a new Deutschmark.

3 THE BERLIN BLOCKADE (1948–9) AND ITS RESULTS

From the Berlin blockade sprang the 'two Germanys' (East and West), the North Atlantic Treaty Organisation and the Warsaw Pact military alliance.

Note how Stalin weighed up the situation. He could see that it was only a matter of time before the West formed a new Germany out of their zone. The one place he could bring pressure on the West was in Berlin, if he could force them out of the German capital he would win an immense propaganda victory.

Read the following extract:

> *General Clay, commander in Berlin, realised that one day Stalin might blockade the city and he had drawn up a plan to cope with this. So he was ready when, on 24 June 1948, the Russians announced that 'technical difficulties' had suddenly stopped all road, rail and canal traffic into Berlin. Simultaneously, they warned Berlin housewives of immediate water and power failures. Americans*

The UN, alliances and arms talks

countered this – and prevented a panic – by broadcasting a statement that there was plenty of water and that every mother should give her baby a bath! On 25 June the first American Skymaster touched down at Tempelhof airport bringing in the first food supplies. Military and civilian aircraft flew 270,000 sorties and carried nearly 2.5 million tons of coal and food in their cargo holds. Not even the Russians could invent 'technical difficulties' to prevent aircraft flying down the three air corridors to Berlin. Inevitably, some aircraft crashed and seventy airmen died in the cause of preserving an Allied foothold in Berlin. On 12 May 1949, Stalin agreed to end the Berlin blockade. It was an admission that he had suffered his first major defeat in the Cold War contest to win political control of Germany.

1. How many sectors were there in occupied Berlin?
2. Were military personnel allowed to move from one sector to another?
3. Look at the map below. What was the name of the French air base in Berlin?
4. Why do you think the Russians said there had been water and power failures?
5. How long did the Berlin blockade last?

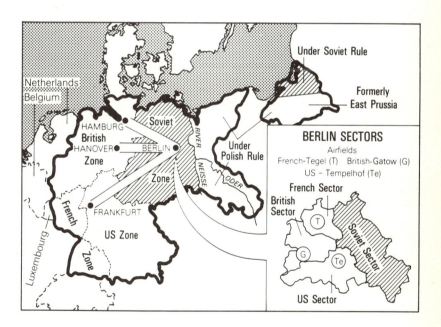

Germany: Zones and air corridors

Results of the Berlin blockade
The Western allies announced the formation of the Federal German Republic (West Germany); Stalin's retort was to proclaim his zone the German Democratic Republic (East Germany).

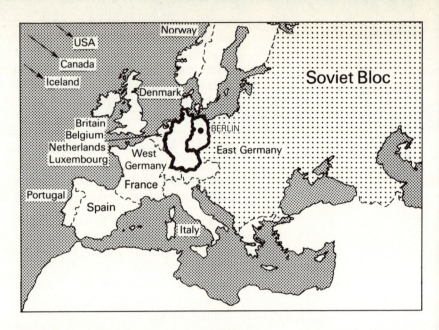

The two Germanys, in the middle of a divided Europe

Later crises involving Berlin:

◊ 1956 crisis: coincided with the Suez Crisis (page 219) and the Hungarian Uprising (page 176). Infuriated West Berliners rampaged through the city and tried to invade East Berlin.
◊ 1958: 'Khrushchev crisis' when the Soviet leader offered to sign a separate peace treaty with East Germany (ended 1961).
◊ 1961: Checkpoint Charlie crisis, after the building of the Berlin Wall. Soviet and US tanks faced one another at Checkpoint Charlie.

Even before Stalin had lifted the Berlin Blockade, Truman had decided to create a permanent military alliance in the west. This was the North Atlantic Treaty Organisation (1949) consisting of the USA, Britain, France, Canada, Iceland, Denmark, Norway, Luxembourg, the Netherlands, Belgium and Portugal. Greece and Turkey joined in 1952; the Federal German Republic joined in 1955; Spain joined in 1982 (France left the military command structure in 1966). When West Germany joined NATO the Soviet Union and her satellites met in Poland to sign the Warsaw Pact.

Now you can see that within ten years of the end of the Second World War two military alliances:

(a)   NATO: the North Atlantic Treaty Organisation
(b)   The Warsaw Pact

symbolised the divided world of western capitalism and eastern communism, a world made far more dangerous now that Russia had exploded an atomic bomb (1949).

4 THE WAR IN KOREA, 1950–53

When Soviet and American troops arrived in Korea 1945 to disarm the Japanese forces stationed there, they divided the country into two separate occupation zones along the 38th Parallel. The original plan was to repatriate the Japanese and then hold free elections so that the Korean people could create their own democratic state. But neither the Russians nor the Americans could agree on how this should be done and so the UN decided to take over the problem and organise free elections inside the two occupation zones. This they did in 1948; but the Russians refused to let UN teams enter the northern zone. This was why the UN allowed a 'South Korean' government to be set up under the leadership of Syngman Rhee; while in the north the Russians encouraged Kim Il-sung to set up his 'North Korean' government. Both leaders believed they had a right to rule over both parts of Korea and they immediately began to hurl insults at one another.

How these two Koreas came into conflict with one another is a matter of historical controversy. Some historians believe that when Stalin withdrew his troops in 1948 he beefed up North Korea's army, notably with T-34 tanks. Others point out that the Americans were worried about Syngman Rhee's aggressive tone and in 1949 they defined Korea as outside the 'main US defence perimeter'. US troops left in 1949 and went to bases in Japan. The weight of the evidence seems to be that North Korea was relatively well equipped for an attack; but South Korea was not.

Document 1

The invasion is a classic example of the type of incident which endangers world peace when the world is divided into two armed camps. The procedure for dealing with it is also familiar from past experience. The objectives are the cessation of hostilities, withdrawal of troops and, above all, the exclusion of the Great Powers from the conflict. These must be the aims of the Security Council.
Manchester Guardian, 26 June 1950.

Document 2

On 25 June 1950 North Korean troops crossed the 38th Parallel; four days later they were in Seoul. On this occasion the United Nations acted swiftly, calling for a cease-fire and the immediate withdrawal of the North's forces. When this demand was ignored, American troops under the flamboyant General Douglas MacArthur were sent to support the armies of the South. The first two months were marked by communist victories and by August the defenders were hemmed in round Pusan. Primarily as a result of a daring and successful sea-borne attack on Inchon, MacArthur was back in Inchon by September.
A. J. Barker, *Fortune Favours the Brave*. Leo Cooper, 1974, page xiv.

Document 3

On 26 June 1950 the UN Security Council ordered the North Koreans to withdraw – significantly the Russian delegate was absent from this session and thus unable to veto these instructions. The next day the Council asked member states of the UN to send aid to South Korea; the Russian delegate was still absent.
British textbook

Document 4

The barbarous action of American imperialism and its hangers-on seriously threatens the security of China. It is impossible to solve the Korean problem without the participation of its closest neighbour, China. North Korea's enemy is our enemy. North Korea's defences are our defences. North Korea's victory is our victory.
World Culture. Vol XXII, No.8, 26 August 1950 (This was in fact the first Chinese warning to the UN.)

1. In Document 1, how do you think the UN Security Council could have brought about a 'cessation of hostilities' and 'the withdrawal of troops' without using the aid of the Great Powers (i.e. the Superpowers). Bear in mind the UN had no army of its own.
2. What evidence is there in Document 2 that the North Koreans were prepared for a rapid advance into South Korea?
3. Name the UN military commander.
4. In Document 3, why do you think the Russian delegate absented himself from this crucial UN session?
5. Why did the Russian delegate fail to attend the session on the following day?
6. Why was it impossible for the UN delegates to discuss the Korean problem directly with the Chinese? (Remember that the Communist Revolution in China had taken place in 1949).
7. In Document 4, is there a hint that the Chinese (then neutral) might intervene in the Korean problem?
8. In November fourteen divisions of the Chinese People's Volunteer Army attacked the UN troops and MacArthur told the UN that it faced 'an entirely new kind of war'. What did the Chinese achieve by the beginning of 1951?

Read the following account:

MacArthur urged President Truman to let him use maximum firepower to push the Chinese out of Korea and to enable him to carry the war into China – and to use anything within America's huge military arsenal to force the Chinese to surrender. Truman was horrified. On no account, he said, was MacArthur to cross the Yalu. No US aeroplane must fly over China. It must be a 'limited war', using a restricted number of weapons with the minimum number of troops required. To ram home his point, Truman dismissed MacArthur in 1951 and replaced him with General Ridgeway.

The UN, alliances and arms talks 165

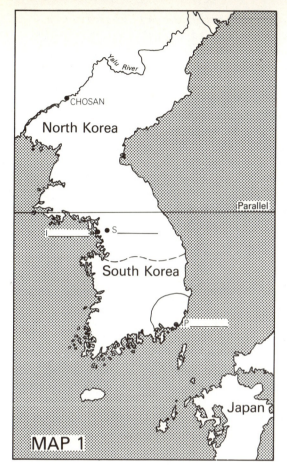
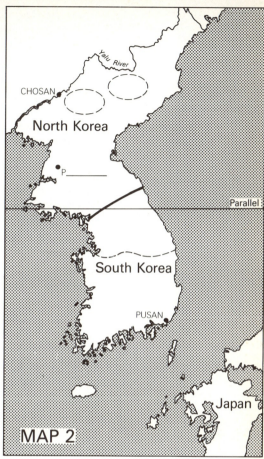

The war in Korea 1950–53

1 Why was Truman horrified by MacArthur's ideas?
2 What did Truman mean by 'a limited war'?
3 Did the Chinese have similar restrictions placed upon them?
4 How did the nature of the war change in 1951?
5 Find out the name of the Chinese commander at this time.

Key words have been omitted from the following passage. They are:

  Main Line of Resistance;   Jets;   North Korean;
  UN tanks;   PVA artillery;   fighting;   delegates.

Insert these key words to complete the sense of the passage:

A _____ stretched across the peninsula. High above the troops, dug in among the brown hills of Korea, droned the B-29s en route for their _____ targets. _____ screamed in *low level passes, blanketing the Chinese positions with napalm. Infantry patrols cautiously probed No Man's Land, their 'snatch squads' on the look-out for isolated soldiers. _____ artillery swamped the UN positions with barrages comparable with those of the Second World War. _____ tanks, hull-down in sandbagged entrenchments, replied with round after round of high explosive. Peace talks began at Kaesong in 1951 and then moved to Panmunjom. For two years the _____ from the two sides talked and as they talked the _____ went on.*

1. On map 1
   (a) Indicate the 38th Parallel.
   (b) Mark Pusan, Seoul and Inchon.
   (c) Draw arrows to show the North Korean advance to Pusan.
   (d) Mark the landings at Inchon and the advance to Chosan on the Yalu River.
2. On Map 2
   (a) Shade the two staging areas secretly occupied by the Chinese 13th Army Group.
   (b) Shade in the area *not* occupied by the Chinese in 1951.
   (c) Label the Main Line of Resistance.
   (d) Label the North Korean capital of Pyongyang.

In May 1953 the Chinese launched their biggest attack in the Main Line of Resistance, on the hill known as the Hook. They were repelled. In the same month America exploded a hydrogen bomb (test firing). Stalin had died on 5 March 1953 and Dwight D. Eisenhower, the former Supreme Commander of the Allied invasion of Europe (1944), was the US President and said that his priority was peace in Korea.

Which of these events do you think most influenced the Chinese to agree to an armistice?

They did agree on 27 June 1953, and the fighting ended with the Chinese and UN troops dug in roughly along the line of the 38th Parallel. Well over thirty years later, that armistice was in force – the longest in recent history.

Significance

The War in Korea was the first in which the UN had taken sides. Yet the UN had prevented the expansion of communism.

5 INTERNATIONAL CRISES AFTER KOREA

Although the UN acted as a forum for the settlement of international disputes, it did not represent the entire world during the period known as the 'First Cold War':

e.g. People's Republic of China voted in 1971; East and West Germany voted in 1973; divided Vietnam couldn't join until the North Vietnamese Army reunified the country in 1975.

Consequently, the UN tried to intervene in those 'trouble spots' where the superpowers were not directly committed, e.g. the Middle East, Africa and the Indian sub-continent. After the Anglo-French-Israeli attack on Suez (1956) the UN formed its own Emergency Force (UNEF) and UN troops served in Kashmir, Sinai, the Congo, Cyprus, the Golan Heights and the Lebanon. But there was no UN involvement in the two most dangerous international crises of the Sixties – Berlin (1961) and Cuba (1962).

Nikita Khrushchev

He emerged as the leading Soviet figure after the death of Stalin in 1953. His policies, reactions against America's attempt to 'contain' communism, twice led the world to the brink of nuclear war.

Note that his tactics were quite different from those of Stalin. He called Berlin 'the bone that stuck in the gullet of communism' and he was very worried by the thousands of East Germans who were escaping to the West via the western sectors in Berlin. This was the root cause behind the Berlin crisis of 1958–61.

THE BERLIN CRISIS, 1958–61

- The Khrushchev threat: he told the West to quit Berlin within six months; otherwise he would sign a peace treaty with the East Germans.
- He visited Eisenhower at Camp David (1959) and promised to attend a summit meeting the following year in Paris.
- He arrived in Paris but announced that Soviet gunners had shot down an American U-2 spy plane and captured the pilot Gary Powers.

Note what Khrushchev did then: he accused the Americans of treachery and unreliability, and stated that there was no point in discussing Berlin.

Significance

Khrushchev now had no need to come to a compromise over the allied sectors in Berlin. Tension grew and did not lessen when the new US President, John F. Kennedy, met Khrushchev in Vienna (June 1961). The young President was aware that his own international status was low since the affair of the Bay of Pigs (see page 168) and took Russian threats (that there would soon be a peace treaty with East Germany) quite seriously. Kennedy thought that war was imminent. So did many Americans – 'nuclear-bomb-proof shelters' achieved record sales in the USA!

However, Khrushchev had overplayed his hand. The Americans expected war; so did the East Germans, thousands of whom fled their homeland into the West via Berlin.

13 August 1961 Ulbricht (East German leader) sealed off East Berlin with the 'Berlin Wall'.

Kennedy accepted it as the price of preventing

> *'a spark from setting off . . . World War III'.*

THE CUBAN MISSILE CRISIS, 1962

The Cuban missile crisis of 1962 was the first nuclear crisis in world history and one in which the firm line of President Kennedy forced the Russians to withdraw, defeated. This is one aspect of its importance. The second is that the Russians were determined that the Americans would never do that to them again.

THE BACKGROUND TO THE CRISIS

- America acquired commercial control of Cuba after the 1898 Spanish-American War (when she also won Guam, the Philippines and Puerto Rico) and stationed her marines permanently at Guantanamo base. Any Cuban government supporting US interests secured US support; and America traditionally bought most of the island's main export – sugar.
- 1952–8: President Batista governed Cuba, salting away a great deal of dollar aid into his own bank account and ruling the island with terror tactics. Fidel Castro's guerrilla movement overthrew Batista in 1959. Castro infuriated the Americans by confiscating many US-owned plantations. When he asked for dollar aid neither the USA nor the International Monetary Fund would lend him money.
- This was why Castro approached the Soviet Union for help; why he nationalised the rest of the US-owned investments in Cuba.
- It was also the reason why President Eisenhower planned an invasion of Cuba to overthrow Castro.

Such was the situation at the end of 1960 when Kennedy inherited the problem.

- Kennedy authorised the invasion of Cuba (April 1961).
- US-supported Cubans attacked – completely defeated. This was the fiasco known as 'the Bay of Pigs'.
- Soviet freighters now arrived in Cuba and unloaded huge, mysterious crates.
- 16 October 1962: McGeorge Bundy told the President:

> *'Mr President, there is now hard photographic evidence that the Russians have offensive missiles in Cuba!'*

Kennedy's quandary was that he was uncertain what the Soviet move meant. He decided to throw a 'quarantine' around Cuba to prevent the Russians shipping in more missiles; and then to launch a full-scale invasion of Cuba if Khrushchev refused to withdraw the ones already installed.

Khrushchev's reaction:

> *Your rockets are in Turkey. You are worried by Cuba. You say that it worries you because it is ninety miles from the American coast. But Turkey is next to us!*

Kennedy's answer:

> *It shall be the policy of this nation to regard any nuclear missile launched from Cuba against any nation in the western hemisphere as an attack by the Soviet Union on the United States, requiring a full retaliatory response upon the Soviet Union . . . let no one doubt that this is a difficult and dangerous effort on which we have set out. No one can see precisely what course it will take or what cost or what casualties will be incurred . . .*

Meanwhile, about twenty-five Russian ships were strung out across the Atlantic, all heading for Cuba.

Kennedy offered Khrushchev a way out:

> *I call upon Chairman Khrushchev to halt and eliminate this clandestine, reckless and provocative threat to world peace and to stabilise relations betweeen our two nations. I call upon him further to abandon this course of world domination and to join in an historic effort to end the perilous arms race and transform the history of man. He has the opportunity now to move the world back from the abyss of destruction.*

The first Soviet ship to reach the US quarantine was a tanker and Kennedy ordered the US warships to let it through. Petrol wasn't on the list of embargoed goods!

This was when Khrushchev lost his nerve. The other Soviet ships turned back and the Russian leader agreed to move the rockets and Soviet warplanes from Cuba.

Results

◊ By 19 November 1962 the Russians had removed their offensive weapons from Cuba and the missile sites had been ploughed up.

◊ As one Soviet diplomat said, 'Cuba was a very painful experience for the Russian people. It is the last time the US will be able to do that to the Soviet Union.'

◊ After 1962 the USSR set out to build a huge conventional navy and to seek bases all over the world; while at the same time developing a Strategic Rocket Force backed up by strategic bombers and ballistic submarines.

◊ Cuba 1962 may have ushered in a long period of truce between the superpowers; it also began an unprecedented arms race using the most sophisticated technology – an operation that would drain the resources of both the superpowers.

◊ On the map (page 170):
   (*a*)   Circle the numbers 1 to 9 to indicate the missile bases.

History 1: World History since 1914

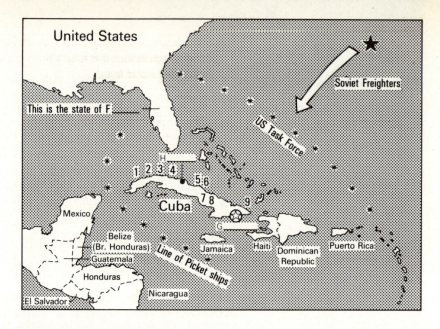

The 1962 Cuban missile crisis

(b) Label the US marine base at Guantanamo.
(c) Label the capital of Cuba.
(d) Insert the name of the nearest American land.

6 PEACEFUL CO-EXISTENCE, 1963–1979

Both the superpowers wanted to avoid a repetition of the near-catastrophe of 1962 and in April 1963 they agreed to set up the famous 'hot line' – a direct telephone link between the Kremlin and the White House.

August 1963: They signed (with Britain) the Partial Test Ban Treaty.

1968: The three powers signed the Nuclear Non-Proliferation Treaty.

The Russians said that this 'marked a shift from the Cold War to a reduction in international tension'. This 'reduction in tension' between the superpowers became known as 'détente'. Khrushchev fell from power (1964) to be replaced by Leonid Brezhnev (First Secretary of the Communist Party) and Alexei Kosygin (Soviet Premier). From now on the policies of the Soviet Union underwent subtle change.

◊ She did not want to end the arms race or limit in any way her status as a superpower.

The UN, alliances and arms talks

- She began to intervene in areas where the US and Britian exercised minimum influence.
- She gave aid to peoples seeking their own independence and freedom from western domination.
- One example: when India and Pakistan failed to solve their problems over Kahmir, Kosygin offered himself as a mediator and provided a conference venue at Tashkent (page 199).
- And over Vietnam: Kosygin said he would send all the help he could to Ho Chi Minh: 'The US cannot defeat Vietnam. We, for our part, will do all we can so that the US does not defeat Vietnam.'
- So it became possible, between 1963 and 1979, for the superpowers to create their own 'spheres of influence' in which they could expect to meet plenty of criticism and clandestine aid from their opposite number but no direct confrontation.

Gradually, the tensions of the Cold War receded and it is usual to date the beginning of détente from the signing of a Franco-German declaration (Moscow 1966) when both countries called on all European states to settle their differences irrespective of the political beliefs.

- This was not an easy task. It became especially difficult when the Soviet Union sent in tanks to crush the liberally minded Dubcek government (Czechoslovakia 1968).
- Great progress made under the leadership of Willy Brandt (Chancellor of the Federal Republic of Germany 1969) with his 'new eastern policy' or Ostpolitik. He accepted the Oder-Neisse line as the frontier between East Germany and Poland – and this led to the 1972 Basic Treaty recognising 'a new quality of political understanding . . . on both sides'.

SALT 1, 1972

1971: Sea-bed Treaty banned the siting of nuclear weapons on the sea-bed.

In the same year the superpowers converted the 'hot line' into a sophisticated satellite communications system.

1972: The first Strategic Arms Limitation Treaty (SALT 1) comprised two agreements:

- Treaty on the Limitation of Defence Anti-Ballistic Missiles.
- Interim Agreement on Certain Measures with respect to the Limitation of Strategic Arms (designed to last to 1977).

Permitted:

- Soviet Union to have 1618 land-based missile carriers.
- Americans to have 1008.

Brezhnev visited Washington in 1973. Over television he told the American people: 'Mankind has outgrown the rigid armour of the Cold War.'

THE 1975 HELSINKI CONFERENCE

In 1974 President Ford of the USA visited Brezhnev in Vladivostok and agreed to hold a Conference on Security and Co-operation in Europe. This conference met in Helsinki in 1975. The Conference made many recommendations and its famous 'Final Act' (1975) stressed that:

> Nations should respect all basic human freedoms; there should be no discrimination on grounds of race, sex, religion or language.
> Europe's existing frontiers are the legal frontiers.

Such was the level of goodwill in 1975. Unfortunately, détente was only too easy to damage and even destroy.

Document 1

Source: BBC TV booklet, *History 1917–67*.

Document 2

The UN, alliances and arms talks

Document 3

Source: BBC TV booklet, *History, 1917–67*.

Document 4

The Soviets argue that success in war goes to the side with the biggest resources at its disposal. In the event of war, the USSR had to be able to survive the first nuclear strikes and then retaliate with her own missiles against the West. Their numerical superiority in ICBMs convinced the Russians that they had deterred the Americans from making a pre-emptive strike on the USSR; while their twenty divisions (450,000 men) and 8,000 tanks in East Germany had prevented a 'conventional' war.
British textbook.

Document 5

The Americans argue that they have sought to contain communism ever since the proclamation of the Truman Doctrine. They ringed the USSR with allies who either adopted US policies or allowed US bases on their soil. As there have been nineteen divisions (350,000 men) stationed in Western Europe since the 1950s, peace has existed there if nowhere else in our violent world. A graduated (sometimes the word 'flexible' is used) nuclear deterrent would back up these forces to contain superior numbers to Soviet tanks should they advance across the river systems of Western Europe. The ultimate deterrent – Polaris Submarine Launched Ballistic Missiles and Minutemen ICBMs – was the last resort, designed to counter a Soviet strike in the West.
British textbook.

1   In Document 1, what does the photo depict?

2 When was this constructed?
3 Why did President Kennedy consider it to be a device to prevent 'a spark from setting off . . . World War III'?
4 Name the Russian leader depicted in Document 2.
5 Why and for what reason did he fall from power?
6 Name the Soviet leader who succeeded him.
7 What does Document 3 depict?
8 What cargo is it carrying?
9 What was its original destination?
10 In Document 4, explain the meaning of ICBMs.
11 Explain the term 'pre-emptive strike'.
12 Why do the Russians believe they had prevented a 'conventional' war from breaking out in Europe?
13 Does Document 5 provide evidence that the Americans are equally confident that their policies have guaranteed peace in Europe?
14 Name one ally in Europe that has provided bases for the USA.
15 Have such bases ever been used for offensive action against a hostile nation?
16 Explain the phrase 'a graduated nuclear deterrent'.

SALT 2

When Jimmy Carter became US President in 1976 he made the renewal of SALT 1 conditional on Russia's granting human rights to oppressed peoples. His move startled the Russians.

Multiple-choice questions

1 The Russians rounded on President Carter and accused him of undermining SALT by manufacturing
☐ A stealth bomber
☐ Chemical weapons
☐ The neutron bomb
☐ The Star Wars system

2 Eventually Carter met Brezhnev to sign SALT 2 in
☐ Berlin
☐ Vienna
☐ Ottawa
☐ Vladivostock

3 This event took place in
☐ 1976
☐ 1977
☐ 1978
☐ 1979

4 The treaty defined the weapons the two superpowers would have up to
☐ 1981
☐ 1982
☐ 1985
☐ 1986

The UN, alliances and arms talks

Then, in 1979, two events occurred that, between them, seemed to undermine and almost destroy the years of effort that had gone into the creation of détente. These events heralded the 'Second Cold War'.

The NATO decision, 12 December 1979
Western scientists detected the arrival of the SS-20 as the latest weapon in the Soviet armoury. It was an ICBM capable of carrying three nuclear warheads over a range of 1,700 miles (2,736 km). 200 SS-20s were targeted on Western Europe by 1979. The NATO governments agreed that it was time to update their own short-range weapons. They therefore asked the US government to station Pershing IIs and Tomahawk Cruise missiles in five West European countries.

1 Who was the Soviet leader at that time?
2 Who was the US President at that time?

The Soviet invasion of Afghanistan, 24 December 1979
Russia invaded Afghanistan to save the communist Afghan government from total defeat at the hands of the Muslim resistance movement – the Mujahideen. The Russians killed the Afghan President and appointed Babrak Kamal his successor. Babrak Kamal then asked the Russians for aid under the 1978 Soviet-Afghan Treaty of Friendship.

		YES	NO
1	Was Afghanistan a Soviet satellite in the sense that East Germany and Hungary are Soviet satellites?	☐	☐
2	Was the invasion of Afghanistan the first deliberate act of aggression by Soviet armed forces since 1945?	☐	☐
3	Some people tried to justify the invasion on the basis that it was a variation of the Brezhnev Doctrine (promulgated in 1968). But this related to the defence of Eastern bloc unity – so was it fair to quote the Brezhnev Doctrine in connection with the invasion of Afghanistan?	☐	☐

President Carter endorsed the decision by Congress *not* to ratify the 1979 SALT 2 Treaty. He also boycotted the 1980 Moscow Olympics and banned the sale of 'high-technology goods' and desperately needed grain to the Soviet Union.

7 THE SUPERPOWERS AFTER 1979

The ill-health of Soviet leaders made further discussions difficult and for a time the new missile sites became the target for western European supporters of unilateral nuclear disarmament:

Brezhnev died in 1982

Andropov died in 1984
Chernenko died in 1985

START talks (i.e. Strategic Arms Limitation Talks) began in 1981, stalled over the imposition of martial law in Poland the same year and resumed in 1983. The new Soviet leader, Mikhail Gorbachev, met President Reagan in Geneva (1985). The Russian said, 'the world has become a safer place'; the US leader spoke of a fresh start to US-Soviet relations, despite the disagreements over the proposed US Strategic Defence Initiative (SDI) – better known as 'Star Wars'. To try to reduce the nuclear armouries held by the two superpowers, Gorbachev and Reagan held a 'mini-summit' in Reykjavik, Iceland (October 1986).

Source: *The Times*, 30 December 1985.

1. Name the leader on the left.
2. Name the leader on the right.
3. The cartoon was drawn in 1985 – what do you think the artist is trying to say?

8 COMECON AND THE EEC

Stalin secured economic control over his East European satellites through the Council for Mutual Economic Assistance, known either as COMECON or the CMEA. This occurred in 1949, when political control was all important. Since then COMECON has developed into a huge agency responsible for co-ordinating all of Eastern Europe's trade, much of which is now with Western Europe. COMECON has survived political crises such as the 1956 Hungarian Uprising (crushed by Russian tanks) and the 1968 Soviet invasion of Czechoslovakia.

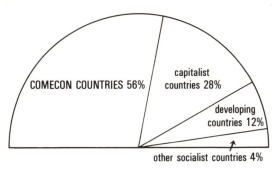

Soviet trade c.1980.

The pie-graph shows the importance of COMECON to the Soviet Union.
1   With what group of countries does the Soviet Union carry out most of its trade?
2   What is the total percentage of trade with capitalist countries and developing countries?
    COMECON countries enjoy many benefits from their trade with the Soviet Union, e.g.

◊   Cheap oil via the Friendship pipeline.
◊   Cheap electricity from the MIR grid.

Western Europe's economic community developed rather more slowly. During 1948 the US Secretary of State, George Marshall, begun funnelling dollar aid to the OEEC (Organisation for European Economic Co-operation) formed to oversee the rebuilding of Europe's trade and industry.

◊   March 1984: Belgium, Netherlands and Luxembourg formed their economic union – Benelux.
◊   1951: France, West Germany, Italy and the Benelux countries formed the European Coal and Steel Community (ECSC).
◊   1957: They signed the Treaty of Rome and created the EEC (European Economic Community) generally called the Common Market. This was a free trade area:
    (a)   it levied taxes on imports coming from outside the community;
    (b)   it then redistributed much of this revenue to subsidise CAP – the Common Agricultural Policy. This enabled the EEC to sell its surpluses on the world market often lower than market prices, which was beneficial to those countries that produced their own food.
◊   The Six rapidly became Twelve:
        1973: Britain, Ireland and Denmark joined.
        1981: Greece joined.
        1986: Portugal and Spain joined.

(For further details, see History 2, Section II, *British and European History since 1789*).

CHAPTER EIGHT

INDEPENDENCE IN AFRICA, ASIA AND THE CARIBBEAN

CONTENTS

- **Africa** — 181
- **Asia** — 195
- **The Caribbean** — 204

Independence in Africa, Asia and the Caribbean

1 AFRICA

THE PRE-COLONIAL EXPERIENCE

Until about 1880 the European powers had spent 300 years nibbling at the map of Africa. Remember that, although they had removed millions of Africans to slavery on the other side of the world, the actual amount of African territory under their control was relatively slight. In 1880 over eighty per cent of African territory was under African control. African kings, queens, clan chiefs and lineage heads ruled their own people, operating a range of political systems as varied as anywhere else in the world.

The location of European rule, c. 1880

South of the Sahara, the only strong European presence was in Cape Colony, Natal, the Orange Free State and the South African Republic (the Transvaal). None of East Africa was ruled by whites. Of all the European countries, France had made the greatest number of conquests:

- ◊ North Africa (essentially an agricultural region) provided French people with the chance of setting up their own estates. Morocco, Tunisia and Algeria also represented a source of cheap immigrant labour and cheap raw materials, e.g. iron ore and phosphates. Algeria had a special status: it was an integral part of France and French people settling there were known as *les colons*.
- ◊ In West Africa, France explored the coastal and river regions and then began a series of trans-Saharan expeditions so that she acquired eight distinct colonies: Mauritania, Senegal, French Soudan, French Guinea, Upper Volta, Ivory Coast, Dahomey and Niger. There was no local government, no 'indirect rule' on the British model. French policy rendered Africans into sources of cheap *primary* products (cotton, timber, oil) and markets for cheap French *industrial* products.
- ◊ Britain was well established in four sections of the West African coast: The Gambia, Sierra Leone, Gold Coast and Lagos. When these blossomed into four colonies (the Gambia, Sierra Leone, Gold Coast and Nigeria) they absorbed about twenty per cent of West Africa and became the greatest source of mineral wealth in the region.
- ◊ Portugal possessed remarkably little. This might come as a surprise. After all, Portugal was the first European power in Africa. In fact, Portuguese rule ran rather shakily along the coastal stretches of

Angola and Mozambique, plus a tiny section of the West African coast.

Africa's pre-colonial weakness

Africa's fundamental weakness at this critical stage in her history was over-confidence. Why was this so? After all, this was the most crucial point in her history.

▷ Perhaps Africa believed that she had already made sufficient adjustment to the presence of European soldiers, traders and missionaries. In the past, many African rulers had based their wealth on the export slave trade. Now they had made a dramatic change to export cash crops, but they refused to let Europeans take over their plantations and palm oil projects. They did not give way when Europeans arrived with more and more soldiers. After all, they had been dealing with Europeans for over 300 years. They had stockpiles of muskets and plenty of ammunition.

▷ This was the flaw in Africa's history. The African leaders in the nineteenth century simply did not understand the immense technological advances made by the European powers – the new 'imperialists'. As the satirical British poet, Hilaire Belloc, wrote:

> *Whatever happens we have got*
> *The maxim-gun and they have not.*

CONDITIONS IN THE TWENTIES AND THIRTIES

The administrator who had the most influence on government in British Africa was Lord Lugard (1858–1945). He had developed the system of *indirect rule* in Northern Nigeria after 1900 and had come to believe that a colonial power had a double responsibility when running the lives of millions of African people.

(a)   responsibility for guiding the people
(b)   towards ultimate self-government; responsibility for developing the colony's resources, human as well as material.

Lugard published his definitive work, *Dual Mandate in British Tropical Africa*, in 1922 and this book had a great deal of influence on British governors up to 1939. Unfortunately, Africa in common with the rest of the world was hit by the social and economic problems following on after the First World War, e.g.

(a)   epidemics
(b)   heavy taxation
(c)   declining trade.

A Nigerian might dearly want to participate in self-government and move his country towards independence. But he would find it hard to do this through the agencies set up by the British government. If he lived in Lagos he had to have an income of £100 a year to qualify for the vote. Only a few – the African elite – could afford this. Entrepreneurs (businessmen) found it hard to compete in the world where

Independence in Africa, Asia and the Caribbean

cash crops such as cocoa depended entirely on the willingness of big European firms such as Rowntree's or Cadbury's to pay a reasonable price.

Generally speaking, African colonies depended almost entirely on the aid that their governors could scrounge from mother countries – and in the years of the depression, inevitably, that wasn't very much.

Although Britain did give to Egyptian nationalists their own independent nation state in 1922 (on condition that Britain could keep her armed forces there – limited in 1936 to the Canal Zone), this was not characteristic of Africa.

▷ When the new colony of Rhodesia came into being the political hopes of the Shona and Matabele peoples were ignored and all power passed to the 33,000 white settlers.

▷ The British stated that in East Africa (Kenya, Uganda and Tanganyika) 'the interests of the African natives must be paramount and that if and when these interests and the interests of the immigrant races (i.e. the whites) should conflict, the former should prevail.'

But the British simply could not afford to provide education, health and welfare services on the scale that was needed by the African peoples. There simply was insufficient aid for long-term projects in British East Africa.

AFRICAN COLONIES DURING THE SECOND WORLD WAR

It is hard to overestimate the importance of these colonies to the British war effort. In terms of raw materials, West Africa responded magnificently to demands for rubber, bauxite, manganese and tin. During 1939–45 the famous Royal West African Frontier Force (RWAFF) expanded to over 176,000 men. Nigeria mobilised fifteen battalions and, with other units from Sierra Leone, the Gambia and Gold Coast, saw action in the Middle East, in Africa and in the Far East. The RWAFF's greatest campaign was in Burma from 1943 to 1945, fighting in the Arakan – some of the toughest territory in the world. Nigeria's crack battalions served with the famous Chindits. Altogether, the RWAFF provided 'the largest colonial army in the history of the British Empire ever to serve as an expeditionary force.'*

*F. M. Bouret, *Ghana*, OUP, 1960, p. 145

Multiple-choice questions

1 The French colonial empire in Africa included all but one of the following:
- ☐ Mauritania
- ☐ Senegal
- ☐ Ivory Coast
- ☐ Dahomey
- ☐ Angola

2 The British administrator who developed the system of indirect rule in West Africa was:
- ☐ Lord Baden Powell

- [ ] Lord Lucan
- [ ] Lord Kitchener
- [ ] Lord Lugard

2 Lagos formed the nucleus of the colony of
- [ ] The Gambia
- [ ] Sierra Leone
- [ ] Nigeria
- [ ] The Gold Coast

3 British East Africa included three of the following
- [ ] Rhodesia
- [ ] Transvaal
- [ ] Kenya
- [ ] Uganda
- [ ] Tanganyika

5 Tanganyika had formerly belonged to
- [ ] Spain
- [ ] Germany
- [ ] Italy
- [ ] France
- [ ] Portugal

6 The campaigns for which the RWAFF were the most famous in the Second World War were in
- [ ] India
- [ ] Vietnam
- [ ] Burma
- [ ] Germany

African feelings after the war

The African experience of travelling abroad, serving with white men and learning scores of new skills had distinct political effects. These are summed up admirably in a famous story told by the African nationalist leader, Ndabaningi Sithole:

> A British recruiting officer was trying to persuade Africans to join the army in the war against Hitler. 'But what's wrong with Hitler?' asked one African. The British officer chose his words carefully, hoping to pick ones the African would easily understand. He said, 'Hitler wants to rule the world.' 'What's wrong with that?' said the African. 'He is a German,' said the officer, 'and it isn't good for one tribe to rule another. Each tribe should rule itself. A German must rule Germans, an Italian, Italians, and a Frenchman, French people – that's only fair.'

Africans took the hint and realised that the Second World War marked the end of the myth of white supremacy and the beginning of the end of the colonial rule.

On the map of Africa:
1 Shade in the colonies belonging to France (1945). The British Empire in Africa is already shaded in.

Independence in Africa, Asia and the Caribbean

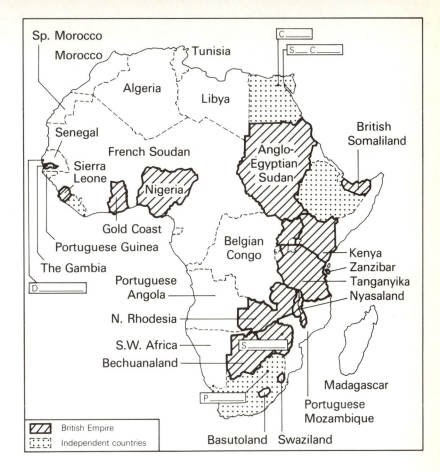

Africa in 1945

2 Note that in 1945 there were only four independent countries in Africa (they are dot shaded). Name these.
3 Within the Union of South Africa, mark the capital, Pretoria.
4 Label:
   (a) the Suez Canal
   (b) Dakar
   (c) Cairo
   (d) Salisbury
5 By what name is Salisbury known today?
6 For a period in the Second World War, one of the three independent states lost its independence. Which one was this?
7 Name its ruler in 1945.

INDEPENDENCE FOR THE FRENCH COLONIES

Even before the end of the Second World War, General de Gaulle had visited Brazzaville (1944) and there assured West African leaders that they would have representative government and economic aid once the war against Germany had been won. But de Gaulle was not the French leader *after* the war – he had to wait until 1958 before he became the leader of the French Fifth Republic. Meanwhile, the French Fourth Republic had to contend with many problems in the colonies. It gave Tunisia and Morocco (both strongly nationalist and Muslim) their independence in 1956. Sandwiched between them was Algeria. One million French *colons* lived there and enjoyed almost total political and economic power over seventeen million Algerian Muslims. The *colons* had no intention of granting independence to a part of France!

Now read this extract from a British textbook:

*See p. 279

> *Algerian nationalists thought differently and their FLN (National Liberation Front) began attacking French targets on 1 November 1954. The armed services of France, barely recovered from the hammering they had taken in Indo-China,* deployed* Les Paras, *the French Foreign Legion and the French Air Force to crush this nationalist uprising (1954–5). But the FLN survived and the fighting in Algeria continued. General Massu's 10th Parachute Division then moved in and used the most brutal methods imaginable to extract information from FLN suspects. The para units gradually came round to the view that the French Fourth Republic was losing interest in keeping 'Algérie Française'. That was why the Commander in Chief, Algeria, General Salan, threatened to invade France unless a new government was forthcoming and willing to help its people in Algeria. This threat helped to bring down the French Fourth Republic and in 1958 General de Gaulle formed a new government. But he wasn't prepared to commit himself to Algérie Française. In fact, he had no wish to retain the French Empire in the face of growing African nationalism.*

1. What had been General de Gaulle's role during the Second World War?
2. When had the French Third Republic collapsed?
3. When was the French Fourth Republic formed?
4. Why didn't Algeria get its independence at the same time as Morocco and Tunisia?
5. How many French *colons* lived in Algeria.
6. What does the expression Algérie Française mean?
7. What do the initials FLN mean?
8. When did the FLN begin its revolt against the French?
9. French West Africa began securing its independence as soon as de Gaulle came to power. Give the dates on which the following won their independence:

   Guinea _____   Senegal _____
   Ivory Coast _____   Mauritania _____
   Mali _____   Niger _____
   Chad _____   Volta _____

Independence in Africa, Asia and the Caribbean

10 Many French people now wanted to cut the links with Algeria. In desperation the army and the *colons* formed a secret organisation called the OAS. What does this expression mean?

Terrible fighting resulted. Altogether, about 17,000 French soldiers, 3,000 *colons* and over one million Algerian Muslims were killed in the bloodbath that preceded Algerian independence.

Results

▷ The Evian Agreement gave Algeria total independence in 1962.
▷ 1962–3: most *colons* left Algeria.
▷ Ben Bella became the first President of Algeria in 1963.
▷ In the same year his government confiscated all agricultural land held by foreigners.

THE BRITISH COLONIES WIN THEIR INDEPENDENCE

British colonies won their independence between 1957 (Ghana) and 1980 (Zimbabwe). By then there was universal black majority rule throughout Africa except in the Republic of South Africa and in its former League of Nations mandate, South-West Africa (Namibia).

Black people from many parts of the world met in Manchester to hold their 1945 Pan African Conference. Kwame Nkrumah and Jomo Kenyatta were both there and helped pass a famous resolution that 'The peoples of the colonies have the right to elect their own governments ... colonial and subject peoples of the world, unite!' When Nkrumah returned to the Gold Coast he formed his own political party – the CPP Convention People's Party. He began campaigning for independence, and soon landed in jail! No African colony won its independence between 1945 and 1951 apart from Libya, which was created an independent sovereign state by the UN on Christmas Eve, 1951.

1 What was Ghana's name before it won independence?
2 What was Zimbabwe's name before it won independence?
3 Which colony did Jomo Kenyatta represent at Manchester?
4 Name Nkrumah's political party.
5 To which country had Libya formerly belonged?

Ghana

The CPP won thirty-four out of the thirty-eight seats in the 1951 Gold Coast elections. The British Governor, Sir Charles Arden-Clarke, therefore released Nkrumah from jail. At the 1956 election the CPP won an overwhelming victory and on 6 March 1957 Gold Coast became independent Ghana. On Independence Day its leader said, 'We have a duty to prove to the world that Africans can conduct their own affairs with efficency and tolerance and through the exercise of democracy. We must set an example to all Africa.'

Document 1

Source: BBC TV booklet, *History 1917–67*

1. This photograph shows the leader of Ghana in 1957. What was his name?
2. Why do you think he chose the name Ghana for his new country?
3. His rule came in for a great deal of criticism. Look back to remind yourself of his words on Independence Day. Do you think he lived up to his promises?

Document 2
See opposite.

4. Document 2 is a monument to the fate of so many African leaders. Nkrumah fell from power in 1966.
5. To which country did he flee?
   Document 2 is reminiscent of many photos from Eastern Europe. Had the scene been Budapest (Hungary) 1956, whose statue would have been overturned?
6. The flag of Ghana consists of three horizontal stripes (red, yellow, green) with a star in the centre. What colour is the star?

Nigeria
Nigeria had three major political parties and was huge in size. It was unlikely that independence could come as quickly as it did to Ghana. Fortunately, Dr Azikwe, destined to become governor (1961) and first president of the Republic of Nigeria (1963), sought to make haste slowly: 'Self-government in our lifetime.'

Independence in Africa, Asia and the Caribbean

Document 2

Source: BBC TV booklet, *History 1917–67*

In 1956 Queen Elizabeth II visited Nigeria: 'They know what they want: they are pushing ahead with education and schools are multiplying.'

All of Nigeria's political parties met at Lancaster House (1957) and agreed that Nigeria should be a federation. This meant there would be a Federal Prime Minister and Abubakar Tafawa Balewa formed a coalition government.

In 1958 the Nigerian armed forces came under Federal control and in 1959 the new Nigerian currency was created. In 1960 Nigeria became the independent Federation of Nigeria; in 1963 it became a republic and stayed within the Commonwealth.

The Times commented (1 October 1960) that 'rarely, if ever, can the end of empire have been announced with so much dignity and good will.'

Sadly, it was not long before simmering ethnic hostility surfaced in the terrible Nigerian Civil War 1967–70.

The Civil War, 1967–70

Most people disagreed with the federal organisation (the country had been divided into four regions), e.g. during 1966 there had been bitter clashes between the Ibo and Hausa. Eventually, the oil-rich eastern region, home of the Ibo, decided to form a 'break-away' state under the leadership of General Ojukwa. From Kaduna and Lagos, federal troops attacked the new state of 'Biafra' and by the end of the year they had captured Enugu – Biafra's capital. Then the rebels fell back to Umuahia and held on to this for a year.

General Obasanjo took command of the federal offensive and split the rebels in two, forcing Ojukwa to surrender on 12 January 1970.

The rebellion was over. The federal government announced that it would now 'assert the ability of the Black man to build a strong, progressive and prosperous nation.'

British East Africa

Constitutional arguments raged in East Africa as to the type of government the colonies should have on independence. But these arguments became insignificant with the outbreak of the Mau Mau rebellion in Kenya (1951).

Mau Mau insurgents always called themselves the 'Land and Freedom Armies'. In 1952 they began a systematic campaign against the white settlers and set fire to buildings and slaughtered cattle. The Nairobi government arrested Jomo Kenyatta, leader of the Kenya African Union (KAU), suspected of being in charge of Mau Mau policies. There was no widespread killing of whites – the Mau Mau favoured arson and sabotage. The Mau Mau's major blunder was to kill a very respected Kikuyu chief and many Kikuyu in the Lari Massacre (1951).

Note the enormous firepower assembled by the British to wipe out Mau Mau:

(a) Numerous British infantry battalions.
(b) Royal Air Force heavy and medium bombers.
(c) The King's African Rifles (recruited mainly from Uganda, Tanganyika and Mauritius.

By 1956 the British had handed over the struggle to Kikuyu loyalists, by which time African political parties were allowed to function normally – polarising in KANU and KADU – the Kenya African National Union and the Kenya Democratic Union. Popular clamour led to Kenyatta's release (1961) and he became president of Kanua and, in 1962, Prime Minister of Kenya.

Note that the two parties merged in 1963 on the grant of independence and Jomo Kenyatta became president of a one-party African Republic in 1964.

Tanganyika became independent before Kenya – in 1961. Obviously, the British were not anxious to repeat the Mau Mau-type of experience elsewhere. Julius Nyerere, an Edinburgh University graduate, always argued that Tanganyika was a UN mandate and that the British should not block his country's independence. His well-organised TANU (Tanganyika African National Union) was overwhelmingly popular and Tanganyika became independent in 1961. The island of Zanzibar won its political freedom in 1963 and in 1964 united with Tanganyika to form a new nation – Tanzania.

Uganda became independent in 1962. Interestingly, the Ugandan people had kept most of their lands; the British administrators said it was best if Ugandan peasants kept control of their own production (unlike decisions made in Kenya and Tanganyika). The main conflict was between the kabaka (ruler) of Buganda and the British: the

Independence in Africa, Asia and the Caribbean

kabaka demanded independence for his own kingdom. This led to the formation of several political parties demanding varieties of independence. Eventually, Dr Milton Obote emerged as Prime Minister and led Uganda to independence on 9 October 1962.

Note how stormy Uganda's history was after independence:

- Major General Idi Amin overthrew Obote (1971).
- Amin driven from power by the Tanzanian invasion (1979).
- Obote restored to power (1980).
- Obote overthrown (1985).

These political upheavals were accompanied by unparalleled suffering for the Ugandan people.

Document 1

We have seen the awakening of national consciousness in peoples who have for centuries lived in dependence upon some other power. Fifteen years ago this movement spread through Asia. Many countries there of different races and civilisations pressed their claim to an independent life. Today, the same thing is happening in Africa and the most striking of all impressions I have formed since I left London a month ago is of the strength of this national consciousness. The wind of change is blowing through this continent, and, whether we like it or not, this growth of national consciousness is a political fact, and our national policies must take account of it.
(British Prime Minister)

Document 2

The three colonies of Nyasaland, Northern Rhodesia and Southern Rhodesia presented one of Britain's most difficult problems. In 1953 the British united them into the Federation of Rhodesia and Nyasaland. This infuriated six million Africans who had nine representatives in the new federal parliament – whereas the 200,000 white settlers had twenty-six! Dr Hastings Banda demanded an end to federation (1959) and free democratic elections in Nyasaland.
(British textbook)

Document 3

We can stand on our own feet and do not have to go round the world with a begging bowl in our hands – a truly rare bird among the post-war independent nations of the world.
(Ian Smith)

Document 4

Rhodesia today is a police state so far as black Africans are concerned. Arbitrary arrest, detention without trial and denial of ordinary political rights are the characteristics of their life.
(British Secretary of State, 1967)

Document 5

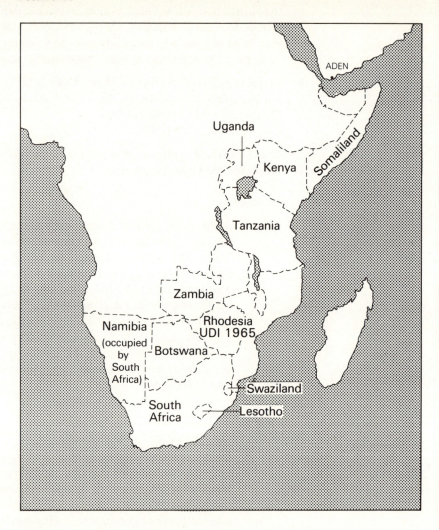

British colonies become independent (up to 1979)

1. Document 1 is an extract from the famous 'wind of change' speech. Name the British Prime Minister who uttered it in 1960.
2. To whom was he talking?
3. Was he in favour of African national independence?
4. Document 2 refers to the short-lived Central African Federation. Nyasaland became independent in 1963. What was the name of this new African state?
5. Northern Rhodesia became independent in 1964. By what name is it known today?
6. Document 3 refers to the illegal state of Rhodesia formed by Ian Smith via his Unilateral Declaration of Independence (UDI) in 1965. Who was Britain's Prime Minister at that time?

7 How did he react to Ian Smith's UDI?
8 Was his policy popular with the Africans?
9 He had two conversations with Ian Smith. They are called the *Tiger* and *Fearless* talks. Explain these terms.
10 Document 4 refers to a speech made by Secretary of State Thomas, a Labour Minister. Did he change the policies adopted by Britain towards Rhodesia?
11 On the map of Africa, shade in all the British colonies that had won independence by 1979.
12 Label Lusaka.

The creation of Zimbabwe

By 1979, when Commonwealth leaders met in Lusaka to discuss the Rhodesian problem, the affair had all the makings of a world crisis.

◊ Guerrilla groups had blossomed among the frustrated Africans, e.g. Robert Mugabe's ZAPU (Zimbabwe African People's Union); Joshua Nkomo's ZANU (Zimbabwe African National Union).
◊ Consequently there was a significant patriotic front formed by Africans against the illegal Smith regime. Its members went on battle courses in the Soviet Union and North Korea and came back well trained and with the latest weaponry. There was a danger that Cuban troops might be involved. South African troops had already been helping Smith since 1969.
◊ Commonwealth leaders put enormous pressure on Margaret Thatcher to resolve the problem and she agreed to do this during the Lusaka meeting.
◊ She arranged the Lancaster House talks between Lord Carrington and the Patriotic Front. ZANU and ZAPU agreed to stop fighting, come out of the bush and hold free elections supervised by British policemen and Commonwealth soldiers. It was a daunting task, superbly accomplished.
◊ Robert Mugabe formed a government in March 1980 and the next month Rhodesia became independent Zimbabwe. Why do you think the Africans wanted their new nation to have this name?

Independence for the Belgian Congo

Belgium was too small to cope with a colonial war and in 1960 she told her African peoples they could have instant independence! This meant that the Congolese were totally unprepared for the responsibilities of self-government.

◊ The Congolese soldiers mutinied against their white officers.
◊ White settlers fled – to become refugees, many of them in Katanga Province where they had to be rescued by Belgian paratroopers.
◊ Amidst the chaos, Moise Tshombe, Governor of Katanga, seceded from the Congo and declared his province an independent state. The Prime Minister of the Congo, Patrice Lumumba, asked both the UN and the Soviet Union for help.

- Russia sent transport aircraft to help ferry loyalist troops around the Congo; the UN airlifted 3,500 soldiers (drawn from Ghana, Ethiopia, Morocco, Tunisia and Sweden).
- The UN concentrated on defeating Tshombe and returning Katanga to the Congo. Secretary-General Dag Hammarskjöld flew out to arrange a cease-fire but died when his aircraft crashed at Ndola.
- By 1964 Tshombe was acting as Prime Minister of the Congo, bolstered up by Belgian paratroops and white mercenaries. The UN had withdrawn – almost in despair.
- Elections (1965) led to Tshombe's defeat. General Mobutu became President and renamed his country Zaire in 1971.

Independence for the Portuguese colonies

Portugal was the first European power to colonise African territory; it was also the last imperial power to leave Africa. The nationalist revolt against Portugal exploded in 1961, and the Portuguese decided to fight the different guerrilla groups (see the table below).

The anti-Portuguese guerrilla groups

Guinea	PAIGC: African Party for the Independence of Guinea and Cape Verde (1956)
Mozambique	FRELIMO: Mozambique Liberation Front (1962)
Angola	MPLA: Popular Front for the Liberation of Angola (1956) FNLA: National Front for the Liberation of Angola (1956 – split 1962) UNITA: United National Party for the Total Independence of Angola – founded by Jonas Savimbi in 1966

The Portuguese fought a war not dissimilar from the one fought by the Americans in Vietnam (see Chapter 9) and with similar results. All the firepower they could mobilise (helicopters, napalm, defoliants) could not defeat the Africans. In 1974 the Portuguese president, General Spinoza, decided to grant independence to the nationalists:

    1974: the PAIGC took over Guinea.
    1975: FRELIMO took over Mozambique.
    1975–6: MPLA formed the government of independent Angola.

SPECIAL POINTS TO NOTE IN THE STORY OF AFRICAN INDEPENDENCE

1. Apart from the special case of Zimbabwe (unresolved until 1980) the African peoples had managed to throw off colonial rule by the beginning of 1976.
2. It had not been a particularly peaceful affair.
3. The reason for this was that no white settler community was ready to give up its power without a fight.

Independence in Africa, Asia and the Caribbean

4 This had caused a very heavy price to be paid:
(a) The history of the French in Algeria and the Portuguese in their African colonies led to the deaths of literally millions of Africans.
(b) It often cost the colonial powers heavy casualties e.g. Portugal lost 11,000 young conscripts.

▷ Particularly significant was the fact that for the first time the Soviet Union had established a presence in Africa
(a) via military advisers and
(b) via 'proxy' soldiers – she arranged for Cuban troops to help the guerrillas in Angola.

When Russia made Treaties of Friendship with Somalia (1974), Angola (1976) and Mozambique (1977) it provoked Zambia's leader, Dr Kenneth Kaunda, to comment:

> '. . . a plundering tiger, with its deadly cubs, is now coming through the back door.'

It was a new development in African affairs and caused a great deal of concern to that already worried group of Afrikaner leaders in the Republic of South Africa (see Chapter 11).

2 ASIA

INDIA

Two nationalist movements existed in British-ruled India before 1914:
(a) The Indian National Congress (founded 1885 – the 'Congress Party').
(b) The Muslim League (opposing the Hindu National Congress) founded 1906.
After 1918 Jawaharlal Nehru (1889–1964) became the leader of Congress; Muhammad Ali Jinnah (1876–1948) became the leader of the Muslim League.

Striving to heal the differences between Muslim and Hindu was Mahatma (the Great Soul) Gandhi (1869–1948), the greatest Indian of them all.

Britain was anxious to move India towards dominion status (see inset) and had already agreed to integrate Indians into the process of government. But India was a huge sub-continent and frequently torn by riot and demonstrations (notably in the restless Punjab). Britain had passed the 1919 Rowlatt Acts (tough security measures) and Gandhi was beginning to counter these with 'hartal' (peaceful demonstrations to disrupt Indian economic life) when one of the most horrific acts in British colonial history occurred – the Amritsar Massacre.

THE DOMINIONS

Self-governing colonies (Canada, Australia, New Zealand and South Africa) were already called dominions. They had taken part in the 1919 Peace Conference and were members of the League of Nations. In 1923 Canada began making her own treaties with the USA; in 1924 the Irish Free State began sending its own ministers to foreign capitals.

The 1926 Imperial Committee (under Lord Balfour) came up with this definition of the Commonwealth of Nations

> Great Britain and the Dominions are autonomous communities within the British Empire, equal in status, in no way subordinate to one another in any aspect of their domestic or external affairs, though united by common allegiance to the Crown and freely associated as members of the British Commonwealth of Nations ... In the sphere of defence the major share of responsibility rests, and must for some time continue to rest, with HM Government in Great Britain.

This definition became part of the 1931 Statute of Westminster which, on face value, did not seem to transform the Commonwealth nations into a tightly knit power bloc. There was no 'Commonwealth Navy', no 'Commonwealth Customs Union', no 'Commonwealth Defence Plan'. People in Quebec agitated for an independent 'French Republic'; the South Africans hinted that they might remain neutral in any future European war.

So: it was understandable that foreign powers might have misjudged the hidden strength of the bonds that held the Commonwealth together.

The Amritsar Massacre, 13 April 1919
General Dyer ordered a party of Gurkhas to fire on a crowd that had gathered to demonstrate (in defiance of orders) in the Sikh holy city of Amritsar. Dyer's troops blocked the only exit so that 'peaceful dispersal' was impossible. Gunfire slaughtered 279 people and wounded over 1,200 others.

- ◊ It permanently damaged relations between Britain and India.
- ◊ Congress intensified its demand for Swaraj (independence) and Gandhi decided to begin his own programme of civil disobedience (satyagraha).

Independence in Africa, Asia and the Caribbean

▷ Gandhi's views seemed extraordinary in the 1920s. He said that the answer to famine and unemployment was self-help and supervised the distribution of two million spinning wheels to the peasantry. 'Independence', he said, 'is an attitude of mind'. He came to Britain in 1931 for the 'Round Table Conference' on India's future. He aroused a great deal of interest but won very little political support. He was, of course, a pacifist and was indignant that the British Viceroy in India should declare war on Germany (3 September 1939) on behalf of 400 million Indians!

India during the Second World War

In 1942, when Britain was reeling under savage Japanese attacks, the Congress Party began a 'Quit India' campaign. Churchill's response was to arrest Gandhi, Nehru and most of the prominent Congress leaders. There was intense civil disobedience all over the sub-continent – it ended when a very ill Gandhi was released in 1944. He then discovered that Jinnah was hoping for a separate Pakistan on independence and became very depressed.

Independence, 1947

> 'At the stroke of the midnight hour, when the world sleeps, India will wake to life and freedom . . . it is fitting at this solemn moment we take the pledge of dedication to the service of India and her people . . . We end today a period of ill-fortune and India discovers herself again.'
> (Nehru, 14 August 1947)

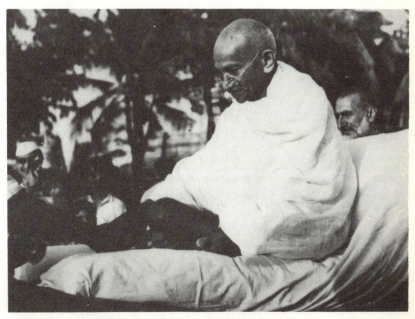

Source: BBC Radio *Man*. 1969/71

On 15 August 1947 India and Pakistan became independent and both remained members of the Commonwealth.

1. Gandhi had been sure that Churchill would never allow India to be partitioned. Name the Prime Minister who agreed to the partition.
2. Who was the Viceroy whose job was to oversee independence and partition?
3. Many fanatical Hindus could not understand Gandhi, could not understand a leader who could say:
'I am a Muslim, a Hindu, a Buddhist, a Christian, a Jew, a Parsi.'
Explain this statement.
4. Name the man who assassinated Mahatma Gandhi (30 January 1948).

MAHATMA GANDHI, 1869–1948

Married at thirteen, he studied law in Britain and practised in South Africa where (1893–1915) he first experienced open racial contempt and discrimination. He was in India after 1915 and demanded Swaraj (independence) from the British. He devised *satyagraha* (non-violent civil disobedience) in 1921; was arrested and jailed in 1922. He led the Dandi Salt March in 1930, another year of satyagraha. He attended the 1931 Round Table Conference in London, fasted on behalf of the harijans (untouchables) in 1932 and devised his rural constructive programme in 1934. He urged his followers to spin and weave cloth and thus become self-sufficient. In 1936 Gandhi went to live in his religious settlement at Sevagram and did not become prominent again until 1942, when he opened his 'Quit India' campaign. He was in jail from 1942 to 1944 and in all spent 2,089 days of his life in prison. During 1946–7 the Mahatma walked barefoot from place to place preaching brotherly love. He achieved the 'Miracle of Calcutta' in 1947 and then went to Delhi to restore harmony in the turbulent capital – 'Gandhi's noblest hour'. He was assassinated on 30 January 1948.

The sub-continent since independence

As well as a major law and order problem, both India and Pakistan had to contend with a breakdown in a previously stable agricultural economy.
Why? Because of:

- Food shortages.
- Masses of refugees.
- A creaking transport system.
- Overcrowding in towns and cities.

◊ No sound industrial base on which to build a new prosperity.
◊ Coincidentally, both countries were experiencing a population explosion.

Both countries had limited resources and both wasted them in three Indo-Pakistan wars. Fundamentally, these wars were fought over the division of the subcontinent. Initially, however, they concerned the ownership of Kashmir.

The Kashmir dispute (first Indo-Pakistan War, 1948)
About seventy-five per cent of Kashmiri were Muslim; their ruler was a Hindu Maharajah. It was rumoured that Muslims were maltreated by the Hindu minority and so Pakistan invaded Kashmir. India retaliated but the Pakistani government appealed to the world to allow Kashmiris the right of self-determination.

1. Why did they do this?
2. How did the UN react?
3. The UN cease-fire came into effect 1 January 1949. Is the UN Kashmir Observation Force still in existence?

The Second Indo-Pakistan War, 1965
India and Pakistan managed to settle their dispute over the control of the Indus waters quite peacefully (1960 Indus Waters Treaty). But both sides clashed in the salt marshes of the Rann of Kush (April–June 1965) though they agreed to a UN truce. Then patrols clashed in Kashmir and India launched a full-scale invasion. The UN arranged another truce; and then the Russians stepped in with the offer of Tashkent as the venue for a peace treaty. Within hours of signing the treaty, India's Prime Minister Shastri died of a heart attack and Mrs Indira Gandhi (daughter of Nehru and unrelated to the Mahatma) became India's first woman Prime Minister.

The Third Indo-Pakistan, War 1971
This arose from a civil war that flared in East Pakistan (March 1971). Why was there a civil war?

◊ There was nothing in common between East and West Pakistan apart from the fact they were both Muslim.
◊ There was no sense of national unity.
◊ They spoke different languages, had different customs and a different economy.
◊ There were three times as many East Pakistanis as there were West Pakistanis, yet the western wing had most of the political power and a much higher standard of living.

These factors explain why Sheikh Mujibur Rahman and his Awami League wanted a federal government for Pakistan. But President Ayub Khan arrested him! East Pakistan demanded a general election:

◊ Ayub Khan fell from power.
◊ Yahya Khan succeeded him.

- He held a general election and was appalled when the Awami League won a majority.
- He postponed parliament and sent troops into East Pakistan – that was when the fighting began. Thousands of East Pakistanis joined the guerrilla movement called Bangla Desh.
- Literally millions of East Pakistanis fled from the fighting – into India.
- At this stage Mrs Indira Gandhi decided to fight a war on two fronts, against both wings of Pakistan but in support of Bangladesh. The two sides were evenly matched on the ground but India had overwhelming air superiority.

The war was over swiftly – an Indian victory. Pakistan formally surrendered on 17 December 1971. She had lost the eastern wing, now the independent state of Bangladesh.

New leaders in Pakistan

Zulfiqar Al Bhutto had founded the PPP (Pakistan People's Party) in 1967. He replaced President Yahya Khan at the end of 1971 and withdrew Pakistan from the Commonwealth (1972). Bhutto took office as Prime Minister (1973–7) and began his programme of social reform: land redistribution, minimum wages, old-age pensions. He was much criticised by political rivals and the army. General Zia ul-Haq led a coup against Bhutto and accused him of many crimes. He executed Bhutto in 1979.

General Zia became president of Pakistan, determined to improve the security of his country and to rebuild his armed forces after their shattering defeats in the Third Indo-Pakistan War. Pakistan traditionally supported Western alliance systems (though she had left the South East Treaty Organisation in 1972). Moreover, her geographical location was now even more significant after the proclamation of the Islamic Republic of Iran (1979) and the Soviet invasion of Afghanistan. US President Reagan was particularly keen to update Pakistan's armoury; and it was natural for Mrs Indira Gandhi to assume that this was a new threat in the battered Indian sub-continent.

India's problems

India faced the problem of how to feed her expanding population and Indira Gandhi concentrated on improving agricultural output and reducing poverty. She flew to the USA to secure wheat and financial aid:

> *'Today democracy implies social welfare, equality of opportunity, reasonable living standards and the dignity of the individual. Man does not live by bread alone. But equally he needs bread to enjoy liberty.'*

Her reforms made headway and her scientists exploded a nuclear device at the Pokharan test centre (1974). She justified this on the grounds that India was a poor country and atomic power was the energy of the future. However, the years 1975–7 were critical –

Independence in Africa, Asia and the Caribbean

drought, starvation, inflation. She ruled by decree during the 'Emergency' and was voted out of office in 1977. She returned to power in 1980 and by now the people of India referred to her as 'Indira Raj' or as 'the Shekinah': the only person capable of leading India out of poverty and disorder. She never had the chance. Indira Gandhi was assassinated in 1984.

Source: BBC TV booklet *History 1917–67*

◊ Name the leader depicted in the photograph on page 200.
◊ What was his reaction when Bhutto's daughter returned to Pakistan in 1986?
◊ Name the leader shown in the photograph opposite.
◊ She was especially concerned for the future of the people of Assam. Why were they so rebellious during 1983?
◊ Why were many Indians worried by President Zia's plans to build a nuclear enrichment plant in 1979?

Independence for Burma

Burma became independent on 4 January 1948 and left the Commonwealth. A wealthy, literate country, self-sufficient in oil and with a rice surplus for export, Burma has been the classic example of a non-aligned country in the Asian world. The one exception involved the assassination of seventeen South Koreans at the Martyrs' Museum, Rangoon in 1983. Burma concluded that this was the work of North Korean terrorists and severed diplomatic relations with North Korea – the first time she had ever done this to another country.

1 What was the name of the distinguished Burmese who was UN Secretary-General from 1962–71?
2 Explain the term 'a non-aligned country'.
3 Name one other Asian country that claims to be this.

Independence for Ceylon

In 1947 Britain agreed to give Ceylon her independence – granted on 4 February 1948. Prime Minister Solomon Bandaranaike tried to adopt policies similar to those of Burma, but he was assassinated in 1959. His widow, Mrs Sirimavo Bandaranaike was twice Prime Minister from 1959 to 1965 and from 1970 to 1977. In 1972 Ceylon became a republic and took the name Sri Lanka – the Resplendent Island. her recent history has been marred by conflict between the native Sinhalese people and the immigrant Tamils, which reached a peak from 1983 to 1987. This is partly a culture conflict (Tamils speak a different language and worship a Hindu god) and partly an economic struggle – the Sinhalese fear that the forty million Tamils still in India might want to come to Sri Lanka.

Independence for Indonesia

For a time after 1945 the Dutch tried to hang on to their empire in the East Indies. But they faced an Indonesian resistance movement led by

Achmad Sukarno (1901–70). By 1949 the Dutch were ready to concede independence and Sukarno became the first president of Indonesia.

Independence for Malaysia
The Malayan Communist Party had formed the core of the resistance against the Japanese during the occupation (1942–5). They formed an Anti-Japanese Army, backed by the British. After the war the British planned to make Malaya an independent country but to keep Singapore as a colony. The Malayan Communist Party (MCP) opposed this and, led by Chin Peng OBE, they formed ten resistance regiments (nine of which were Chinese). Malaya was a 'guerrilla's paradise' and it was very difficult to eliminate the 'bandits' as the MCP fighters were called.

General Sir Gerald Templer arrived in 1952 to drive the MCP into the wilderness and win the hearts and minds of the Malayan people. He was remarkably successful, though when he retired in 1954 6,000 guerrillas were still at large. The state of emergency finally ended on 31 July 1960. Over 3,200 civilians died. The Malay police lost 1,346; the British 350, the Gurkhas 159. Some 10,000 MCP men had been killed, 1,287 were prisoners and 2,702 surrendered.

On 31 August 1957 the Federation of Malay came into existence; in 1963 it joined with Borneo (Sabah) and Sarawak to form the Federation of Malaysia. Singapore became a separate independent nation state.

Confrontation between Malaysia and Indonesia
President Sukarno was enraged by all these changes and threatened a 'terrible confrontation'. His main complaint was that Malaysia was occupying lands belonging to Indonesia.
Read the following account:

> *His agents encouraged the crowds in Jakarta to attack the British embassy; his army raided Sarawak; his air force buzzed British troop positions with their ancient Mustangs inherited from the Dutch. Then his daring commandos landed in Singapore and his paratroopers dropped in Johore. Sukarno was using all of his resources and there was no doubting the courage of the Indonesian combat troops whose remarkable forays were skilfully contained by British and Commonwealth troops. Sukarno's reign ended in 1966 when he was overturned by General Soeharto. The Treaty of Kuala Lumpur ended a three-year struggle that could easily have grown into a major war involving the British armed forces. As it was, the fighting ended with minimum casualties: the Gurkhas lost 43; the British lost 32.*

1. By what name was Jakarta previously known?
2. What common defence policy formed the basis of the Treaty of Kuala Lumpur?
3. Why was that Treaty so important?
4. Name the British government in power in 1966.

5   Its Defence Minister said this about the confrontation:

> 'In the history books it will be recorded as one of the most efficient uses of military force in the history of the world.'

Who was he?

ASEAN

Five nations – Thailand, Indonesia, the Philippines, Malaysia and Singapore – met in Bangkok 1967 to set up the Association of South East Asian Nations (ASEAN).
The **aims** were:

- All five nations should live in peace and security.
- All opposed the expansion of communism into the ASEAN region.
- All were worried that the War in Kampuchea would spread into their region (1979 onwards).

Its **resources** were enormous:

- 253 million people.
- Two Commonwealth countries (Malaysia and Singapore).
- Huge potential wealth (gas, oil, rubber).
- A massive market for the new industrial nations of Japan, South Korea, Taiwan and Hong Kong (the last, of course, is still a British colony until its lease from China expires in 1997).

Map work

1   The Indo-Pakistan Wars
    See map on p. 204.

   (a)   Label the UN cease-fire line in Kashmir
   (b)   Label the main Indian attack on Lahore 1965.
   (c)   Label the Indian attacks on East Pakistan 1971.
   (d)   Mark Delhi.
   (e)   Indicate Bangladesh.

2   The ASEAN nations
    See map on p. 205.
   (a)   The ASEAN nations are shaded in. Insert their names.
   (b)   Mark Jakarta and Bandung on the island of Java.
   (c)   Label Kuala Lumpur.
   (d)   Label Bangkok in Thailand.
   (e)   Shade in the People's Republic of China.
   (f)   The disputed frontier between Malaysia and Indonesia was the Borneo-Sarawak frontier. In the blank box insert notes to show that

- the dispute lasted 1963–6
- that it was settled 1966.

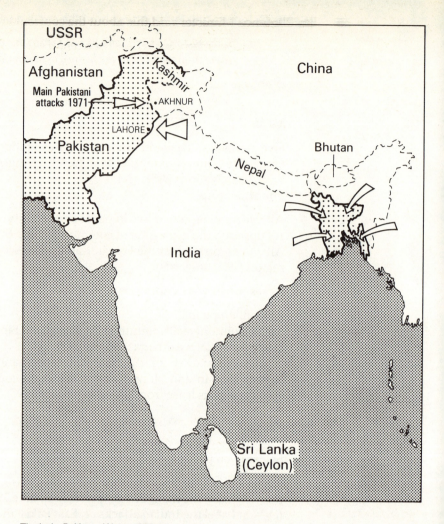

The Indo-Pakistan Wars, 1948–71

3 THE CARIBBEAN

THE WEST INDIES

Since the 1890s the West Indian population had expanded rapidly and people who couldn't find jobs on the islands emigrated to Brazil, Honduras, Costa Rica, Cuba and – most popular destination of all – the USA.

Two factors radically changed the situation:

- ◊ 1924 saw a US clamp-down on West Indian immigrants.
- ◊ The sugar industry declined in Brazil and Cuba. This meant that many West Indians came home at the precise moment when job opportunities were contracting.

Independence in Africa, Asia and the Caribbean

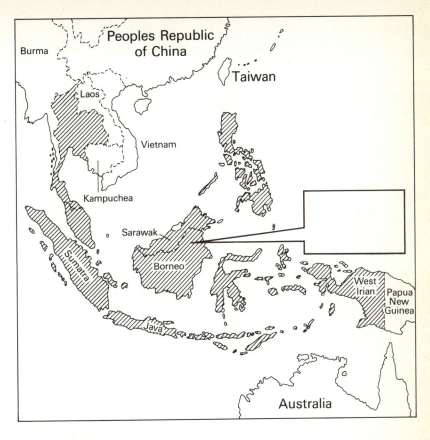

The ASEAN nations

Result: wages went down and there was a marked drop in living standards. This began the West Indian protests against the British Crown Colony system of government:

- They had no political parties to represent them.
- They had no union protection against wage cuts and redundancies caused by the dramatic fall in world sugar prices.
- They had a poor system of education and felt underprivileged in view of their common background of slavery.

New trends

- Some islands turned to new export products. Trinidad was lucky. It had started exporting oil to the US in 1912 and by 1936 its earnings were worth £3.8 million – over half of the island's export earnings for that year. However, most islands depended on exporting cocoa, cotton and limes, and were either undercut by foreign competitors or crippled by crop disease.
- Some people turned to the teachings of Marcus Garvey (recently

returned to Jamaica having been deported from the US). Garvey persuaded workers to join trade unions and fight for 'a dollar a day'.
- Strikes began in 1934 and became serious between 1935 and 1938:
  (a)   St Kitt's riot, 1935.
  (b)   Uriah Butler's attack on Trinidad oil wells, 1937.
  (c)   The Tate and Lyle Frome estate clash (4 killed), 1938.
  (d)   The Kingston waterfront battle (8 killed and 171 wounded), 1938.

The British reaction
Alarmed by the disorder, the British set up the Moyne Commission to investigate conditions in the West Indies. Its preliminary findings were that conditions were appalling and that the Crown Colony government had failed to honour its responsibilities. It did not recommend independence, and its final report didn't appear until after the Second World War had begun.

So the West Indians had very real grievances by 1939, but these did not impair their loyalty towards their 'Mother Country' – Britain. Many West Indians played a significant role during the Second World War, often in the European theatre.

The importance of the Second World War, 1939–45
The war years were in sharp contrast to the depression of the thirties. Now the British government bought sugar at prices that guaranteed workers a reasonable wage. Britain wanted all the oil that Trinidad, Aruba and Curaçao could produce. Freighters and tankers – prime targets for German U-boats – constantly visited the region and their presence created many new jobs. And when President Roosevelt offered Britain fifty old destroyers in exchange for bases in the Bahamas, Jamaica, St Lucia, Trinidad, Antigua and Bermuda there was an enormous demand for dock-workers, construction workers and truck drivers. Migrants to the new oil refineries sent money back to their families – sometimes enough for a new house. Thousands of people volunteered for the armed services and West Indians made a notable contribution to the Royal Air Force. For those who were lucky enough to return, the war had been an education. For those who stayed behind the influence of Bustamente's Labour Party, the Harlem Renaissance and the teachings of Marcus Garvey made a profound impact. By 1945 there was a demand for independence.

Changes
Many trade unions blossomed during the war and these protested against the continuation of Crown Colony government. So the British decided to transfer certain posts to elected West Indians. This began in Jamaica (1944) when a House of Representatives was added to the nominated Legislative Council. All thirty-eight members were elected by universal adult suffrage – one of the most significant developments in the British Caribbean islands during the Second World War.

Independence in Africa, Asia and the Caribbean

The idea of federation

The British (and some West Indian leaders) liked the idea of a federal government for the widely scattered islands. Members of the 1947 Montego Bay Conference through it might be a short cut to independence; and that it might lead to dominion status. A new 'Federal Labour Party' won the 1958 elections and formed the first West Indian Federal Government (April 1958).

The Federation of the West Indies, 1958

Read the following extract:

> Grantley Adams of Barbados became the first Federal Prime Minister as neither Norman Manley (Prime Minister of Jamaica) nor Eric Williams (Prime Minister of Trinidad) would take on the job. There were ten member states: Jamaica, Trinidad, Tobago, Barbados, Antigua, St Kitts, Dominica, Grenada, St Vincent and St Lucia. British Guiana and British Honduras refused to join. Adam had little hope of success. His federal government had no authority, little or no practical political power and no federal police or federal military organisation. Jamaica and Trinidad disliked their heavy federal taxes and wanted to restrict immigration and protect their own developing industrial base. In 1961 Norman Manley held a referendum: should Jamaica stay in the federation? Fifty-four per cent of Jamaicans voted to come out.

1. Who was the first Prime Minister of the Federation?
2. Why do you think that others refused to take on the job?
3. Why did British Honduras and British Guiana refuse to join the Federation?
4. What were the weaknesses of the Federation?
5. Eric Williams' famous statement, arithmetically wrong but politically correct, was;

    > 'One from ten leaves nothing.'

    What did he mean?

Significance

Why did the Federation fail?

- There was no pre-existing sense of unity at the time.
- There were deep suspicions about Britain's intentions when she applied to join the EEC (1961).
- West Indians were influenced by the success Castro had achieved in developing Cuban nationalism.
- Individual island nationalism was stronger and more meaningful than any sense of 'West Indian unity' at this stage of Caribbean history

In 1962 Britain formally abolished the Federation and granted independence to Jamaica and Trinidad (now linked to Tobago).

Some problems of independence

◊ Trinidad and Tobago had enormous advantages over other islands: oil, asphalt and natural gas industries.
◊ Asian immigrants demanded higher wages on the sugar plantations.
◊ Modern technology threw many manual workers out of their jobs.
◊ Jamaica (with a population of 2.2 million – twice the size of Trinidad's) was hard hit and depended on US and Canadian support for bauxite processing (alumina became the island's most valuable export).
◊ Jamaica's Rastafarians: a special religious and social problem. Rastafarians were followers of the cult of Ras Tafari (Haile Selaisse) whom they regarded as the 'living god' or Jah. One of their first leaders, the Rev. Howell, founded a commune known as Pinnacles in 1940 which was the first and only 'Rasta Republic'. Dispersed by the police, the Rastas went to live in Kingston (1954).
◊ Fear of Rastas increased after 1962 (many saw them as political revolutionaries) and in 1966 lecturers at the University of the West Indies urged the government to regard Rastas as an important and valuable part of Jamaican society.
◊ Perhaps the reggae superstar, Bob Marley, did most to project a peaceful image of Rastafarianism. He intervened in the political rivalry going on between Michael Manley (Norman Manley's son) and Edward Seaga during the seventies, rivalry that embraced gang warfare and gun battles. Marley held his famous 'peace concert' in 1978, patched up the quarrels and convinced Jamaica's leaders that Rastafarianism was a peaceful ideology that wanted to change society so that everyone would benefit. Marley died in 1981 and the two political leaders attended his funeral.

Bob Marley

A new sense of economic unity
1968 CARIFTA: the Caribbean Free Trade Area.

1973 CARICOM: the Caribbean Community and Common Market.
This new-found economic unity did not encourage further thoughts of federation – as evinced by tiny St Kitts and Nevis, the forty-eighth independent Commonwealth member in 1983.

Grenada
Originally named Conception by Columbus in 1498, Grenada became independent in 1974. In 1979 a revolution overthrew Prime Minister Sir Eric Gairy. Some of the revolutionaries were US Black Power-leaders and Rastafarians – but the man who came to power was Maurice Bishop, founder of the New Jewel Movement. He set up a People's Revolutionary Government with the help of Cuban advisers. The presence of Cubans, plus the new runway at Pointe Salines, alarmed the US.

Independence in Africa, Asia and the Caribbean

Multiple-choice questions

1. The man in the photo on page 208 is
   - [ ] Ray Charles
   - [ ] Maurice Bishop
   - [ ] Bob Marley
   - [ ] George Benson

2. The New Jewel Movement stood for
   - [ ] Joint Endeavour for Welfare, Education and Liberation
   - [ ] Union with Cuba
   - [ ] Union with the EEC
   - [ ] Union with the United States

3. 'Grenada is a Soviet-Cuban colony being readied for as a major military bastion to export terror' was said by
   - [ ] Sir Eric Gairy
   - [ ] Margaret Thatcher
   - [ ] Ronald Reagan
   - [ ] Sir Paul Scoon

4. The request put forward to the USA for American troops to land on Grenada (1983) was made by
   - [ ] Margaret Thatcher
   - [ ] Sir Eric Gairy
   - [ ] Dennis Healey
   - [ ] Sir Paul Scoon

5. The number of Caribbean island states that supported the US landings was
   - [ ] Nine
   - [ ] Eight
   - [ ] Seven
   - [ ] Six

6. After the US troops left Grenada, the Caribbean islands based troops on the island to help the restoration of a normal state of affairs. Most came from
   - [ ] Trinidad
   - [ ] Jamaica
   - [ ] St Vincent
   - [ ] St Lucia

Map work

See map on p. 210.

1. What is the modern name for British Honduras?
2. What is the modern name for British Guiana?
3. From which country was Marcus Garvey returning?
4. Insert the Panama Canal.
5. What is the capital of Jamaica?

In the following passage describing Crown Colony government certain key words have been omitted. These are:

Whites; designed; inappropriate; executive; members; expansion

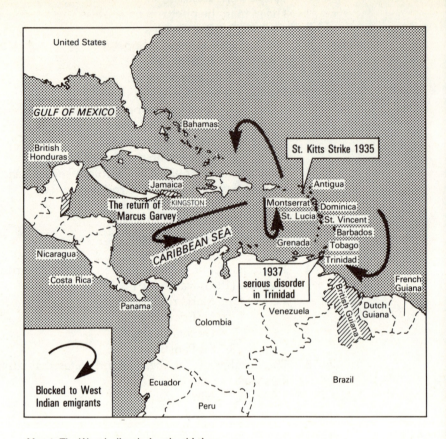

Map 1 The West Indies during the thirties

Crown Colony Government

Britain's colonial _____ 1763–1815 brought people of many different languages and cultures under her control, e.g. Spanish Creoles in Trinidad and French Creoles on many other West Indian islands. Representative government (i.e. government in which _____ alone were represented) was _____. So the British _____ the Crown Colony system in which all _____ power was in the hands of the Governor and his Council. Though the Governor usually nominated his Council _____. Council's composition could – and often did – take many forms, especially in the West Indies.

Independence in Africa, Asia and the Caribbean

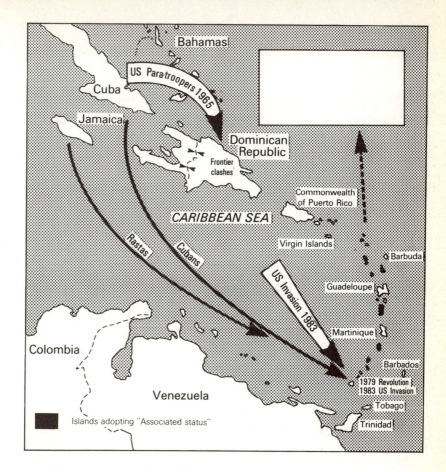

Map 2 Clashes in the Caribbean 1965–83

1 Label Grenada.
2 Mark Haiti.
3 Under the heading 'Emigrants to Britain' insert notes to explain that emigration was blocked by the 1962 Commonwealth Immigrants Act.
4 The Commonwealth of Puerto Rico sends a Commissioner to which House of Representatives?
5 After the failure of the West Indies Federation certain islands (shaded on the map) chose 'associated status' by which Britain retained responsibility for defence and external affairs. Name each of these islands/island groups.

CHAPTER NINE

THE ARAB–ISRAELI CONFLICT

CONTENTS

- The origins of the conflict — 215
- The British mandate, 1920–48 — 217
- The First Arab–Israeli War (the War of Liberation), 1948 — 219
- The Second Arab–Israeli War (Suez 1956) — 219
- The Six Day War: the Third Arab–Israeli War — 222
- The War of Yom Kippur, 1973: the Fourth Arab–Israeli War — 225
- The Israeli–Egyptian peace treaty, 1979 — 226
- Israel and the Lebanon — 227

The Arab–Israeli conflict

1 THE ORIGINS OF THE CONFLICT

PALESTINE – THE PROMISED LAND

Substantial numbers of Jews were in Palestine before the First World War. They came for several reasons:

- They regarded Palestine as their traditional home – the Jews lived in Palestine (then the Israelite Kingdom of David and Solomon) around 1000 BC.
- They were harried by persecutors in many European states, where anti-Semitism increased during the late nineteenth century.
- They dreamed of setting up a modern Israel, a nation state that would be able to hold its own against the other nation states of newly industrialised Europe.
- It was fairly easy to buy land in Palestine and to find work in Jerusalem and other cities. The kibbutz, or collective community, was an established feature of Palestine by 1914.

However, by then there were at least half a million Arabs living in Palestine – Arabs whose help the British needed in the war against Turkey.

- 1915 saw the British promise the Hashemite Arab leader, Sharif Hussein, the principle of Arab independence provided he would head the 'Arab Revolt' against Turkey in 1916 (in this connection he had the help of T. E. Lawrence – Lawrence of Arabia).
- Possibly the British did not have Palestine in mind when they made this agreement, but the Arabs assumed that the idea of 'Arab independence' would include the Promised Land.
- Certainly the other promises made in the 1917 'Balfour Declaration' conflict with the 1915 promises: Arthur Balfour promised the Zionist Federation that there would be a 'national home' for Jews after the war.
- There was also the problem of the secret Sykes-Picot agreement of 1916 (leaked by the Russians in 1917) in which Britain and France planned to carve up the Middle East into their own 'spheres of interest'.

Document 1
The famous letter from Balfour to Lord Rothschild (2 November 1917) emphasising the 'promise':

Dear Lord Rothschild

I have much pleasure in conveying to you, on behalf of His Majesty's Government, the following declaration of sympathy wtih Jewish Zionist aspirations, which has been submitted to and approved by the Cabinet.

> *'His Majesty's Government view with favour the establishment in Palestine of a national home for the Jewish people and will use their best endeavours to facilitate the achievement of this object, it being clearly understood that nothing shall be done which may prejudice the civil and religious rights of the existing non-Jewish communities in Palestine, or the rights and political status enjoyed by Jews in any other country.'*

I should be grateful if you would bring this declaration to the knowledge of the Zionist Federation.

Yours sincerely

Arthur Balfour

Document 2

We oppose the pretensions of the Zionists to create a Jewish Commonwealth in the southern part of Syria, known as Palestine, and oppose Zionist migration to any part of our country; for we do not acknowledge their title but consider them a grave peril to our people . . .
(Published by the General Syrian Congress, July 1919)

Document 3

It looks as though Britain has promised the Promised Land to more than one country.
(Contemporary comment)

Document 4

The League of Nations granted Britain the mandate to Palestine in 1920 and ordered her to co-operate with the Zionist Organisation to set up a Jewish national home: The Administration of Palestine, while ensuring that the rights and position of other sections of the population are not prejudiced, shall facilitate Jewish immigration . . .

1. Explain the term 'Zionist'.
2. Did the British support a Jewish national home in Palestine in 1917?
3. Had the Arabs reason to expect that they too would govern Palestine after the war?
4. Do you think Document 2 is a fair reaction to the views expressed in the Balfour Declaration?
5. Would you agree with the opinion expressed in Document 3?
6. Do you think the Zionists gained more than the Arabs?

7 Do you think that Britain went some way to meet Arab nationalist aspirations when she created Trans-Jordan (modern Jordan)?

2 THE BRITISH MANDATE, 1920–48

British troops and police found themselves compelled to keep the peace between rival groups of Arabs and Jews. Frequently, the clashes were caused through religious conflict and commercial hostility – at first there was little of the traditional 'anti-Semitism' in the European sense.

Examples

- 1921 Jaffa riots.
- 1929 riots (more widespread – including Jerusalem), with over 140 deaths.

The British were now anxious to keep Jewish immigration into Palestine down to a minimum but the anti-Semite policies of Adolf Hitler (he came to power in Germany 1933) made this impossible. Over 100,000 Jews arrived to swell the existing 150,000. Many of these Jews had savings and could readily acquire land. Significantly, the first Arab guerrilla raids on Palestine from Lebanon began at this time, under the leadership of Fawzi el Kawakji. This led to the formation of a Jewish terrorist group, the Irgun Zvei Leumi.

By 1937, therefore, Jews and Arabs were ready to fight one another for the right to be in Palestine. Terror and assassination thus began before the Second World War – with the Jewish Defence Force (Haganah) playing a leading part.

Palestine during the Second World War, 1939–45

- About 130,000 Jewish men and women volunteered to fight against the Nazis. They served in all branches of the British armed forces and in 1944 small Jewish units were parachuting into occupied Europe to organise local resistance movements.
- Some extremists carried on the war against the British in Palestine, notably Abraham Stern (founder of the Lehi Stern Gang) who was killed by the British in 1942.
- Ben Gurion had emerged as the Jewish national leader and he formally abandoned terrorism in 1944 – handing over lists of Irgun and Stern members to the British.

The end of the British mandate, 1948

By 1945 Palestine seemed to be the most dangerous Middle East trouble spot. Bear in mind that the victorious western allies were very conscious of the importance of the Middle East:

(a)   As a source (then) of very cheap oil.

(b) As the crucial strategic zone – location of the Suez Canal and the 'exit' for Russia from the Black Sea.

Palestine was still under the British mandate and it seemed an insoluble problem to the post-war Labour government headed by Clement Attlee.

◊ Britain's original promise that Palestine would be a national home for the Jews (Balfour Declaration) couldn't be reconciled with the British assurance that Arabs would always be in the majority within the lands of the mandate.

◊ Hitler's holocaust had exterminated six million Jews; but another million still survived in the DP camps (camps for displaced persons) scattered across Europe. Of these, 250,000 wanted to settle in Palestine.

◊ President Truman urged Ernest Bevin (British Foreign Secretary) to allow 100,000 Jews to settle immediately.

Read this account of the events that followed:

> When Bevin refused to let the Jews come to the Promised Land, the Jews resorted to the tactics they had perfected against the Nazis during the war. They attacked British soldiers inside Palestine and blew up the British headquarters housed in King David Hotel (1946). Then they whipped up international sympathy by chartering some old merchant ships and filling them up with Jewish DPs. These then ran the gauntlet of the British naval blockade. The world was therefore deeply shocked when the British turned away the Exodus, packed with 4,500 Jews who had survived the Nazi death camps and now had to return to live as stateless people in the depths of Europe. Some blockade runners were sunk; a few – such as the Holgana and the San Dimitrio – got through. But the British had had enough. On 18 February 1947 they handed over the Palestine problem to the UN and told them that they would end their mandate in 1948. The UN formed UNSCOP (UN Special Commission on Palestine) and charged it with finding a solution. Predictably, UNSCOP came up with the idea of partition: divide Palestine between the Jews and Arabs and let Jerusalem become a Holy City for everyone.

1 Why do you think that Bevin refused Jewish immigration in 1945–6?
2 Where was the King David Hotel?
3 What was UNSCOP?
4 Do you think its ideas were constructive?
5 Do you think, as UNSCOP thought, that Jerusalem should be an 'international city' under UN control?

Results

By November 1947 Palestine was in a state of civil war. The British had the thankless task of trying to separate the warring groups and preventing atrocities. So they pulled out and on 10 May 1948 Ben

The Arab–Israeli conflict

Gurion proclaimed the independence of Eretz Israel – the State of Israel.

3 THE FIRST ARAB–ISRAELI WAR (THE WAR OF LIBERATION), 1948

It is important to remember that, within hours of Ben Gurion's announcement, both the USA and the USSR had recognised the sovereignty of Eretz Israel.

Almost as quickly, the armies of Egypt, Syria, Jordan and Iraq invaded the new Israeli state. Backed by aid from Saudi Arabia, Morocco and – indirectly – by the arms and ammunition the British had left behind, the Arabs had superiority in tanks, machine-guns, armoured cars, artillery and aircraft. They expected to crush Israeli resistance within a few weeks and re-establish Arab rule in Filastin Arabiyah – an Arab Palestine. But the Jews drew on reserves of experienced soldiers from all over the world and bought up surplus warplanes. Before long, the Israelis had driven back their enemies and expanded their territories.

Some results of the War of Liberation

- The Israelis forced all attacking Arab states (apart from Iraq) to sign an armistice.
- No Arab state recognised Israeli sovereignty, however.
- The Israelis retained their occupied territories.
- 100,000 new citizens had come to live in Israel.
- To make room for these people, the Israeli troops evicted thousands of Palestinians who had to live in camps along the Israeli–Jordanian border or else find a home in a foreign country.
- The plight of the Palestinian refugees would dog Middle East history for decades.

4 THE SECOND ARAB–ISRAELI WAR (SUEZ 1956)

THE SUEZ CRISIS, 1956

Egyptian soldiers blamed their 1948 defeat by Israel on the corrupt rule of King Faruk. In 1952 army officers led by General Neguib forced Faruk to abdicate. Neguib was a popular President but commanded little support from his officers. From March 1954 General Abdel Nasser had effectively replaced Neguib. Nasser was a man with a mission: to unite millions of Muslims throughout the world; to reassert their pride in traditional Muslim values; and to bring them to a stage of development equal to that of the superpowers and the nations of Western Europe. First, he had to reassert pride in Egypt and to drive the British from their bases in the Suez Canal Zone.

In a carefully controlled election – ninety-seven per cent of the Egyptian people voted for him – Nasser became President of Egypt (1956). Now he would harness the waters of the Nile and build a vast dam at Aswan. He hoped that the US would provide the cash and weapons to carry on the fight with Israel. But the Americans were suspicious:

- Nasser was also asking the Soviet Union for aid.
- Was he really a communist?
- What would happen if the US withdrew dollar aid?

The Americans soon found out: Nasser nationalised the Suez Canal (26 July 1956), a month after the British quit. The British Prime Minister, Sir Anthony Eden, (he had succeeded Churchill in 1955) believed that Nasser was behaving in the same way as Hitler – and no one had bothered to stop the German dictator. His Foreign Secretary,

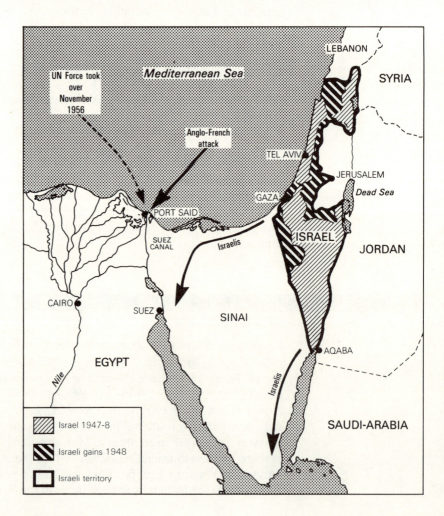

Israel, 1948–56

The Arab–Israeli conflict

Selwyn Lloyd, felt that 'this great waterway is not to be left at the mercy ... or hatred of one power or one man'. So Britain and France conspired with the Israelis to take 'energetic action' against Nasser.

- On 29 October 1956 Israel attacked Egypt.
- Britain and France vetoed a UN proposal that members should not intervene.
- Britain sent an ultimatum to Israel and Egypt ordering them to withdraw troops sixteen km each side of the Canal.
- Nasser refused and on 31 October Anglo-French aircraft began bombing Egyptian targets.

Read this account of the attack on Suez:

> *This act of aggression was universally condemned and there was no international recognition of the courage displayed by Anglo-French soldiers, sailors and airmen. Egyptian forces fought well against the Israelis but had to fall back to the Suez Canal where the Anglo-French invaders were making surprisingly slow progress. Obviously, the invasion was going horribly wrong and there seemed little chance that President Nasser would be forced to give up the Suez Canal, especially after the US strongly condemned the fighting that was going on. It certainly stirred the UN into action. For the first time since Korea it supported military intervention; only this time it created its own UNEF – the United Nations Emergency Force. The UNEF troops swiftly took over and the UN followed these up with a promise to help clear the Suez Canal, blocked by Nasser during the fighting. Undoubtedly, the Suez affair was a failure for Anglo-French policies. For the Israelis, it represented their second Arab–Israeli War. For Nasser, it represented a moment of pure triumph.*

1. Why do you think the invasion of Suez was so widely condemned?
2. What do you think the invaders hoped to achieve?
3. Why was the UN so hostile to the British and French involvement?
4. What was the UN's response?
5. Who gained the most from this affair?

Now read these statements about the Second Arab–Israeli War (i.e. the Suez affair of 1956) and decide which of the following said them:

- A An Israeli soldier
- B The British Government
- C President Nasser
- D President Eisenhower (USA)

Then tick the appropriate box beside each statement.

A	B	C	D

We request that Anglo–French forces be allowed to move temporarily into key positions at Port Said, Ismailia and Suez in order to guarantee freedom of transit in the Zone.

Dear Mr Prime Minister

I have just learned from the press of the twelve-hour ultimatum which you and the French government have delivered to the government of Egypt under threat of forceful intervention . . . I feel I must urgently express my deep concern at the prospect of this drastic action . . .

A	B	C	D

We flew out across Sinai and dropped just below Suez. We thought the British might be there but they hadn't come. So we had to trek miles through the desert to make contact with one or two isolated Egyptian outposts. Then we came back to our home base. It hardly seemed worthwhile, especially as we had to evacuate Sinai shortly afterwards.

A	B	C	D

We fought Israel, Britain and France – three aggressors – single-handed and relying on nobody except God and ourselves.

A	B	C	D

Over the next ten years the Arab states lacked unity and argued fiercely among themselves. The United Arab Republic (the union between Egypt and Syria) proclaimed in 1958 lasted three years. During 1958 there were revolutions in Iraq and the Lebanon. Civil war tore the Yemen apart in 1961. Syria's government fell in 1963; the same year saw a revolution in Iraq. There was little evidence of Arab unity in 1967 – the year in which Israel decided to launch her remarkable 'Six Day War'.

4 THE SIX DAY WAR: THE THIRD ARAB-ISRAELI WAR

THE CONDITION OF ISRAEL, 1967

Nineteen years had passed since Ben Gurion had proclaimed the Israeli state. Since then, Israel had fought and won two wars against her Arab nations and survived countless guerrilla raids across her totally indefensible borders. She had no guarantee that her future would be secure as no Arab state recognised the legality of those frontiers. Additionally, the Palestine Liberation Organisation (PLO), and the best organised of the forty or so Palestine resistance movements, had stated categorically:

> 'The partition of Palestine in 1947 and the establishment of Israel in 1948 are entirely illegal, regardless of the passage of time.'

But the real reason for Israel's anxiety in 1967 was Nasser's decision to move his troops into Sinai (currently held by the UNEF as a buffer zone between Egypt and Israel) and to block the Strait of Tiran. Moreover, Nasser announced that the previously disunited Arab states were about to create a unified military command in order to bring about the destruction of the Jewish state.

Israel's military commanders decided that they must:

(a)   secure space in which to manoeuvre their newly equipped tank forces;
(b)   advance to frontiers capable of easy defence;
(c)   wipe out, in a series of pre-emptive strikes, the huge air superiority enjoyed by Egypt, Syria and Jordan.
Israel's political leaders agreed that this would mean occupying Sinai, the Gaza strip, the West Bank of the River Jordan and the strategically important Golan Heights in Syria.

The Israeli defeat of Egypt, 5–8 June 1967
On 5 June 1967 the Israeli Air Force rocketed and bombed seventeen Egyptian airfields and destroyed 300 aircraft including all of Egypt's Russian-supplied heavy bombers. Israeli armour raced across Sinai, destroyed seven Egyptian divisions and inflicted 10,000 casualties.

The Israeli defeat of Jordan, 5–7 June 1967
Smothered by napalm and showered by rocket missiles, the main Jordan defence positions were quickly overrun. But there was fierce hand-to-hand fighting for the Holy City of Jerusalem. Apart from Jerusalem, air power was the key to Israeli success.

The Israeli defeat of Syria, 9–10 June 1967
Syria had the best natural defences in the shape of the Golan Heights and the Israelis naturally assumed that the war against Syria would be the toughest of all. That was why they sent in more air strikes here. The Syrians fought for thirty-six hours, and then retreated. The Israelis took the Golan Heights – where the Syrians had prepared their defences for the previous ten years.

Now the Israelis believed themselves to be in a strong negotiating position and calculated that, over the next ten years, they ought to be able to trade back Sinai in exchange for full Arab recognition of the legality of Eretz Israel.

However, they underestimated the Arabs:
◊   They were not prepared to accept the 1967 defeat as final.
◊   They rebuilt their armed forces with the new 'high technology' of modern warfare – notably the powerful Soviet SAM (surface-to-air) missiles.
◊   They felt even more strongly about the plight of the Palestinian refugees now that thousands of other Arabs had become refugees as a result of the Six Day War. The estimated total of homeless Arabs was now 3.7 million! Yet Jews coming in from Asia and America could get instant citizenship. As Professor Said has said:

> 'Why is it right for a Jew born in Chicago to immigrate to Israel, whereas a Palestinian born in Jaffa is a refugee?'*

◊   Al Fatah, the PLO's military wing, insisted that Israel must be exterminated, but President Nasser didn't think this could be done by terrorism. He thought Israel should be worn down by constant military attrition.

*In his *The Question of Palestine*. Routledge & Kegan Paul, 1980, p. 234

Nasser's war of attrition

World opinion did not approve of Israel's military conquests. The UN passed several resolutions:

> Resolution 242 (1967): Israel should evacuate the occupied territories.
> Resolution 2534 (1969): the UN deplored the loss of Palestinian civil rights.
> Resolution 2627 (1970): Palestinians should have equal rights and political self-determination.

This was the situation that Nasser exploited:

(a) by bombarding the Israelis from the east side of the Suez Canal.
(b) by protecting his guns with a curtain of SAM missiles.
(c) by using his new Russian-supplied fighters to intercept patrolling Israeli aircraft.

There was a major air battle in July 1970 and the US stepped in to arrange a cease-fire. Suddenly, President Nasser died. His successor was Muhammad Anwar el Sadat who became President of Egypt in 1970.

The PLO

The PLO saw themselves as the equivalent of wartime resistance fighters, as partisans or maquis. But few countries wanted to host them as their actions always brought Israeli reprisals. That was why Jordan decided to evict Al Fatah from its bases in September 1970 – which they did, after very heavy fighting. The PLO moved to the Lebanon and from these events the international terrorist group Black September took its name.

International terrorism

PLO groups adopted these tactics in the early seventies as a response to:

(a) Israeli tactics and
(b) to focus world attention on the plight of the Palestinian refugees.

They justified their actions by reminding the world that on 9 April 1948 members of the Irgun gang had murdered 250 innocent Arab villagers at Deir Yassin – one reason why so many Arabs decided to flee Palestine.
So:

- the PLO hired Japanese gunmen to kill twenty-eight people in the Lod airport massacre (May 1972).
- Black September killed eleven Israeli athletes at the 1972 Munich Olympics.
- Israeli fighters shot down a Libyan airliner (1973) and killed 104 people – most of whom had no connection with terrorism.
- An Israeli terrorist commando entered a Beirut hotel (1973) and murdered some PLO leaders.

The Arab–Israeli conflict

Such was the undeclared war of (*a*) attrition and (*b*) terrorism in the early seventies; it was only a matter of weeks before it flared into open hostilities.

5 THE WAR OF YOM KIPPUR 1973: THE FOURTH ARAB–ISRAELI WAR

President Sadat was highly conscious of his destiny: 'From the day I took office on President Nasser's death, I knew I would have to fight. It was my inheritance.'

How could he overwhelm the Israelis without giving them the chance of using their remarkable air power?

Operation Badr – the plan

Sadat decided to attack Israel without warning on 6 October 1973 – the anniversary of the Prophet Muhammad's victory at Badr in the year 637; it was also Yom Kippur, the Holy Day of the Atonement in the Jewish calendar when the Israelis would least expect an attack. Egyptian troops would cross the Suez Canal on mobile pontoon bridges, specially supplied by the Russians; there would be a massed tank assault under the cover of SAM missiles; the infantry would have RPG–7 grenade launchers capable of penetrating Israeli tank armour. Simultaneously, 1,200 Syrian tanks would move across the Golan Heights under the cover of SAM missiles and then smash through the Israeli defences using their own firepower.

Operation Badr – the attack

Operation Badr was essentially a missile war designed to combat the flair of the Israeli fighter pilots and the drive of Israeli tank commanders. The attack went in as planned. Sadat's troops crossed the Canal and entered Sinai. As expected, the Israeli jets hurtled overhead. Then the SAM missiles rose to meet the enemy, their infra-red sensors homing in on the Israeli exhaust nozzles. For the first three days the Arab tactics met with brilliant success and fifty Israeli jets fell in combat.

The Israeli response

The Israelis fought a bitter war on the Golan Heights, 'trading space for time' in the Sinai desert. Israeli tanks defeated the Syrians; in the desert they detected a gap between two Egyptian armies. Israeli tanks poured through, defeated the Arabs at the Battle of Chinese Farm, crossed the Canal and circled round to trap the entire Egyptian Third Army. It was at this critical point of the war that Saudi Arabia used a new economic weapon: she stopped oil exports to the USA as a retaliation against American arms supplies to the Israelis.

The danger of a major war

Huge American aircraft ferried in tanks to the Israelis; and the Americans actually let the Israelis have active combat aircraft – all the

Israelis had to do was change the markings! At the same time, the Russians operated a daily airlift to Egypt and Syria. There was a real risk of military confrontation and both Russia and America thankfully supported a UN cease-fire (22 October 1973). When the Israelis broke this, Egypt asked Brezhnev for aid and President Nixon (perhaps thinking that this Middle East crisis was as dangerous as the Cuban crisis exactly eleven years earlier) placed US armed forces on nuclear alert.

A second cease-fire (24 October) received Soviet support and the Israelis ceased fighting. Nixon cancelled the nuclear alert on 31 October 1973.

6 THE ISRAELI–EGYPTIAN PEACE TREATY, 1979

Mrs Golda Meir was Prime Minister of Israel from 1969 to 1974 and had led her country during the War of Yom Kippur. Once the fighting was over she hinted that Israel would be open to negotiation:

> *'We will not descend from the Golan, we will not partition Jerusalem and we will not agree that the distance between Netanya and the border shall be eighteen km . . . But if we want a Jewish state we have to be prepared to compromise on territory.'*

On the map of the Yom Kippur War (page 227) mark Netanya, note the location of the Golan Heights and Jerusalem.

1   In what territories do you think the Israelis would be prepared to negotiate?
2   What would the Israelis expect in return?

When Menachem Begin became Prime Minister of Israel (1977) he discovered that President Sadat was equally anxious to reduce hostility between the two countries. Begin invited Sadat to Jerusalem (November); he visited Egypt (December). In 1978 President Jimmy Carter (USA) invited the two leaders for a conference at Camp David, Washington. Here a 'framework for peace' in the Middle East was worked out and the agreements were called the 'Camp David Accords':

◊ Israel would work towards autonomy for the West Bank and Gaza.
◊ Israel would progressively withdraw her troops from Sinai.
◊ Egypt would recognise the sovereign independence of Eretz Israel.

For the first time, an Arab country had accepted Israel. In 1979 Sadat and Begin returned to the USA and there signed the Israeli–Egyptian Peace Treaty. Egypt formally recognised Israel in 1980; Israel withdrew the last of her troops from Sinai during 1982.

But Sadat was now an outcast in the Arab world and the PLO demanded that a new 'Arab Palestine' be created out of the West Bank and Gaza. Sadat was assassinated in 1981.

The Arab–Israeli conflict

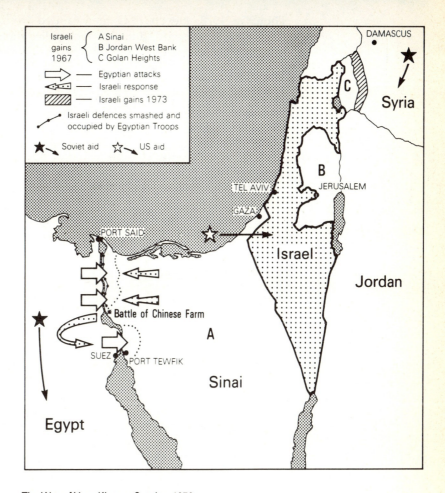

The War of Yom Kippur, October 1973

7 ISRAEL AND THE LEBANON

THE LEBANON: A PLO BASE

The arrival of the PLO and its leader Yassir Arafat in the Lebanon created a completely new Israeli security problem, for the PLO was quite unlike any other terrorist organisation in the world.

◊ The UN had recognised the PLO as a legal government in 'Palestine' (1974).
◊ The Russians supplied the PLO with sophisticated weapons: tanks, heavy artillery, rockets.
◊ The PLO could count on Syrian support and Syria was one of the best armed Arab nations. When civil war broke out in the Lebanon (1975) Syria offered 'protection' and in 1977 moved its Arab Deterrent Force into the country.

Then, in 1978, eleven PLO men landed from the sea and killed thirty-four Israelis and, though Israeli police shot nine of them, Prime Minister Begin decided to wipe out the PLO bases in the Lebanon.

- The 1978 invasion: 20,000 Israeli troops moved into the Lebanon.
- The UN decided to separate the PLO and Israeli forces.
- It created UNIFIL (UN's Interim Force in the Lebanon) and this soon became involved in the complex religious and civil strife of the Lebanese people.
- UNIFIL failed to prevent the 1982 Israeli invasion – caused by an abortive attempt to assassinate the Israeli ambassador in London. Now the Israelis moved north of the UNIFIL positions and entered Beirut.
- It was here that the terrible Chatila and Sabra camp murders took place (September 1982), supposedly the work of Phalangists.

THE MILITIAS OF THE LEBANON

Druze: form about ten per cent of the population and split away from the Muslims in the eleventh century to live as a separate sect in the Chouf Mts.

Maronites: form about twenty per cent of the population; they are Roman Catholics.

Shi'ites: form about thirty per cent of the population; they are Islamic Fundamentalists.

Phalangists: orthodox Christians and Maronites whose main aim was to drive the Palestinians and the Syrians out of the Lebanon.
Note that this complicated population mix derives from the French decision, in 1920, to split the Lebanon away from the other part of its League of Nations mandate, Syria.

The Multinational Force (MNF)

Israel had gained some advantages from the 1982 invasion in that the PLO had to leave its Beirut base (they evacuated their other bases in 1983 and went to Tripoli). Meanwhile, a growing conflict between the Lebanese government and the Syrian-backed Druze persuaded four countries (USA, Britain, France, Italy) to send a multinational force of 5,400 men to bolster up the authority of the Lebanese Prime Minister, Amin Gemayel. However, neither this force nor the Israeli presence made any significant difference to the warring factions inside the Lebanon.

By 1984 the multinational force (MNF) had left and after this the Israelis also began evacuating the Lebanon. Two reasons for this were:

- The very high cost of mounting an occupation force at a time when the Israeli economy was suffering from its perpetual war expenditure.

◊ The growing unpopularity of the Lebanon affair among the Israeli people.

However, the Israelis remained intolerant of PLO activity and in 1985 their jets bombed the PLO's new headquarters in distant Tunisia.

So the great issues of the Middle East had not been settled. The issue of the Palestine refugees, the future of Israel and the unity of the Arab world remained major problems. Moreover, the terrible Gulf War that began in 1980 between Iraq and Iran complicated the situation. During 1986 the Israelis considered widening the opportunities for discussing a 'Middle East peace settlement' and actually made contact with the Soviet Union after many years of hostility.

However, the attitudes of the Arabs and the Israelis remained largely unchanged.

The consistent Israeli view

Most Israelis do not see the Palestine refugee problem as the great issue in the Middle East. They accept in principle the idea of the creation of a independent Palestine but only in the context of a negotiated peace settlement that would guarantee the survival and security of Eretz Israel. They argue that the Palestinian refugee problem, for which they take partial responsibility, was the product of the four Arab Israeli Wars: the War of Liberation 1948, Suez 1956, the Six Day War 1967 and Yom Kippur in 1973. They say that the Arab states never had any intention of setting up an independent Palestine. They could have done this, had they so wished, at any time between 1948 and 1967 by giving them Gaza and/or the West Bank. Israelis are convinced that the Arab states have always manipulated the PLO for their own ends and that the Arab leaders didn't see any value in Al Fatah until after Egypt and Syria suffered defeat in the Six Day War.

The consistent Arab view (at least up to the 1979 Israeli-Egyptian Treaty)

When the state of Israel emerged in 1948, about fifty per cent of the Arab population had to flee. They had no alternative. Even before the fighting was over Israeli troops were evicting Arabs, demolishing their dwellings and replacing them with Jewish settlements. After the Six Day War the refugee problem worsened. About 1.7 million Arabs still stayed on inside the Israeli state; but over 2 million had moved to other Middle East countries and Western Europe. By 1969–70 the number of stateless Palestinians exceeded 3.7 million. There could be no denying the fact that these people were entitled to a homeland, and the implication was that their homeland was within the present frontiers of the Israeli state. The Arabs quote two important UN resolutions:

1. **No. 2535 B (1969)**: this regretted that the Palestinians had lost their civil rights.

2. **No. 2627 C (1970)**: this confirmed that the Palestinians were entitled to

equal rights and political self-determination according to the terms of the UN Charter.

During the period 1985–6 many more Arab terrorist groups were active in the Middle East and Western Europe, Increasingly, Israelis saw themselves as part of a 'siege society' not only in their own country but whenever they boarded a jet airliner. Yet they were still prepared to take part in audacious enterprises, as Operation Moses (their rescue of 25,000 Falashas – black Ethiopian Jews) demonstrated.

Consider the following passage:

> In September 1982 President Reagan suggested some ideas for a homeland for the Palestinian refugees. He thought the Israeli-occupied West Bank might be the best place and was pleased when King Hussein of Jordan and Yassir Arafat reached some agreement. Then in mid-1983 there was a rebellion within the PLO, challenging the leadership of Yassir Arafat. Four thousand Arafat supporters were evacuated from Tripoli under the UN flag and eventually made their headquarters in Tunis. But Arafat was determined to assert his leadership and in 1984–5 he held a series of talks with King Hussein of Jordan who was quite positive in his approval of President Reagan's original plan. By February 1985 Arafat and Hussein had drawn up proposals for a Middle East peace plan.

Yassir Arafat

Source: Bill Mandle, *Conflict in The Promised Land*. Heinemann Educational Books, 1976

The Arab–Israeli conflict

1. Do you think Yassir Arafat is a relatively moderate leader of the Palestinian people?
2. Why are the Israelis still distrustful of his leadership?
3. Where do you think the best place is to resettle the Palestinian people in their homelands?
4. How would you answer Fouzi El Asmar, a Palestinian in an Israeli prison during 1971, and the author of this poem:

> I was raised
>   under an olive tree.
> I ate the figs
>   of my orchard
>   drank wine from
>   the sloping vineyards
> Tasted cactus fruit
>   in the valleys
> more, more.
>
> The nightingale has sung
>   in my ears
> The free winds of fields and cities
>   always tickled me
> My friend
> You cannot ask me
>   to leave my own country.

Fouzi El Asmar (a Palestinian), *Poems From an Israeli Prison*, March 1971, quoted by Bill Mandle, *Conflict in the Promised Land*. Heinemann Educational Books, 1976, p. 53

Multiple-choice questions

1. The leader of the PLO, formed in 1964, was
   - ☐ Gamal Nasser
   - ☐ Sharif Hussein
   - ☐ Fawzi al Kawakji
   - ☐ Yassir Arafat
2. The United Nations force in the Lebanon is known as
   - ☐ UNSCOP
   - ☐ UNEF
   - ☐ UNIFIL
   - ☐ UNDOF
3. Jordan forced the PLO to leave in
   - ☐ 1970
   - ☐ 1971
   - ☐ 1972
   - ☐ 1973
4. Israel's leader during the War of Yom Kippur was
   - ☐ Ben Gurion
   - ☐ Ariel Sharon
   - ☐ Menachem Begin
   - ☐ Golda Meir

5 The 1979 Israeli-Egyptian Peace Treaty was signed in:
- ☐ The USA
- ☐ The Soviet Union
- ☐ Egypt
- ☐ Israel

6 During Lebanon's agony (1982–3) the US battleship that shelled the Lebanon coast was called
- ☐ *New York*
- ☐ *Manhattan*
- ☐ *Missouri*
- ☐ *New Jersey*

7 The Shi'ite Islamic suicide squad that attacked the MNF headquarters in 1983 and killed 241 US marines and 58 French soldiers was called
- ☐ The Red Army
- ☐ Black September
- ☐ Islamic Jihad
- ☐ Al Fatah

8 The 1981 attack by Israeli jets on the Osirak nuclear reactor took place in
- ☐ Iran
- ☐ Iraq
- ☐ Lebanon
- ☐ Tunisia

9 The 1985 attack by Israeli jets on the PLO headquarters took place in
- ☐ Tunisia
- ☐ Libya
- ☐ Algeria
- ☐ Morocco

10 The country that began the oil sanctions against the USA in 1973 was
- ☐ Egypt
- ☐ Kuwait
- ☐ Syria
- ☐ Saudi Arabia

CHAPTER TEN

RACE RELATIONS: CONTRASTS BETWEEN THE UNITED STATES AND SOUTH AFRICA

CONTENTS

- **The United States** — 235

- **South Africa** — 245
  Before the white men 246
  The political problem, 1910 onwards 248
  Apartheid 249

- **Namibia** — 259

Race relations: the US and South Africa

THE UNITED STATES

Slavery was a permanent feature of West African society which for centuries had been divided up into changing groups of states and empires, frequently at war with one another. Africans expected that prisoners of war and criminals would become slaves; but it was rare for an African king to enslave a whole people or even an entire village. African rulers had never practised slavery on the scale demanded by the American market from the seventeenth century onwards.

Why didn't the early plantation owners enslave the native Indians? Because the Indians fought back and never accepted the idea of slavery.

Why didn't they enslave white criminals? Because everyone thought it was immoral to enslave white people.

Why were West Africans enslaved? Because businessmen accepted the expenses and inconvenience of turning West Africa into a permanent source of slaves – they had thirty per cent profit on every boatload crossing the Atlantic.

As far as North America was concerned, the slave trade began in 1619 when a Dutch ship anchored in Chesapeake Bay with twenty 'negars' for sale.

It is very important to understand that these blacks (there may have been a few women) didn't arrive as slaves. The citizens of Jamestown, Virginia, hired them as indentured servants. Exactly how these servants turned into slaves is obscure; but it happened. It seems that when colonies such as Virginia, Maryland and Massachusetts passed their first slave laws in the 1660s they were simply legalising a well-established social practice begun by the first English settlers living in America. But not all blacks were slaves. There were at least 3,000 free blacks living in the English colonies by 1670. So from very early days the basic problem, the co-existence of two free races, one white, one black, has beset the American people.

The black population explosion
- 1800   About a million blacks
- 1840   2,328,000 blacks
- 1860   4,441,000 blacks

The American Civil War
This began on 12 April 1861 after seven states had seceded from the

American Union. Lincoln's objective was to preserve the Union. In 1862 he wrote:

> *If I could save the Union without freeing any slave, I would do it; and if I could save it by freeing all the slaves, I would do it; and if I could do it by freeing some and leaving others alone, I would also do that.*

But he didn't have these alternatives and on 1 January 1863 he issued the Emancipation Proclamation. On 31 January 1865 (before the Civil War ended) the US Congress passed the *Thirteenth Amendment*:

> *Neither slavery nor involuntary servitude, except as a punishment whereof the guilty party shall have been duly convicted, shall exist within the United States . . .*

The whites' dilemma

White Americans were alarmed by the speed at which blacks sought to enter politics, the church, industry, commerce, education and the arts. They looked for ways of containing the blacks. They sought methods to control them in order to replace the lost discipline of the slave plantations.

Black codes and Jim Crow laws

From the 1860s onwards various states enacted special codes of law to deny blacks their basic civil rights. Some actually were contrary to the US Constitution, e.g. when they prohibited blacks from having firearms (this was an infringement of the Second Amendment).

- Blacks not to marry whites.
- Blacks not to have licences for the sale of liquor.
- Vagrancy laws often prevented blacks from entering city limits.

The Jim Crow laws specifically excluded blacks from white society.

- In many Southern towns blacks had to ride in segregated street-cars.
- Blacks could be whipped if they tried to participate in any white assembly as an equal; so churches, theatres, hotels and libraries were closed to blacks.

But despite the threats, the tarring and feathering, the lynchings, the house-burnings (much of this was instigated by the Ku Klux Klan, founded in 1865), the blacks' demand for civil rights was never crushed. In 1887 a group of black Nashville businessmen defined what they wanted:

> *We want to be treated like men, like anybody else, regardless of colour . . . We want public conveyances open to us according to the fare we pay; we want the privilege to go to theatres, operas and places of amusement . . . we cannot go to the places assigned to us in concerts without loss of respect.**

*Quoted by Howard N. Rabinowitz, *Race Relations in the Urban South*. OUP, 1978, page 195.

Black culture

Blacks found their self-respect and their own sense of identity through the church. They established their own churches after 1865. Remember: a church could easily become a school, a drama centre, a lecture theatre, a concert hall. From the 1880s there was a flowering of black religion and black music. As segregated communities arose in the cities and black worshippers attended segregated churches so the black preacher became the leader of the black community. Black dancing and black music became the most remarkable expressions of black culture. Jazz and its many offshoots were hard to date precisely. Hoagy Carmichael's famous approximation probably owes more to rhyme than to chronological accuracy, but it can't be far wrong:

> *Along about 1917*
> *Jazz has come upon the scene.*
> *Then about 1935*
> *You begin to hear swing, boogie-woogie and jive.**

*Hoagy Carmichael, *The Old Music Master*, Coral Record, 1971.

Jazz produced musicians whose names become more illustrious as the years go by: Bessie Smith, Big Bill Broonzy, Big Maceo Merriweather and Earl Fatha Hines sang of the deprivation, the misery and hopes of the black people. And it wasn't long before their music made an enormous appeal to whites and attracted white musicians such as Benny Goodman and Bix Beiderbecke.

This is a quotation from a British text:

> *Jazz created a compromise between black and white musicians and pointed one way through the fog of racial prejudice that blanketed the United States of America.*

Explain precisely what the author means by this statement; and point out any other areas in which black Americans were making their mark before 1939.

A glimmer of political hope, 1914–45

Since 1909, when W. E. Du Bois founded the National Association for the Advancement of Coloured Peoples (NAACP) – a movement dedicated to gaining civil rights for the blacks – slow progress was made in the political world. President Roosevelt tried to ensure that blacks had a fair share of the national recovery programme during the depression and his 1935 Social Security Act enabled three million blacks to go on the welfare scheme.

- Eleanor Roosevelt, the President's wife, was a strong supporter of civil rights for the blacks.
- Black gratitude – when it had the chance – showed itself through the ballot box. Many Southern states excluded blacks from voting by imposing very high literacy tests. By 1936 most blacks were voting for the Democrats; and by the time of Roosevelt's third Presidential victory (1940) blacks held the decisive vote in ten of the forty-eight

states of the American Union, and about seventy per cent of their votes were in favour of the President.

Segregation during the two World Wars

Segregation persisted in the US armed forces during both World Wars. The bravery of all-black regiments in the final offensives on the Western Front (1918) did not change racist views. Segregation operated in Britain from 1942 to 1945 when thousands of black soldiers helped build the American bomber bases there. It operated in the Pacific, and in Italy where the all-black 332nd Fighter Group pilots flew their Mustangs during the Second World War.

THE CAMPAIGN FOR CIVIL RIGHTS AFTER 1945

De-segregation in the armed forces

President Truman seemed sympathetic to the NAACP (it had written many moving appeals to the United Nations) and began the abolition of Jim Crow segregation in the armed forces. Integrated units came into being after 1948 and some fought in the Korean War, 1950–53. By 1955, there wasn't much to stop an able black officer from reaching high command (e.g. Major-General Benjamin O. Davis, USAF, had his HQ in the Pentagon during the 1960s).

Brown v. Board of Education

It was much harder for the mass of black civilians to struggle against discrimination and segregation.

Read the following account:

> The ghettos of the northern cities were perhaps the worst example of segregation. Here the employers had a vested interest in keeping a pool of unpaid labour to do the dirty jobs and consume the flood of cheap, low-quality manufactured goods. Individual ghettos had no political organisation capable of challenging discrimination and segregation sanctioned, as they were, by American law. However, the Plessey v. Ferguson test case (1896) defined segregation as legal as long as the facilities provided were equal. This led the NAACP to hit on a brilliant idea: why not challenge education, where they had proof that much less was being spent on black pupils than on white pupils? Guided by Thurgood Marshall, himself destined to become the first black member of the US Supreme Court, the NAACP petitioned several Federal Courts to rule that segregation was both unequal and illegal. Their victory was complete in the Brown v. the Topeka Board of Education, Kansas. In 1954 the Supreme Court ruled that segregation was contrary to the Fourteenth Amendment. Now every state would have to de-segregate its schools.

1. Why were the ghettos in the northern cities said to be 'the worst example of segregation'?
2. What was the main weakness of the ghettos?

Race relations: the US and South Africa

3 What American test case defined segregation as legal?
4 Who was the first black member of the US Supreme Court?
5 Why was segregation in education held to be illegal?

The white backlash: Little Rock, 1957

Few Americans were prepared for the white backlash that followed the Supreme Court decision. In Arkansas, Governor Faubus called out the National Guard rather than let nine black students enter the all-white Central High School. President Eisenhower couldn't tolerate this defiance of Federal law and directed the US army to escort the 'Little Rock Nine' to school.

De-segregating buses; Montgomery, 1955

On Thursday afternoon, 1 December 1955, Mrs Rosa Parks had taken her usual bus home from work in Montgomery, Alabama. Before she reached her front door Mrs Parks had won her place in American history by refusing to give up her seat to a white man. Hustled off to jail as a communist agitator, Rosa Parks was the signal for the rest of Montgomery's blacks to boycott the buses. On Monday they all walked to work! That evening they met their new Baptist minister, Dr Martin Luther King, to form the Montgomery Improvement Association. As the blacks represented seventy-five per cent of the city's commuters the bus company surrendered. In 1956 the segregation of blacks on municipal transport in the entire United States became illegal – a great victory for the policy of peaceful protest.

Read the following statements and then answer the related questions:

> *We have decided and we have done it, I think very effectively, to base our whole protest on the philosophy of non-violence. As we move on we will only use the weapon of love.*

This was said by Martin Luther King.   YES ☐   NO ☐

> *The famous song that became synonymous with black protest was the spiritual 'We shall not be moved'.*   TRUE ☐   FALSE ☐

> *The anthem of the civil rights movement was 'We shall overcome', a song based on the nineteenth-century spiritual, 'I'll be all right'.*   TRUE ☐   FALSE ☐

De-segregating the lunch-counters: Greensboro, 1960

On 1 February 1960 black students from Greensboro's Agricultural and Technical College for Negroes sat down at a Woolworth's lunch-counter – and the manager refused to serve them. The blacks refused to leave and their famous sit-in was the first of thousands up and down the country. Sit-ins and peaceful pickets disrupted the US catering services and forced many firms to de-segregate or face bankruptcy. Civil rights workers and demonstrators were often beaten up and most went to jail. And it was still something of a gesture: the blacks needed to make a bigger impact than this before they could capture the conscience of American whites.

Aspects of the Civil Rights Movement in America

Black demonstrator forced to leave a Massachusetts sit-in.

Source: Brian Catchpole, *A Map History of The United States.* Heinemann Educational Books, 1973.

1. Not all protests were successful, as this photograph shows. Here a black demonstrator is being led away from a 'sit-in' in Massachusetts. Note the salute he is giving, returned by one of his friends.
   What does this salute signify?
2. A higher proportion of blacks than whites found themselves drafted to serve a tour in Vietnam. These two black veterans of the Vietnam war are demonstrating in Washington for full civil rights.
   (*a*)   Why do you think they chose to wear their uniforms?
   (*b*)   Why did they paint their faces white?

Black veterans demonstrating in Washington.

Source: Brian Catchpole, *A Map History of The United States,* Heinemann Educational Books, 1973.

Freedom Riders and the March on Washington

James Farmer, Director of CORE (Congress of Racial Equality) had been the brains behind the sit-ins. Now he planned the freedom rides across state boundaries to challenge the legality of segregated waiting rooms. The first freedom ride was in 1961 to test the levels of racial hatred. The freedom riders found all they wanted in Anniston, Alabama, where a white mob burnt the bus and attacked the blacks. Said Farmer:

> *One of our purposes was to show the nation the real nature of segregation, with its violence, its idiocy, its brutality and its illegality. I think we have succeeded in showing that. I do not think that any man who can call himself human can forget the burning bus of Anniston. I think that consciences have been aroused . . .*

Eventually, Martin Luther King led the remarkable 1963 Washington Peace March. The sight of thousands of well-ordered, articulate and highly professional black leaders, seen by the nation on television, made a great impression.

1. Name the director of CORE.
2. Where did the 'burning bus' incident take place?
3. Put these events, critical in the story of the black struggle for civil rights, in their correct chronological order:
   - Brown *v.* Topeka Board of Education
   - Little Rock
   - The Montgomery bus boycott
   - Greensboro
   - The Freedom Riders
   - The Washington Peace March

Legislation and violence

President Johnson, unpopular for his policies in Vietnam, was a progressive in civil rights. Three major laws were passed:

- **1964** Civil Rights Act
- **1965** Education Act
- **1965** Voting Rights Act

all designed to end discrimination.

These proved inadequate and extremist black leaders emerged e.g.

Malcolm X:

> *Revolution is never based on begging somebody for an integrated cup of coffee.*

Hosea Williams:

> *Black power is when black people respect themselves. Black power is when we refuse to fight thousands of miles away from home for freedoms over there that we cannot enjoy here.*

Everything pointed to a clash between blacks and whites in America.

In 1965 10,000 blacks ran amok in the Watts District of Los Angeles and lifted the television sets and washing machines out of shop windows. Violence destroyed the black leadership as well as white property:

1966 Malcolm X assassinated

1968 Martin Luther King gunned down
Hurried Federal legislation (1968)
(a) guaranteed protection of civil rights workers;
(b) made incitement to riot a Federal offence, but could not contain the violence sweeping America.

1967 100+ US cities experienced race riots: 83 dead, 1,897 people injured.

1968 Fresh riots – people began to realise that racial discord was linked with urban poverty and rural decay:

*1968 National Advisory Commission on Civil Disorders.

> 'Just as Lincoln, a century ago, put preservation of the Union above all else, so should we put the creation of a true union – a single society and a single American identity – as our major goal.'*

America, it seemed was at last groping her way towards a tolerant, plural society.

Read this extract:

> Whites now began to accept black people in positions of authority and trust. Television had spent years focusing on the horrors of Vietnam and the recent race riots. Now the mass media were quick to weigh up the commercial possibilities of integration. So they soon beamed out programmes highlighting the capabilities of black people. Television heroes such as Starsky and Hutch, who accepted the authority of a black police captain and depended on the co-operation of Huggy Bear, made their own kind of important and none too subtle impact. State legislatures passed 'open housing laws' when blacks began playing a full part in local government. The first such law was in Virginia (1973).

1 Can you think of other television programmes or films that have helped to project the identity and competence of American blacks?
2 Do you think they had as much impact on the mass of the people as the Civil Rights movement?

An attitude change

Prejudice and discrimination were difficult to root out overnight. But a change had overtaken America by the 1980s.

◊ Great progress made by
  (a) 'political will' in the White House;
  (b) far-reaching Civil Rights legislation
  e.g. Industrial and commercial firms had to keep careful records of their ethnic employment policies.
  Federal contractors had to be seen giving equal opportunities to all, irrespective of race or colour.

◊ In 1983 Vanessa Williams became the first black Miss America. Said

Shirley Williams (black and a former Congresswoman): 'My first reaction is that the inherent racism in America must be diluting itself.'

The American Indians

American Indians enjoyed less spectacular success. About one million survive. Most live in or near towns; the rest occupy reservations and the 482 tribes or bands have access to ninety million acres of land. However, their living standards are the lowest in the US and they have suffered because of the radical changes in US government policy since 1934. Until then, the Bureau of Indian Affairs was supposed to 'terminate' (i.e. 'assimilate') all the tribes and integrate all Indians as US citizens. Termination reared its head under President Eisenhower (1953–61) and sixty-one tribes were terminated. Later presidents reversed this policy and Indians have managed to preserve their own way of life and win economic returns for the wealth hidden below the ground in their reservations. It was an uphill task and their AIM (the American Indian Movement) had to resort to a violent occupation of Wounded Knee on Pine Ridge Reservation (1973) to secure nationwide television coverage and make people conscious of their plight. Since then they have supervised the oil wells and coal mines on their reservations with a certain amount of financial success.

1 How many American Indians survive?
2 Explain the policy known as 'termination'.
3 Name the last US President to advocate termination.
4 Explain the meaning of AIM.
5 Why did the Indians occupy Wounded Knee in 1973?

The problem of poverty

Between 1955 and 1961:

▷ the US became the world's biggest property-owning democracy;
▷ the average US family was earning over 6,000 dollars annually;
▷ twenty per cent of US citizens lived in poverty.

Overwhelmingly this twenty per cent was made up of:
Black Americans
Indians
Puerto Ricans
Mexican immigrants
Poor whites (mainly ex-farmers)
The sick and elderly from all walks of life.

Neither President Johnson (despite his 1964 Appalachian Recovery programme and his 1965 Medicare scheme) nor President Nixon (despite his 'Six Great Goals': prosperity, new welfare schemes, environmental improvement, health improvement, local and central government reform) made sufficient impact. Certain ethnic groups, notably black Americans, suffered from the unemployment that peaked after 1973. Unemployment among blacks was nearly double that of whites and eighty per cent of teenagers failed to find jobs in the northern ghettos. It was possible to make generalisations about American poverty:

◊ Location was crucial. Black families living in New York State could earn double the income of black families living in Mississippi.
◊ Mexican-American families had lower per capita incomes than most because they had larger families.
◊ Yet Indians remained the most poverty-stricken even though they, together with Puerto Ricans, tended to have smaller families.

One organisation in the US (PUSH = People United To Save Humanity) was dedicated to the improvement of blacks' living conditions. Led by the Rev. Jesse Jackson, PUSH threatened to stop buying popular products such as Coca-Cola unless 'big business' began to trade with 'black business' – and thus create more job opportunities for black citizens.

Multiple-choice questions

1 Laws specifically made to exclude blacks from white society were called
- ☐ Slave laws
- ☐ Jim Crow Laws
- ☐ Settlement laws
- ☐ Liquor laws

2 The US President who issued the Emancipation Proclamation was
- ☐ Lincoln
- ☐ Washington
- ☐ Johnson
- ☐ Nixon

3 The movement dedicated to winning civil rights for blacks was
- ☐ AIM
- ☐ PUSH
- ☐ NAACP
- ☐ KKK

4 This American black leader ran for President
- ☐ James Meredith
- ☐ James Farmer
- ☐ Martin Luther King
- ☐ Jesse Jackson

5 The first major 'race riot' during the 1960s was in
- ☐ Los Angeles
- ☐ Topeka
- ☐ Dallas
- ☐ Chicago

6 The most important factor in winning civil rights for the American blacks was
- ☐ 'Political will' in the White House (the determination of US Presidents to change the system)

☐ The widespread media coverage of Civil Rights demonstrations such as Montgomery and Greensboro
☐ The de-segregation of the US armed forces after 1945
☐ The race riots of 1967–8

7 When Hosea Williams spoke of fighting for freedoms 'over there' that 'we cannot enjoy here', he was referring to the war in:
☐ France, 1918
☐ the Pacific, 1945
☐ the Congo
☐ Vietnam

SOUTH AFRICA

1 SOUTHERN AFRICA TO 1910

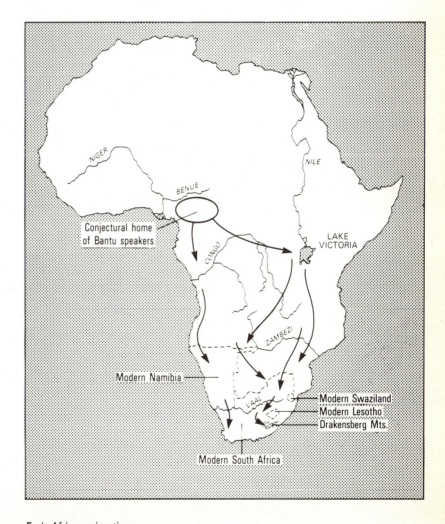

Early African migrations

BEFORE THE WHITE MEN

Archaeology has shown that there were Sotho-Tswana settlements on the Transvaal low veld just after 400 AD and, between 1450 and 1600, some chiefdoms developed into the early kingdoms of southern Africa. These Bantu peoples knew how to build stone houses and they put up some of these near modern Johannesburg. Bantu cattle owners began moving south of the Vaal about 1300 while an off-shoot group, the Nguni speakers, made their way through the Drakensberg Mountains into modern Transkei. In fact, from 1300 onwards there was considerable migration by African peoples into those regions now called Namibia and the Republic of South Africa.

White settlers

Two Dutch ships arrived off the Cape peninsula in 1652 and landed a small party of German, Swedish and Dutch settlers. Their job was to grow fruit and vegetables vital for the Dutch crews sailing round the Cape of Good Hope. These were the 'Boers' (farmers) who used slaves imported from East Africa, Madagascar and the Far East. Over the years more settlers arrived and moved inland either as graziers (trekboers) or as voortrekkers (nomadic farmers). They made contact with Nguni speakers in 1702. These Boers took their slaves with them and evolved the language 'Afrikaans'.

The British arrival

Britain took over the Cape as part of her strategy against the French during the Revolutionary Wars (1795). In 1806 the British turned Simon's Town into a naval base; in 1814 they took over the Cape (paying the Dutch £5 million as compensation); in 1820 4,000 British settlers arrived. The Dutch felt outnumbered. In 1833 Britain outlawed slavery in her colonies and paid the Boers fifty per cent of the market value of their slaves.

Remember: the numbers involved were relatively small compared with the United States. There were no accurate statistics, but it is thought that about 32,000 people were freed in 1833–4.

The Great Trek, 1836–40: results

Boer settlers began moving out of Cape Colony into Natal but the British followed them. The Boers had already made bitter contact with African peoples (especially the Zulu) and now decided to move even further north, ultimately to found the Orange Free State and the Transvaal.

The discovery of gold

In 1867 the discovery of diamonds in Griqualand West (on the Orange River) attracted many European migrants; then the discovery of gold on the Witwatersrand (1886) attracted thousands more. The Boers called the immigrants Uitlanders. Read the following account from a British textbook:

After the discovery of gold in the 1880s thousands of Uitlanders swarmed into the Transvaal where they soon outnumbered the resident Boer farmers. President Kruger forced them to pay heavy taxes, but denied them any civil rights. When the disgruntled Uitlanders planned a revolt against Kruger, Cecil Rhodes decided to lend assistance by sending in a band of armed raiders under the command of his friend, Dr Jameson. Almost immediately, a Boer commando captured the raiders and in the resulting scandal Rhodes resigned his office. Relations between Britain and the Boers worsened . . . and hostilities began on 10 October 1899.

1 Who were the Uitlanders?
2 Who was President Kruger?
3 Who was Cecil Rhodes?
4 What were the effects of the Jameson Raid?
5 During this period more and more Africans came to live and work in the Transvaal. How can you explain this development?

The creation of the Union of South Africa, 1910

After three major defeats, the British managed to wear down Boer resistance and peace was eventually signed in May 1902 (Treaty of Vereeniging). Representatives of the white population in the Cape, Natal, Orange Free State and the Transvaal urged a Union, in which only Africans in the Cape (assuming they possessed the appropriate property rights) would have the vote. But Africans in Natal, Orange Free State would have no political rights whatsoever; and no Cape African would be allowed to stand for Parliament. Britain agreed to these arrangements and the Union of South Africa came into being on 31 May 1910.

Read the following three extracts and identify each of their sources:
(a) Winston Churchill
(b) The original Transvaal constitution
(c) The British government

Extract 1

There shall be no equality in State and Church between white and black. Source ☐

Extract 2

The three British protectorates of Basutoland, Swaziland and Bechuanaland shall not be transferred to the Union until we see how the racial issues are operated in practice. Source ☐

Extract 3

I sympathise profoundly with the native races of South Africa, whose land it was long before we came to force a policy of dispossession on them . . . But I don't believe in politics for them. Source ☐

The 1913 Land Act

The 1913 Land Act stopped any African from buying land outside his own area (as defined by the new Union government). Many of these 'homelands' were unproductive. So the African was at a double disadvantage: no political rights and no freedom to buy land. From 1913 onwards the fate of every African was bound up with the ownership of the land because it was synonymous with their unquenchable desire for national freedom. It was as simple as that and one African neatly summed up his people's frustration:

> *At first we had the land and you had the Bible; now we have the Bible and you have the land.*

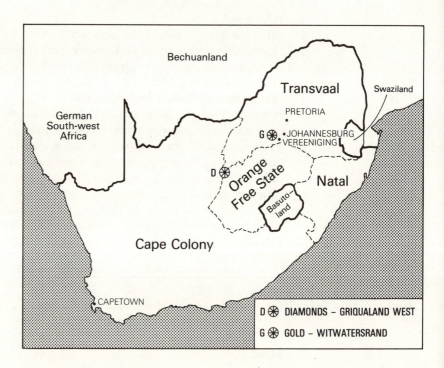

The Union of South Africa 1910

2 TO THE CREATION OF THE REPUBLIC OF SOUTH AFRICA

THE POLITICAL PROBLEM, 1910 ONWARDS

In 1910 the British Parliament at Westminster created the Union of South Africa. Louis Botha, a distinguished Boer general, became Prime Minister. He tried to work out a form of government acceptable to Afrikaners (Boers) and British alike. Few politicians of the day had any interest in the political and territorial rights of the black majority – most politicians held that the blacks didn't have any such rights. In 1912 the Afrikaner Nationalist Party emerged, openly hostile to British ideas and values.

In 1948 this Afrikaner Party won the General Election (in which the majority black population could not participate directly) and held power thereafter. Since 1948 South Africa's leaders have followed a policy of apartheid (pronounced 'apart-hate') or 'separate development'. Apartheid prohibited any mixing of the different ethnic groups then living in South Africa. Apartheid has kept over twenty million blacks in a condition of economic and political servitude to the white minority (less than five million).

Within South Africa the African National Congress (ANC) worked to transform the country into a new 'Azania' where all people had equal rights. Within South-West Africa, the former German colony mandated to the Union after the First World War, the South-West Africa People's Organisation (SWAPO) fought to have the right to represent their people in a new 'Namibia'.

APARTHEID

The 1948 definition

The Nationalist Party put into words ideas that many Afrikaners had felt for over a century. Their historical argument was that South Africa had been created by white people and was the first modern nation state to be formed in the entire continent. In the process, they said, Afrikaners had inherited a historical problem: how to deal with millions of Africans, most of whom had entered South Africa to find work in the coal and gold mines. Just before the 1948 election the Nationalist Party issued this definition:

> The concept of apartheid is a concept historically derived from the experience of the white population of the country.
>
> It is a policy which sets itself the task of preserving and safeguarding the racial identity of the white population of the country; of likewise preserving and safeguarding the identity of the indigeneous groups (i.e. the blacks) as separate racial groups. The policy of our country should envisage total apartheid as the ultimate goal of a natural process of separate development.

This statement took no account of the archaeological, historical and linguistic evidence that Bantu speakers had been settling in and opening up the country south of the River Vaal before the first white man had even arrived in South Africa.

However, having decided on apartheid, the Afrikaners had to create an elaborate structure of:
(a)   apartheid laws and
(b)   security laws
to prevent organisations such as the ANC from challenging it. It also meant (after the other African states won their independence) training and equipping the armed forces to meet attacks from the 'front-line' states in the north and mass insurrection from within.

The apartheid laws

During 1949–50 the Afrikaners physically shifted black populations out of the inner cities into shanty towns and forbade blacks and whites to marry or have sexual relations:

1949 Mixed Marriages Act.

1950 Immorality Act.

1950 Population Registration Act by which one's 'racial' colour was confirmed.

1950 Group Areas Act by which blacks were shifted into new quarters on the outskirts of large towns. Two well-known examples are Sharpeville and Soweto.

It is very difficult to appreciate the sheer size of these townships. Soweto (this stands for 'South-West Township') covers about forty square miles. Over 1.25 million people – mostly Zulus – live there. Its origins date back to 1904. It was designed to discourage settlement; living conditions were appalling as Soweto had none of the amenities one associates with a town. Before 1976 only one home in five had electricity so most people had to use coal for heating and cooking which meant that there was always a blanket of fog over Soweto during the winter. All of Soweto's homes now have electricity but there is still a desperate need for houses. About twelve people live in the average two-bedroomed Sowetan house.

Two Education Acts created separate educational provision for the blacks:

1954 Bantu Education Act, designed to provide minimum educational opportunities so that Africans would remain in a state of economic and political servitude.

1959 Separate Universities Act.

After 1952 and right up to 1986 all Africans had to carry their pass or 'reference book' containing their photograph, details of ethnic origin and work permit. No work permit meant instant arrest and deportation from the area. If blacks had permission to be in a 'white area' they had to sit on different seats in the parks, on public transport and in places of entertainment. Signs reading 'Netblankes' (White Europeans only) sprang up everywhere.

The security laws

1950 Suppression of Communism Act: banned the Communist Party in South Africa, together with any doctrine that advocated 'disturbances or disorder'.

1953 Public Safety Act: enabled the government to call a state of emergency on any pretext and impose martial law.

1953 Criminal Law Amendement Act: made passive resistance to any Union law a criminal offence. All strike actions became illegal in 1956.

1962–4 The General Law Amendment Act enabled the government to hold people without trial for ninety days.

1962 Sabotage Act: made sabotage (however the courts cared to define it) a treasonable offence carrying the death penalty.

1967 Terrorism Act: gave unprecedented powers to the security police who could ban activities under the 1960 Unlawful Organisations Act. At first the police forces were run by BOSS (Bureau of State Security,

1969). BOSS arrested or deported thousands of South African citizens (black and white). Many died in custody. One of the most famous was Steve Biko, the black activist and outstanding writer. Twice detained under the Terrorism Act, he died from 'brain damage' in 1977. Since then his 'Black Consciousness' movement and the Pan African Congress (both banned under the 1960 Act) have won immense support; while BOSS changed its name to DONS – the Department of National Security.

The Bantustans or 'Homelands'
The 1954 Tomlinson Report recommended that most Bantus should live in specially developed Bantustans or in the three British High Commission Territories:
>Basutoland (became independent Lesotho 1966)
>Swaziland (became independent Swaziland 1968)
>Bechuanaland (became independent Botswana 1966).

All surplus Africans had to be shunted into ten Bantustans; and after 1975 the Afrikaners began to grant them a form of independence (not recognised by the outside world):
>1976 Transkei
>1977 Bophuthatswana
>1979 Venda
>1981 Ciskei

Families often had to be left behind in the Bantustan when the breadwinner sought work in a 'white area'. A wife could not follow her husband to Cape Town or Pretoria unless her own reference book contained the magic 'Section 10' stamp.

AFRICAN RESISTANCE

Resistance began within two years of the creation of the Union of South Africa. The ANC was born at the Bloemfontein Conference of African leaders and by 1952 it commonly used strikes and boycotts to improve working and living conditions, even though it knew that, under a 1942 law declaring strikes by Africans illegal, the Afrikaners would use force to disperse them:

- e.g. 1946: African Mineworkers Union on strike – police smashed the strike and the mine owners declared they would not accept the idea of black unions working among the labour force.
- 1950: Transvaal strikes – police killed eighteen Africans.

1952 was the crucial year – the year when the ANC (and the Indian Congress) deliberately broke the pass and segregation laws – but bus boycotts and anti-pass demonstrations had little impact on the Afrikaner authorities. This was the 'Defiance Campaign':
- it produced few tangible results;
- it gave the Africans experience of planning for widespread anti-Afrikaner demonstration and encouraged them to support pass-burning as a basic sign of hostility to white domination.

Sharpeville, 1960

ANC and Pan-African activists organised a peaceful demonstration of pass-burning at Sharpeville.

Read this account from a British textbook:

> Frustrated by poor wages and living conditions, many Africans went on strike, threw away their reference books and marched down to the police station. Here they all demanded to be arrested – they thought this would give the police some difficulties. Crowds now assembled; government Sabre jets whistled overhead; Saracen armoured cars nuzzled the people. There was a scuffle, the police opened fire and sixty-nine Africans died. It was 21 March 1960 – the day of the Sharpeville Massacre. It stunned South Africa; it shocked the world deeply.

1. Do you think that there is any evidence that the Africans provoked the police?
2. Is there evidence that the fact that there would be a demonstration was well known?
3. From whom did the South Africans buy
   (a) their Sabre jets
   (b) the Saracen armoured cars?
4. Why do you think South Africa was 'stunned' by news of the Sharpeville Massacre?
5. What was the South African reaction to international criticism?

The creation of the Republic of South Africa

In 1961 South Africa declared herself a Republic and left the Commonwealth.

3 THE STRUGGLE AGAINST THE REPUBLIC SINCE 1961

After Sharpeville the Afrikaners banned both the ANC and Pan Africanist Movements, both of whom now turned to the idea of an armed struggle against the dominant white minority (the blacks outnumbered the whites roughly 4:1). The Afrikaners then responded with the lists of security laws.

The arrest of Nelson Mandela

Nelson Mandela led the ANC in 1960 and he was arrested, together with many of his senior colleagues, on a charge of treason. In 1964 he was found guilty and given a life sentence (part of which he served on the notorious Robben Island). He has said:

> During my lifetime I have dedicated myself to the struggle of the African people. I have fought against white domination, and I have fought against black domination. I have cherished the ideal of a democratic and free society in which all persons live together in harmony, with equal opportunities. It is an ideal I hope to live for and achieve. But if needs be, it is an ideal for which I am prepared to die.

> **ASPECTS OF APARTHED**
>
> SOUTH AFRICAN PRIME MINISTERS SINCE 1948
>
> MALAN 1948–52
> STRIJDOM 1952–58
> VERWOERD 1958–66 (ASSASSINATED)
> VORSTER 1966–78
> BOTHA 1978
>
> SOME OF THE TERMINOLOGY USED IN APARTHEID
>
> (*APARTHEID* is pronounced 'APART-HATE')
>
> COLOUREDS: These are the 'Cape Coloureds' who have descended from mixed marriages between Europeans, Indians, Malays and Africans from the seventeenth century right up to the race laws of 1949.
> INDIANS: These are the distinct Asiatic groups who live in South Africa and who have special provision made for them by the National government.
> HETEROGENEOUS: this expression is used to mean 'many kinds of people'.
>
> In 1983 Prime Minister Botha appealed to the 2.7 million Coloureds and the 0.85 million Indians to support him in a referendum (it excluded the blacks) on a new constitution. This would give Coloureds and Indians representation in their own 'House of Representatives' and 'House of Delegates', plus the right to be elected to an 'Electoral College' and the Council that advised the President of the Republic. But their political rights would be still very limited as they would be outvoted by the whites.
> Prime Minister Botha won the 1983 referendum.

The riots of 1973

Black workers in Natal and at the Western Deep Mine, Carletonville, went on strike in 1973. Twelve people were killed by the police at Western Deep but significantly the mine owners awarded the black workers a twenty-five per cent wage increase after the shootings.

The Soweto massacre, 1976

On 16 June 1976 children in Soweto demonstrated against the compulsory use of Afrikaans in their lessons. Adults joined in and there was a breakdown in law and order within the township. As at Sharpeville, the Afrikaners intervened with force and several hundred people (the official figure was 180) were killed, including many children. The shootings led to the biggest demonstrations against apartheid and the demonstrators were whites as well as blacks. Many young people had joined the ANC after Sharpeville; the new Azania People's Organisation attracted even more. Guerrilla training camps opened in Botswana, Zimbabwe, Zambia and Mozambique. Among Afrikaners there was now the very real fear that they would be subject to the same sort of terrorist attacks as were the white settlers in Rhodesia.

South Africa's reaction to arms embargoes
Fearing a massive confrontation between blacks and whites, the UN ordered an arms embargo against South Africa. The Afrikaners responded by setting up their own military manufacturing corporation called Armscor (1977). Up to then South Africa was ninety per cent dependent upon arms imports and needed to buy all of its aeroplanes abroad. Since 1977 it has become ninety per cent independent of foreign weaponry and has developed a single-seater interceptor fighter (the Cheetah, based on an Israeli fighter design) and a helicopter gunship called the Alpha XIII.

A new Prime Minister
In 1978 Pieter Botha became the fifth Nationalist Prime Minister. He set out to remove the day-to-day discrimination. He authorised black trade unions and allowed a few integrated sports teams to play in public. However, he had to face the very real issue of black majority rule and a growing hostility from the rest of the world as black anger exploded into violence unprecedented in the history of the Republic. Abolishing pass laws and granting limited political rights (Botha's concessions in 1986) were simply not enough.

Increasing violence
During 1984–6 there were riots all over the country. During 1985 Winnie Mandela became prominent as an ANC leader (though Oliver Tambo had taken her imprisoned husband's place). She was supported by Bishop Tutu (the first African to become Archbishop in South Africa in 1986) and the white activist Helen Suzman.

21 July 1985 — Botha declared a State of Emergency.

February 1986 — Terrible riots in Alexandra, north of Johannesburg. The tension was largely reduced by the personal appearance of Bishop Tutu. But by then over 2,000 blacks had died in over a year of violence.

The EPG (Commonwealth Eminent Persons Group)
This visited South Africa in 1986 and recommended:

- the release of Nelson Mandela;
- that the Commonwealth should take 'concerted action of an effective kind' to avert 'what could be the worst bloodbath since the Second World War'.

The impact of the EPG peace mission was lost when South Africa attacked ANC HQs in Botswana, Zimbabwe and Zambia. Said Shridath Ramphal, Commonwealth Secretary-General, the Afrikaners have 'declared war on peace in southern Africa'.

The demand for sanctions against South Africa
A world-wide demand for sanctions against the Pretoria government was resisted by Britain, West Germany and the US. Japan and the EEC did impose limited sanctions, which were quite insufficient to damage the Republic during 1986. The ANC and Bishop Tutu called for sanctions; some African groups (notably the Zulu led by Chief Buthelezi) opposed sanctions.

Attitude of the OAU (Organisation of African Unity)
Since its foundation at Addis Ababa in 1963 (its President had said that its main role was to help liberate those parts of Africa not yet liberated) the OAU had been bitterly divided over policies and unable to cope with the problem of African famine. In 1986 it merely condemned the South African government for its attacks on the 'frontline states' of Botswana, Zambia and Zimbabwe and urged the imposition of international sanctions.

The attitude of the Afrikaner National Party (1986 Conference)
It defied the rest of the world, saying that there was really little understanding of apartheid:

> *It is a serious misconception that political representation based on race has anything to do with discrimination or the outdated concept of apartheid.*

There was no concession at this conference to the idea of black majority rule.

Look at the map on page 256 of the African homelands.

1. Insert the names of the 'independent Bantustans' listed on page 251.
2. Mark Natal, the Transvaal and the Orange Free State.
3. Mark Robben Island.
4. Name the capital of the Republic of South Africa.
5. Write a paragraph to explain precisely what the intention of the South African government is:
   (a) for the blacks living within the homelands;
   (b) for the blacks living outside the homelands.

Multiple-choice questions
1. The most significant move for the blacks since apartheid was begun was the removal of
   ☐ The pass laws
   ☐ The legalisation of trade unions
   ☐ The visit of the EPG
   ☐ The election of Bishop Tutu as Archbishop
2. The man who took over the leadership of the ANC after Nelson Mandela's imprisonment was

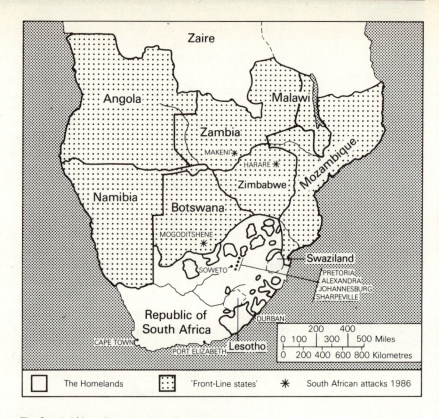

The South African 'homelands' or Bantustans

    ☐ Chief Buthelezi
    ☐ Walter Sisulu
    ☐ Oliver Tambo
    ☐ Kenneth Kaunda

3 The 'Black Consciousness' writer who died in police custody was
    ☐ Lawrence Ndzanga
    ☐ Elijah Loza
    ☐ Albert Lutuli
    ☐ Steve Biko

4 The Bantustans have been used as
    ☐ Dumping grounds for Africans not needed by the white economy
    ☐ Training grounds for democratically elected opposition political parties
    ☐ Areas for the growing of high quality cereals

5 The Commonwealth leader who was *not* a member of the EPG was
    ☐ Malcolm Fraser
    ☐ General Obasanjo
    ☐ Lord Barber
    ☐ Dame Nita Barrow
    ☐ John Malecela

Race relations: the US and South Africa

☐ Sardar Swaran Singh
☐ Rev. Edward Scott
☐ Shridath Ramphal

Look at the cartoon:

Source: *The Observer*, 28 November 1982

1 What is the cartoonist trying to say about Africa's leaders?
2 The cartoonist has split up the map of Africa to form three letters. What are these?
3 What does the African child represent?
4 Would the cartoonist think that African leaders are well organised to deal with the problems of South Africa?
    Overleaf are a dozen comparisons/contrasts between the American blacks and the South African blacks in their quest for Civil Rights. Consider them carefully. How many more significant points of comparison or contrast are there?

United States	South Africa
1 Africans were forcibly brought to America and enslaved by white people. Slavery was not abolished until 1863 and even after that plantation owners secretly replenished their stock of black labour by importing slaves across the Atlantic via Brazil.	Relatively few Africans were enslaved by the Boers. Slavery was abolished in 1833 throughout the British Empire – and this contributed to the Great Trek into Natal, Orange Free State and the Transvaal.
2 Blacks did not willingly come to America to join their colleagues on the cotton plantations in the South or in the factories of the North. America had the advantage of enormous white immigration during the nineteenth and twentieth centuries.	Blacks came from colonies outside South Africa in order to find work in the gold and coal mines, in factories and the service industries. There was steady white immigration into South Africa and Rhodesia in the twentieth century, but not on America's scale.
3 There were no serious restrictions on movement in the USA after Emancipation.	Until 1986 pass laws severely restricted movement in South Africa, with consequent hardship.
4 Blacks are not excluded from any states in the American Union; nor do they have to live in specific parts of the United States. American Indians are not compelled to live on reservations.	The African experience has been totally different. The Afrikaners have set aside parts of the Republic specifically for black peoples. They have given 'independence' to some of these homelands.
5 A strong tradition of segregation developed after 1863. Blacks were seen as a reservoir of cheap labour. Very few states gave them civil rights.	After 1910 the Afrikaner attitude towards segregation hardened, though full apartheid was not introduced until 1948. Blacks were seen as a source of cheap labour after gold was discovered at Johannesburg.
6 Blacks were able to begin their Civil Rights movement through legal processes, by appealing to the US Federal Constitution against the discriminatory actions of individual American states.	Africans had no such opportunity. South Africa was a unitary state with all power centred on Pretoria. There was no standing body of constitutional law to which they could appeal. Pretoria simply made new laws designed to frustrate every black move to win civil rights.
7 The nature of black culture (their way of life) enabled them to find natural leaders among the clergy. There were other sources of leadership (e.g. Black Power) that advocated violence but they made only a brief impact. Dignity, respectability and the sheer intellectual argument of the blacks' case enabled civil rights to triumph.	The black clergy has made an important contribution to the demand for civil rights. But it has not been able to moderate the violence (except in one or two notable cases). Pretoria is rarely impressed by intellectual arguments justifying the case for equal treatment of all peoples.
8 The American conscience was smitten when it realised that race and poverty went hand in hand. The injustice of the ghettos and the nature of racial segregation was brought home to Americans through the race riots of the sixties. Americans went through a dramatic attitude change, made easier, perhaps, because American blacks were in a minority.	The fact that race and poverty are connected in South Africa has made little effect on Pretoria. Life in rural South Africa remains at a very low level; though there has been some improvement in urban conditions. More than anything, the white Afrikaners realise that they are in a minority and the blacks in the majority.

Race relations: the US and South Africa

United States	South Africa
9 Blacks and whites shared a hard, bitter experience in the Vietnam War. There was a sense of community in that special context. It had an effect on white 'Nam' veterans.	The blacks and whites have never shared an important experience in the twentieth century. There is no sense of community in South Africa.
10 Integration in school and public life has become almost universal in America.	Integration is a token gesture in South African sport, hotels. The Afrikaners are determined to encourage separate racial and political development.
11 Organised black groups have exerted financial pressure on American business – to their advantage. These pressure groups operate in a very sophisticated manner and have no need to use violence, e.g. PUSH.	African pressure groups such as the 1955 SACTU (South African Congress of Trade Unions) have organised strikes and boycotts but these have nearly always led to violence and bloodshed; rarely have they led to specific gains to the Africans involved.
12 The overwhelming reason for the success of black civil rights has been the fact that America is a democracy. Once the President of the United States insisted on the equality of blacks and whites before the law, Congress passed the appropriate civil rights legislation. Integration became a federal requirement. Of course, there was never any danger of black majority rule in America.	No Prime Minister in the history of the Union (1910–61) or the Republic (1961–) has ever favoured civil rights for the Africans in the sense the rest of the world understands the term. Had he done so he would have automatically created black majority rule in South Africa at a time when the black population was on the increase and white numbers were falling.

NAMIBIA

Its changing status
- 1880–1915   Imperial Germany ruled South-West Africa.
- 1915–1920   Occupied by South African troops.
- 1920–1966   Governed by South Africa under the League of Nations mandate, having promised in 1945 that Namibians would be fully protected.
- 1966   UN scrapped its mandate and regarded the region as 'Namibia'.
- 1971   UN International Court of Justice ruled that South African occupation of Namibia was illegal.

The extension of apartheid
By the time the UN declared the South African presence illegal, apartheid was already operating inside Namibia.

- 1968   Development of Self-Government for Native Nations in South Africa Act, which created homelands for the non-whites (mainly the Ovambo people).
- 1969   South West Affairs Act, which increased South Africa's political and military control of the region.

South Africa promised the Namibian homelands independence provided that it kept control of the port at Walvis Bay and the Rossing uranium mine – the most important source of this vital element in the world.

Resistance
In 1972–3 Ovambo miners joined with colleagues in Natal in a series of strikes. They refused to take part in local elections and the more militant joined SWAPO – the South West Africa People's Organisation.

In 1973 the UN recognised SWAPO as the representative government of the Namibian people.

Reaction
Prime Minister Vorster challenged this at the Turnhalle Conference held at Windhoek in 1975. Dick Mudge emerged as the leader of the Democratic Turnhalle Alliance – a multiracial group committed to the eventual independence of Namibia. For the time being, it acted as the only government in Namibia recognised by Pretoria. SWAPO's reaction was to plan guerrilla raids on the South Africans and to begin building bases in the 'front line' states. Soviet and Cuban advisers operated in Angola and from 1975 onwards fighting flared along the border between Angola and Namibia.

The contact group
Many western nations found that events in Namibia and South Africa caused a conflict between their moral values and their business interests. South Africa was of tremendous strategic and economic importance. So, in 1977, the USA, Britain, Canada, West Germany and France formed their 'contact group' to bring about a settlement between SWAPO and South Africa. They began drafting constitutions for a new Namibia that would protect the interests of the Namibians as well as those of South Africa and the western nations.

Reduction in warfare
Major battles had been fought in the late seventies between South Africa and Angola. There were also clashes between South Africa and Mozambique. Then, during 1984, the South Africans began talks with both countries and, in particular, created the Pretoria-Luanda Accord.

ASIAN CONTRASTS: CHINA, VIETNAM AND JAPAN

CONTENTS

- **China** 263
- **Vietnam** 279
- **Japan since 1945** 284
  Recovery from war 284

Asian contrasts: China, Vietnam and Japan

1 CHINA

Although China had thrown off the rule of the Manchu Emperors and had the status of a Republic after 1912, she had seen no unity, peace or stability. President Yuan Shih-kai was simply a powerful warlord who wanted to found his own imperial dynasty in China. When he died in 1916, the countryside fell under the control of scores of warlords – not deliberately wicked men but men who had little interest in their people and who usually preferred a constant round of military campaigns in preference to flood control projects and famine relief work. So despite:

(a) the Kuomintang (KMT) Nationalist Party led by Sun Yat-sen and
(b) the CCP (Chinese Communist Party) founded 1920–1

it was the warlords who ran the day-to-day affairs of the Chinese people. On the fringe were the imperial powers – Britain, the USA, Japan, Italy, France – who controlled China's external trade and provided the cash investment for the growth of industry in the great 'Treaty Ports' fringing the coast of China: Tientsin, Tsingtao, Shanghai, Hangchow, Ningpo, Wenchow, Foochow, Swatow and Canton.

The Russian influence

Although the Russians had been instrumental in founding the CCP, they backed the KMT for the time being.

- They thought the KMT had the best chance of defeating the warlords and ejecting the imperialists.
- Sun Yat-sen agreed and worked closely with the Russians; and sent several officers (including Chiang Kai-shek) to study Red Army training methods and tactics (Moscow 1923).
- Russian ships arrived with weapons (Whampoa, 1924) and Sun decided to move north to attack the warlord. The Russians urged him to consolidate his position in the south but Sun – dying of cancer – refused.
- He went north to hold a crucial conference with the warlords in Peking where he died in 1925 – Asia's first great nationalist.

The Northern Expedition, 1926–8

Chiang Kai-shek inherited the leadership of the KMT and drew up his own plan against the warlords – the famous Northern Expedition.

Read the following extract from a British textbook:

> In 1926 two armies left Canton and by March 1927 they had conquered most of southern China. In the midst of the campaign, Chiang decided to dispense with the Communists for ever. They were out in the open, easy to identify and easy to annihilate. He had no illusions about the future. If he let the Communists survive they would one day try to kill him and overturn the KMT. So on 12 April 1927 he ordered the 'White Terror' to begin. KMT troops and secret agents arrested all the Communists in Shanghai – and shot them. Other mass executions went on all along the Yangtse valley but when the KMT tried the same tactics in the southern cities they found themselves up against a tough opposition. For weeks fierce battles raged in Swatow and Nanchang until the Communists realised that their only chance of survival was to retreat into the mountain fastness of Chingkanshan where they lived side by side with the regular occupants, the bandits of the Ko Lao Hui secret society.

1. Why was Chiang Kai-shek so hostile to the Communists?

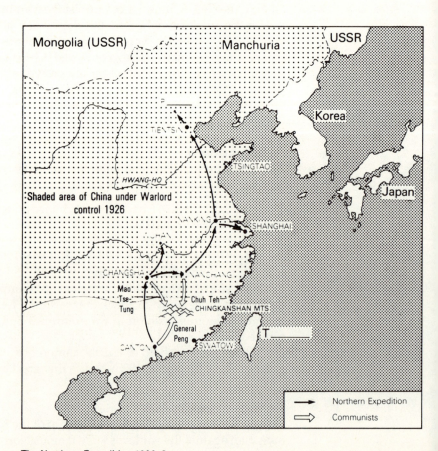

The Northern Expedition 1926–8

2 What was the 'White Terror'?
3 Why do you think resistance was so heavy in the southern cities?
4 What plan did the Communists devise in order to survive?
5 On the map of the Northern Expedition:
   (a) Mark Peking (Peiping)
   (b) Draw an arrow to mark the withdrawal of the Russian advisers from China.
   (c) Label Taiwan (held by the Japanese).
   (d) Name the Yangtse-kiang.

Chiang Kai-shek then moved north, persuaded many warlords to join the KMT and entered Peking (1928). To round off the campaign, he sent his best troops south to exterminate the Communists in Ching-kanshan – and might have succeeded had the Japanese not launched their invasion of Manchuria (1931).

Note that the world's attention was not especially riveted on Manchuria in 1931–2 but on Shanghai. Until then, the advancing Japanese had not seriously threatened the commercial interests of the imperial powers. Then came news of the Japanese air attack on Chapei (north Shanghai):

> *For terrifying ghastliness, the aerial bombardment of Chapei is appalling beyond appreciation except by those who had seen the same in the European war. Hundreds of houses are a wreck and a ruin.*

Chiang Kai-shek sent troops to stem the invasion by Japanese marines and after many days fighting around Shanghai the British patched up a truce between the Chinese and Japanese (March 1932).

1 Why didn't the Western Powers immediately react when the Japanese invaded Manchuria (1932)?
2 Why were they more concerned about the later Japanese attack on Shanghai?
3 What did the war reporter's reference to 'the European war' mean?
4 What was the attitude of Chiang Kai-shek to the Japanese attacks?

The Long March, 1934–5

Chiang Kai-shek was soon reconciled to the loss of Manchuria and quickly resumed his extermination campaign against the Communists. This time he hired German army officers to plan his attacks. One of them, General von Seeckt, tempted the Red soldiers out of their mountain retreat and then defeated them in the Battle of Kuanchang (April 1934). The survivors, including Mao Tse-tung and Chou En-lai, realised their plight was desperate and and decided to break out and head in the general direction of the Soviet Union. On 16 October they slipped away, leaving behind comrades to cover their escape and fool Chiang Kai-shek into believing he had the Communists surrounded. Now read this extract:

> *The Nationalist leader soon realised he had been tricked. Infuriated, he blasted the Communists with artillery fire and harried them with*

ground-attack aeroplanes. The Long Marchers survived these and a pitched battle at the River Hsiang. What to do next? There were so many plans, so many planners. And time was short. Eventually, they decided to choose an overall leader – and they nominated Mao Tse-tung, hereafter known as Chairman Mao. With renewed energy, the Long Marchers crossed the Yangtse and then marched towards the Tatur River – destined to be the scene of their most courageous effort of all: crossing the Luting Bridge. The Nationalists had removed most of the wooden planking suspended from the thirteen huge chains but had failed to dynamite the vital moorings holding the chains on their side of the river. A few brave comrades made their way across under withering rifle fire, held a bridgehead on the far side and enabled their comrades to cross.

1 Did the Long Marchers fight a pitched battle after leaving Chingkanshan?
2 Whom did the Long Marchers nominate as their leader?
3 Where did their 'most courageous effort' take place?
4 Why were the chains still in position?
5 Look at the photograph of the Long Marchers. Would you agree that they had primitive transport.

Source: BBC Radio for Schools pamphlet, 1969

After the successful crossing the Long Marchers pushed north, over the Great Grasslands, across the mountain ranges and into Shensi Province. About one marcher in twenty survived this epic of human endurance.

Was it a success?

Asian contrasts: China, Vietnam and Japan

- Only about 35,000 Red Army men assembled at Yenan, Mao's new headquarters, by the end of 1935.
- Yenan, however, was a much better base than Chingkanshan had ever been.

Look at the map depicting the Long March. Why was the Yenan base so important?

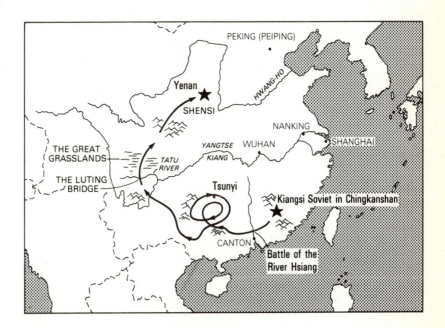

The Long March, October 1934 – October 1935

Chiang Kai-shek's 'New China'

Between 1934 and 1935, while the Long March was in progress, the Nationalist leader tried to modernise China. He funded new industries and brought in new health and education programmes. But he did nothing to make the cherished beliefs of Sun Yat-sen come true: there was no freedom, no democracy and no land reform. In fact, he employed a secret police known as the Blue Shirts and censored the press in order to cut down criticism of his government. Chiang Kai-shek openly admired the techniques used by the European dictators (especially Mussolini), and many army officers feared that he intended to set up a Fascist-style government in China. Some actually kidnapped him (1936) and ordered him to stop fighting the Communists and prepare for the coming war against Japan. Chiang Kai-shek agreed to form a second 'United Front' with Mao Tse-tung, and was allowed to fly out to Nanking.

The Sino-Japanese Incident, 1937

The word 'Sino' used in this adjectival form means 'Chinese'. The incident was a resumption of the original conflict during which the Nationalists had lost Manchuria. The threat from Japan was now so great that Chiang Kai-shek moved his capital to Chungking – and survived on the aid still coming in from Russia, Britain and the USA. There was virtual stalemate during 1939–40 but after the Japanese attack on Pearl Harbor (7 December 1941) China became an ally of America and Britain.

The significance of China in the Second World War

◊ China was tying up about 1.2 million Japanese soldiers. President Roosevelt knew that it took the Japanese only 500,000 men to carry out their Pacific conquests.

◊ Aid to China was therefore vital – but how to get it there?
(a)   Japan cut the Burma Road in 1942.
(b)   So American aid had to come over the 'Hump' – the name given to the mountain ranges on the China-Burma frontier.

◊ American bomber bases were built in China and their presence led to the biggest Japanese offensive of the war – Ichi-go, 1944. The Japanese commander, General Hada, captured most of the eastern bases and overran vast tracts of Chinese territory.

◊ During 1944–5 Chinese troops helped to build the Ledo Road. This linked up with the Burma Road still in Allied hands and enabled Chiang Kai-shek to acquire vast quantities of brand-new trucks, tanks and heavy artillery at the very end of the Second World War – equipment that would enable him to face the Communists with confidence in 1946.

The failure of America's China policies

Meanwhile, the Americans were working hard to bring Mao and Chiang together in a common cause: the creation of a peaceful, united China. They sent missions to Yenan and advisers to Chungking. Ambassador Hurley even managed to set up a meeting between Mao and Chiang in 1945. But it was all in vain. For the Chinese people, the Second World War had simply been an interruption in their long civil war.

◊ Mao never intended to collaborate with Chiang. He regarded the Nationalist leader as the last of the warlords.

◊ Chiang was equally intolerant of Mao. The Nationalist leader had his heart set on regaining Manchuria, built up by the Japanese as the biggest industrial region in the Far East.

◊ In Manchuria 1947–8 the Nationalists occupied many of the industrial centres but failed to gain control of the countryside where the Communists were based.

◊ In 1948 Mao's best general, Lin Piao, killed, wounded or captured 400,000 Nationalist soldiers. Chiang Kai-shek had lost the cream of his fighting men; and at the same time many other Nationalist soldiers were throwing in their lot with the Communists.

◊ In desperation President Truman signed the 1948 China Aid Bill – and the first ammunition ship sailed to China in November. But it was too late. The first Communist offensives that would drive Chiang from the mainland had already begun.

The Communist victory

Mao Tse-tung was principally interested in the social and political conduct of his troops when they were taking part in a military campaign. He insisted that they came as friends of the people, as representatives of a 'People's Liberation Army'. This was in complete contrast to the Nationalists who frequently looted and terrorised the areas they occupied. Consequently, Mao left military operations to his trusted friend Chuh Teh who in turn directed the Communist generals. The photograph below shows Mao – just before the war – in his typical leadership role, a teacher, a speaker.

Mao Tse-tung speaking at the University established in Yenan

Source: BBC Radio for Schools pamphlet, 1969

The capture of Peking (Peiping), 1949

The Chinese Red Army began its general advance towards the Yangtse-kiang in October 1948. The decisive battle was fought just outside the city of Suchow and this great Communist victory persuaded the Nationalist commander of Peking that further fighting was useless.

The Communists cross the Yangtse, April 1949

Mao now demanded unconditional surrender from the Nationalists and after regrouping his forces he ordered his generals to cross the Yangtse. The Chinese Red Army entered Nanking and for many Nationalist soldiers this represented defeat. Over the next few weeks they surrendered to the Communists by the thousand and in one sense the advance of the Red Army southwards was a triumphal 'long march'. In every village and every town the Red soldiers carried out land reform to the benefit of the local peasantry.

Chiang escapes to Taiwan

As the Nationalist government moved from Nanking to Canton and then on to Chungking and Chengtu it was obvious that its days in China were numbered. Chiang Kai-shek decided to abandon the mainland. He still had a strong navy and air force and so began the task of ferrying his supporters across to Taiwan. He also managed to repel Red Army attacks on the two tiny islands of Quemoy and Matsu and so 'Nationalist China' now consisted of three off-shore islands (December 1949).

Document 1

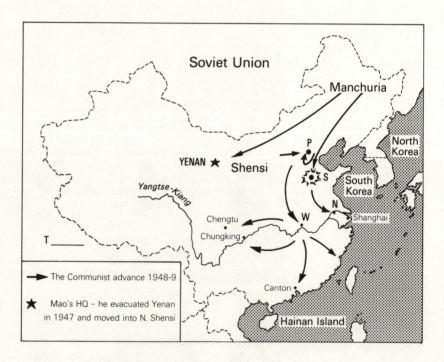

The Chinese Communist victory, 1948–9

Asian contrasts: China, Vietnam and Japan

Document 2

Red Army soldiers resting in Nanking

Source: Brian Catchpole, *A Map History of Modern China*. Heinemann Educational Books, 1982

Document 3 The thought of Mao Tse-tung
In 1949 Mao was very conscious that he stood at a great moment in history, facing the responsibility of rebuilding Chinese society:

> *The Soviet Communist Party has won its victory. Under the leadership of Lenin and Stalin they have shown that, not only are they capable of revolution, but of reconstruction too . . . The Communist Party of the Soviet Union is our best teacher . . .*
> (From Mao's *Concerning the People's Dictatorship*)

Document 4

HMS *Amethyst*

Source: Brian Catchpole, *A Map History of Modern China*. Heinemann Educational Books, 1982, p. 79

1. On the map (Document 1) mark Peking, Wuhan and Nanking.
2. Mark the off-shore islands that make up the territory now known as 'Nationalist China'.
3. Was Hainan included in that territory?
4. Mark the key battle at S. Why was it so important?
5. What was the name of the territory at T_____ ?
6. Shade in the People's Republic of China as it existed at the end of 1949.
7. Document 2 is a photograph of Red Army troops resting in Nanking during the Revolution. Do they give the impression that they are well disciplined?
8. What do you think is going on in the minds of the civilian onlookers?
9. Does Document 3 convey the idea that Mao is about to imitate the policies of the Soviet Union?
10. Name the two Soviet leaders he appears to admire.
11. What quality, apart from revolution, does he stress as important in Soviet history?
12. Document 4 is a picture of the British warship HMS *Amethyst*. What was the *Amethyst* doing in the Yangtse in 1949?
13. What events caused the 'Amethyst incident' to make British people hostile towards the Chinese People's Republic?
14. How did Mao interpret the incident?

Asian contrasts: China, Vietnam and Japan

The Sino-Soviet Treaty of Friendship and Alliance, 1949
In Moscow Stalin promised Mao that he would:

- protect China against the possibility of attack from Japan.
- give China as much economic aid as possible.

The treaty gave Mao immense confidence and he returned to China convinced that he must tell his people

- that they were part of a huge international brotherhood ready to lend a hand at this crucial stage in Chinese history;
- that they must accept the 'thought' of Mao Tse-tung as it was especially worked out to meet the needs of a society in the midst of massive reconstruction.

Mao ensured that key members of the Communist Party (mainly veterans of the Chinese Red Army, now called People's Liberation Army – PLA) trained students and peasants as 'cadre leaders' whose job was to convey the new ideas to the people. These ideas were:
> Hard work, plain living, self-reliance, inventiveness, fearlessness in the face of danger.

Mao had to translate these ideas into propaganda the mass of the people could understand. In this respect he was quite brilliant during the famine period 1949–50:

e.g. 'the single bowl of rice movement' required that everyone lucky enough to escape food shortages should contribute a bowl of rice to their less fortunate comrades – every PLA man would contribute an ounce of rice from his rations. In fact, the Chinese Communist Party (CCP) moved thousands of tons of grain to the eastern cities to which literally millions of starving refugees had flocked.

Learn from Tachai!
This was Mao's best known propaganda exercise. Read this account based on original Communist 'hand-outs':

> *The village of Tachai in Shensi Province had been an underproductive settlement run by a rich landlord and a couple of wealthy peasants. There was the constant problem of soil erosion and the villagers were always in debt. PLA men had liberated the village as early as 1945 and the cadres had worked with the peasants to form a mutual aid team – once they had eliminated the corrupt landowners. Output rocketed and in 1953 the peasants formed themselves into a co-operative farm. This was way ahead of its time – China's first commune. Between 1950 and 1958 Mao constantly urged his people: 'Learn from Tachai!'*

1. What do you think really happened during the 'single bowl of rice movement'?
2. Why were the Tachai villagers always in debt?
3. When did Tachai become 'China's first commune'?
4. What was 'a mutual aid team'?

5 What was the name of the Chinese leader who stated that Mao had exaggerated the story of Tachai and that the village had been carefully subsidised by the CCP to make it a good propaganda exercise for the Communists?

The Great Leap Forward, 1958–60

Mao's Agrarian Reform Law dates from 1950 and the cadres redistributed land to the peasants, three million of whom became modest landowners for the first time in their lives. It was a bloodthirsty process – about two million existing landowners were killed and their lands and effects were then parcelled out among the people. Mao insisted that the people must 'leap from small-scale farming' to form co-operatives – there were 800,000 of these by 1955.

At the same time, Mao adopted Soviet-style Five Year Plans to reconstruct industry and tried to involve everyone in the process of industrialisation. He encouraged people to set up mini steel-furnaces in their back gardens! There were many successes (especially in hydro-electric power) and many failures, which were partly due to the appalling economic conditions of the day and partly to poor planning and administration.

THE GREAT PROLETARIAN CULTURAL REVOLUTION, 1966–76

Since 1956 Mao had tried to involve China's intellectuals in a debate of the Chinese Revolution, and to lead them firmly towards the 'thought of Mao Tse-tung'. This had been the idea behind his famous 'Hundred Flowers' speech:

> 'To the artists and writers we say: let a hundred flowers blossom, let a hundred schools of thought compete.'

Chinese postage stamp

However, this had the opposite effect to what Mao had intended: the debates led to many doubts being expressed about Mao's thought. Later, those people who had voiced such doubts were to be called dissidents and traitors. For a time, Mao disappeared from public view (1961–5) until, suddenly, news reports carried photos of Mao swimming down the Yangtse-kiang! This was supposed to symbolise the seventy-two-year-old leader's determination to make another radical change in the people's way of life. He wanted a classless society; he wanted to eliminate the affluent, privileged bourgeois. So he planned a mass-movement of young people (students and schoolchildren) under the supervision of his wife and former film star, Mme Mao. Schools and universities closed down on 18 August 1966 and a million Red Guards paraded in Peking. The 'Cultural Revolution' had begun.

1 Explain the importance of the 'Hundred Flowers' speech.
2 What effect did it have on the intellectual class in China?
3 How did Mao respond to this?
4 Explain the term 'Red Guards'.
5 The photograph above shows the flag of the People's Republic of

China and the face of Mao. What is the special significance of the single large star and the four small stars?

1967–8 was a year of total chaos inside China:

◊ The Red Guards brought down the Head of State, Liu Shao-chi, and thousands of intellectuals.
◊ Red Guards moved into the farms and factories, where many workers regarded them as dangerous meddlers.
◊ Red Guards fought the Battle of Wuhan against units of the PLA
◊ Military forces seemed to be in control and their leader, Lin Piao, appeared to be the most powerful figure in China – until his mysterious death in 1971 (announced 1973).
◊ Liu also disappeared. He may have died in 1972.
◊ By 1973–4 Mao had regained power with the help of his old friend Chou En-lai. But he was ill and there were rumours that his wife and her own group of advisers were running China.

Changes in China's way of life

◊ By 1974–5 there were about 77,000 communes in China. Some were huge organisations of over 60,000 people; others, especially in pastoral regions, were less than 2,000 in number.
◊ Each commune elected its own Revolutionary Committee and was responsible for communal health.
◊ There was no income tax.
◊ Wages were low; but so were rents. Bearing in mind that in 1975 1 yuan = 15p, rent was 5 yuan and weekly wages were about 35 yuan.

(*a*) Many people saved hard for 'three wheels and a carry'. What were these?
(*b*) Demand for bicycles was immense, especially in the big cities – 160 yuan in Wuhan, where television sets were also on sale at 350 yuan.

◊ The literacy programme was very successful – by 1970 ninety per cent of the population under forty-five could read and write.
◊ One problem was the variety of language used in China: Northern Mandarin, Southern Mandarin, Cantonese and – in the western pastoral zones – Turkic languages and Tibetan.
◊ The CCP experimented with Pinyin (a romanised alphabet) and on 1 January 1979 China adopted it as the national alphabet:
    Mao Tse-tung became Mao Zedong

China since the death of Mao

Mao died in 1976. So did two elderly colleagues, Chou En-lai and Chuh Teh. The new leader was Hua Guofeng and one of his first acts was to arrest the 'Gang of Four':
    Jiang Qing (Mme Mao); Wang Hongwen; Zhang Chinqiao; Yao Wenyuan.

Gradually, criticism of Mao Tse-tung mounted. To a very large extent, Mao's economic policies were discredited. Hua Guofeng resigned in 1980 and the real ruler of China emerged – Deng Xiaoping. Deng allowed the show trial of Mme Mao to go forward in November 1980. She was found guilty, which was Deng's way of telling the people that Mao had been a dictator and that his thoughts and actions had not always been in the best interests of the Chinese people.

Deng's changes included:

- A crack-down on law and order problems. Crimes of violence carried the death penalty – over 5,000 criminals were shot during 1983.
- Support of private enterprise – notably in the 'Special Economic Zones' designed to attract foreign investment into China.

CHINA'S FOREIGN POLICY

Tibet: during 1950–51 the PLA occupied Tibet (declared independent in 1911 but never recognised as such by China). There were many resistance movements; these were not crushed until 1959 when the Dalai Lama (spiritual and temporal leader of Tibet) fled to India.

Korea, 1950–53: China regarded Korea as a buffer state against invasion from Japan (Japan was the main base for the UN during the war). The PLA prevented the UN from returning to the Yalu River.

The Formosan Crises, 1954–5; 1958: China was determined to regain control of the off-shore islands of Quemoy, Matsu and Taiwan. There was brief fighting in 1954–5 but it ceased once China tried to become the Third World leader at the Bandung Conference (Indonesia, 1955). The 1958 crisis was much more serious and the US Navy escorted ships bringing supplies to Taiwan as they passed through the Formosan Straits. China continued to claim Taiwan but it remained in Nationalist hands even after the death of Chiang Kai-shek in 1975.

The Indo-Chinese War, 1962: during 1962 Indian troops began to probe Chinese territory in the Himalayas. This led to a Chinese blitzkrieg at Thag La and in the Aksai Chin, designed to punish the Indians. Some of the fighting took place at heights over 16,000 feet (4,800 metres). The Indians withdrew – it had been a short, sharp lesson to India whose reputation as the great neutralist and pacifist leader of the Third World had taken a hammering.

The Sino-Soviet split

The long quarrel with the Soviet Union began in 1960 over the way in which the two great communist countries approached the 'world revolution'. The Chinese were highly critical of Khrushchev's 'peaceful co-existence' and decided to go their own way:

- Russia withdrew her technicians in 1960.

Asian contrasts: China, Vietnam and Japan

◊ China exploded a nuclear device at Lop Nor in 1964.
◊ In 1969 Chinese and Soviet patrols were in a fire-fight on disputed Damansky Island. President Ho Chi Minh (North Vietnam) made a deathbed appeal to the two 'fraternal nations' to settle their differences. However, Russia stationed about fifty divisions along the Sino-Soviet border and targeted a substantial number of ICBMs on China.

Normalising relations with the US

After China managed to win admission to the UN (1971) she invited President Nixon to Peking (1972). President Ford made his pilgrimage to the Chinese capital in 1975. President Carter sent high-technology aid. China signed a peace treaty with Japan 1978; and attacked Vietnam in 1979, the most unsuccessful operation in the history of the PLA.

Overseas aid

During 1974–5 China sent shiploads of men and materials to help

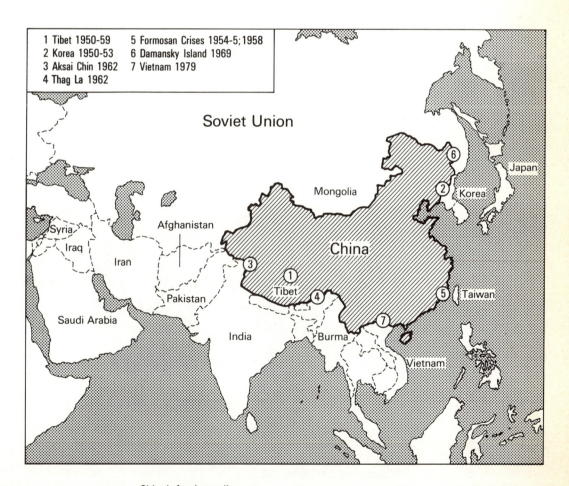

China's foreign policy

build the Tan-Zam Railway (linked Zambia's copper industry with the exporting centres along the African coast). She has sent aid to other countries in Africa, e.g. Egypt, Mozambique, Angola. She has studiously avoided any involvement in African liberation movements or in the Arab–Israeli Wars but it was revealed in 1986 that she is one of the biggest arms exporters to the Gulf War.

CHINA'S SPECIAL RELATIONSHIP WITH BRITAIN

Hong Kong

Over four million people – most of them Chinese – have crowded into the Crown Colony of Hong Kong. The Crown Colony is a thriving business centre and acts as an important centre of foreign exchange for the People's Republic of China. However, Britain's lease on Hong Kong was destined to expire in 1997 when it would revert to China.

Fortunately, China and Britain were able to agree that the handover would proceed peacefully. Good relations were typical of China and Britain, especially after Deng Xiaoping emerged as leader in 1977. His desire to encourage free enterprise was the start of a major revolution in Chinese ideas and values and within a few years he allowed the people to have modest links with western culture as this photograph of a peasant farmer with his 'boom box' indicates.

Chinese farmer with traditional transport and western technology

Source: *The Times*, 20 April 1985

Elizabeth II's visit to China, 1986

Queen Elizabeth II was the first British monarch to visit China; she arrived on 12 October 1986. The visit served to confirm the quality of Anglo-Chinese relations and opened up a brief view of a land about which few outsiders have any understanding. British industry, however, saw the visit as an opportunity to develop business deals, particularly in the growing 'high tech' areas such as telecommunications.

2 VIETNAM

FRANCE AND THE END OF EMPIRE IN INDO-CHINA, 1946–54

Ho Chi Minh

Japanese troops occupied French Indo-China in 1940, over a year before they attacked Pearl Harbor. To oppose them Ho Chi Minh founded a League for Vietnamese Independence – the famous Viet Minh. When the Japanese surrendered in 1945 Ho proclaimed the independence of Vietnam. This was his broadcast from Hanoi (2 September 1945):

> *All men are created equal. They are endowed by their Creator with certain inalienable rights . . . Life, Liberty and the Pursuit of Happiness.*

1. From which other Declaration of Independence were these words taken?
2. To which colonial country was he talking?

France had no intention of abandoning her colonial empire in Indo-China. French troops arrived and forced Ho Chi Minh to take refuge in northern Tonking. But Ho had adopted Mao Tse-tung's teaching on guerrilla warfare:

> *When the enemy advances, we retreat.*
> *When the enemy halts and encamps, we trouble him.*
> *When the enemy seeks to avoid battle, we attack.*
> *When the enemy retreats, we pursue.*

Ho Chi Minh's field commander, General Giap, faithfully followed these tactics until 1954. Then he astonished the French (who had already suffered 100,000 casualties) by attacking the huge fortress at Dien Bien Phu. Ho Chi Minh authorised Giap to assemble 125,000 men with heavy artillery. Giap then surrounded the fortress and in May 1954 overwhelmed the French. France now agreed to dump the entire problem of Indo-China on to the great powers.

The Geneva Conference, 1954

As in Korea, the delegates agreed to partition the problem of Vietnam and divided the country into a communist north and a non-communist south. The dividing line took the form of another DMZ (de-militarized zone), coinciding with the 17th Parallel. This was supposed to last two years; then foreign troops would vacate the country and the people of Vietnam would vote for a new national government. Meanwhile, two neutral states – Laos and Cambodia – would act as a protective pad round the divided peoples of Vietnam.

The South-East Asia Treaty Organisation (SEATO), 1954

In September 1954 representatives of the US, Britain, Australia, New Zealand, Pakistan, France and Thailand met in Manila and there set up SEATO. President Eisenhower said he would protect the off-shore islands of Nationalist China; while the SEATO nations guaranteed to defend Laos, Cambodia and Vietnam against external attack.

'THE LOST CRUSADE': AMERICA'S WAR IN VIETNAM

American intervention

The last French troops left Vietnam in 1955. But there were three reasons why peace could not persist within this battered country:

- Thousands of Viet Minh were still operating south of the DMZ.
- Millions of peasants in the south hated President Diem's government in Saigon because it refused to reduce exorbitant rents and undertake a fair redistribution of the land.
- Ho Chi Minh committed himself to the recapture of the Mekong Delta, the most important source of rice supplies in SE Asia.

Three events then contributed to war:

- The US began sending military aid to prop up Diem's army (the Army of the Republic of Vietnam = ARVINs).
- Ho Chi Minh formed the National Liberation Front for the Liberation of South Vietnam (the Viet Cong or VC).
- The secret US intervention in 1962 when President Kennedy authorised Operation Sunrise – US helicopters airlifted ARVIN soldiers and US jets shot up VC bases.

Two assassinations

- Disgruntled ARVIN troops murdered Diem (November 1963).
- Three weeks later President Kennedy was assassinated in Dallas.

Would the new US President, Lyndon Johnson, remove the 14,000 US 'advisers' from Vietnam? An event occurred that then escalated the war.

The Tonking Gulf Resolution, 1964

According to American reports (often doubted in recent years) several North Vietnamese torpedo boats attacked USS *Maddox* on 2 August 1964. *Maddox* retaliated and when Johnson described the 'Tonking Gulf Incident' to a shocked American Congress it passed the Tonking Gulf Resolution. This allowed him to use fire power against North Vietnamese (NVN) and VC targets north and south of the DMZ. There was no declaration of war against North Vietnam. There was

Asian contrasts: China, Vietnam and Japan

no American attempt to overthrow Ho Chi Minh or to change the boundaries agreed at the 1954 Geneva Conference.

So what was America fighting for? To preserve the status quo; to stop the NVN communists from taking over the south, irrespective of the quality of government there.

Now read the following account of President Johnson's war:

> *Between 1965 and 1968 Johnson fought a typical American war in Vietnam. He brought in overwhelming firepower on land, sea and in the air. He drafted over a million young Americans destined to serve a one-year tour in 'Nam'. Yet all the helicopter gunships, defoliant sprays, search and destroy missions, and B-52 air strikes on the north couldn't bring about an American victory. The VC's Tet Offensive (January–February 1968) proved this. Two thousand VC fighters drove into Saigon in trucks and on Honda scooters. They took over buildings in the city centre and even penetrated the US embassy. Another VC force entered Hué and murdered thousands of pro-American sympathisers. Amidst the chaos, the NVN army attacked and surrounded 6,000 US marines at Ke Sanh. The Tet offensive destroyed all credibility in American strategy. Johnson declined to accept another term as President. President Nixon came forward with his plan for 'Vietnamisation'.*

(Vietnamisation was the term used to bring ARVIN troops up to US standards, put them in the battle line and then withdraw all US troops).

1. How long did American draftees usually serve in Vietnam?
2. What was the Tet Offensive?
3. Where did the NVN army attack the US marines?
4. Did Johnson try to become President again?
5. Who planned the policy of Vietnamisation?

The end of the American involvement, 1973

Nixon gave the American people the impression that the war was running down. So they were naturally astonished when he had to bomb the Ho Chi Minh trail in Cambodia (attacked in 1970) and Laos (attacked in 1971). America had barely recovered from revelations about the My Lai massacre. Many Americans were by now anti-war and relieved when America and North Vietnam signed an armistice at the Paris Peace Talks (1973) and Nixon pulled out most of the US troops stationed in the south.

Consider these extracts:

Extract A

> *The war in Vietnam was the first conflict to be televised in full and the typical American household experienced an endless round of pictures showing death and destruction and, sometimes, of death on university campuses during student protests.*

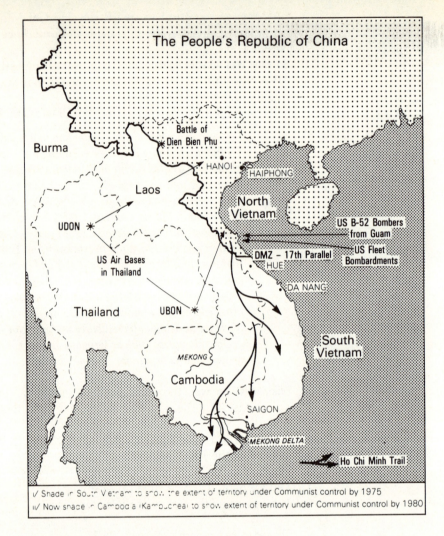

The war in Vietnam

Extract B

> The US media bore a heavy responsibility. It failed to show many scenes of NVN atrocities such as the Dak Son holocaust (250 villagers incinerated by the VC) or dwell on the Hué massacres in which 5,000 people lost their lives. Nor did television mention that when National Guardsmen killed four student demonstrators at Kent State University in Ohio (1970) most young people of call-up age supported Nixon's invasion of Cambodia. The media's coverage was selective. It gave more coverage to Americans than it did to ARVINs and VCs. It presented the anti-war sentiment, the product of a highly articulate minority, as reflecting the average American's view of the war.

Asian contrasts: China, Vietnam and Japan

Extract C

> *Millions of people in the United States did oppose the war for reasons which were sincerely felt, and their activities were an important element in the failure of American involvement.*
> (Sir Robert Thompson, *War in Peace*. Orbis, 1981, p. 219)

1. Would you agree that these comments in Extract A are
    - [ ] untrue
    - [ ] too general
    - [ ] biased against the United States

   Tick the one you think is most appropriate and then write a brief paragraph to support your choice.
2. In Extract B, why is it said that the US media bore a 'heavy responsibility'?
3. Why is it held that the media's coverage of the war was 'selective'?
4. What does the writer claim the media coverage did for the 'anti-war sentiment'?
5. Is there evidence of bias in this extract?
6. In Extract C is there evidence that many American people were deeply opposed to the war?
7. What importance did they have in the history of the War in Vietnam?

Now read the following passage from a British textbook:

> *For the first time in her history America had lost a war. After the armistice she could not resume that war. She had discarded the rhetoric of John F. Kennedy who, back in 1961, had assured the American people that 'We shall pay any price, bear any burden, meet any hardship, oppose any foe, to assure the survival and the success of liberty.' Congress passed the 1973 War Powers Act preventing a future President from exercising the powers Johnson and Nixon had used. When the NVN invaded the south in 1974 President Ford was helpless to prevent the NVN occupation of Saigon in 1975. The last Americans had to clamber on the rooftops to catch the helicopters leaving the city. Off the coast of Vietnam a US fleet took on board thousands of Vietnamese refugees and then sailed away from the long coastline it had shelled and bombed for nearly a decade.*

1. In what context did Kennedy make the speech quoted in this passage?
2. What happened to President Nixon in 1974?
3. What name did the NVN give to Saigon?
4. Why did so many Vietnamese leave with the last Americans?
5. It is sometimes said that a picture is worth a thousand words. What does the photograph on page 284 say?
6. To the North Vietnamese, the long war in and against the south was always a 'War of National Liberation'. To the Americans the war was fought to contain communism, to prevent the countries of South East Asia falling like dominoes before the advancing VC. Construct a short dialogue in which a VC guerrilla tries to convert an American soldier to his way of thinking.

The evacuation of Saigon, 1975

Source: *The Times*, 20 April 1985

7   Has Vietnam occupied another South East Asian country since 1975? If so, which one?

3 JAPAN SINCE 1945

RECOVERY FROM WAR

THE US OCCUPATION

On 15 August 1945 Jiro Horikoshi, designer of the world-famous Zero fighter, sat listening to the recorded voice of Emperor Hirohito. The war was over. 'I thought: this finishes the job to which I have devoted one half of my life . . . what foolish steps Japan had taken! Perhaps Japan was not the only fool, but she had lost millions of valuable lives, not to mention the wasted efforts and assets of those who survived . . . the result of poor political leadership caused by lack of consideration and responsibility. I prayed: let intelligent leaders step forward.'*

*Jiro Horikoshi, *Eagles of Mitsubishi*. Kappa Books, Japan, 1970 (in translation by Shojiro Shindo and Harold N. Wantiez, Osprey Books, 1982)

General Douglas MacArthur

The intelligent leader who stepped forward was the US Supreme Commander of the Allied Powers (SCAP), General Douglas MacArthur. One of his first actions was to bring American-style democ-

racy to the people via the 1945 Japanese Bill of Rights. In effect, this gave the Japanese people the Four Freedoms:
> Freedom from Want
> Freedom from Fear
> Freedom of Speech
> Freedom of Religious Belief

MacArthur also enabled the Japanese people to take part in free, democratic elections (1946).

Significance

This meant that Japan now had a Cabinet government, responsible to the Diet or Parliament. There were a few restrictions on individual rights after the creation of the Chinese People's Republic (1949) – because of the longstanding fear of China.

(*a*)   Strikes forbidden.

(*b*)   Communists placed under police surveillance. But, on the whole, the Japanese people found that MacArthur did not intend to destroy their ancient culture or rob them of their respect for their Emperor and their strong family bonds. So they were ready to accept MacArthur's 'American-style' graft on to their existing way of life, especially when it took the form of popular changes in their education system, in land reform and in opening up opportunities for small businesses.

Education

- All Japanese children now had the right to primary, secondary and further education.
- This education would include economics and management skills.
- It would emphasise individual technical excellence.

Land reform

This freed Japanese tenant farmers from their traditional subservience towards landlords. Tenant farmers started to become freeholders after 1945. Significantly, they tended to run their small farms in exactly the same way as they had always done.

Small business enterprises

Here the Americans tried to break down the monopoly of the traditional 'big business' organisations known in Japan as *zaibatsu* and to allow small business enterprises to compete against them.

The influence of the occupation forces

Thousands of American, British and Commonwealth troops were either based in or took their leaves in Japan. They helped to 'westernise' some aspects of Japanese life-style, especially in the big cities.

Read the following:

Sometimes called the 'Coca-Cola culture', western-style music clothes and values had a marked effect on younger Japanese who hadn't served in the armed forces. This goes some way to explain the extraordinary co-operation between a defeated people and SCAP. This was certainly a characteristic of Japanese history between 1945 and 1950, years in which many of the terribly battered cities were rebuilt and industries restarted.

1. Explain the term 'Coca-Cola' culture.
2. Why were younger Japanese attracted to this?
3. Why do you think the writer uses the word 'extraordinary' to explain the co-operation between SCAP and the Japanese people?
4. What happened in 1950 to involve the Japanese people and Japanese industry in American policies?
5. What role did General MacArthur take in this event?

The 1951 Treaty of San Francisco

The Japanese people had accepted the shock news that their Emperor had renounced his divine status; they accepted the 1946 constitution; they joined in the democratic elections run by SCAP. Now they were willing to sign their peace treaty at San Francisco. They were doing quite well:

- Business was booming because of the demands of the Korean War.
- Prime Minister Yashida was keen to come to terms with the rest of the world, for the sake of Japan's trading future.

By the terms of the Treaty:

- Japan recognised the independence of Korea.
- She surrendered all claims to Taiwan, the Pescadores, South Sakhalin and the Kuriles.
- Japan requested the presence of American troops to guarantee her defence.*

*In a special security pact signed on the same day.

The Soviet Union, Czechoslovakia and Poland refused to sign the treaty which came into force on 28 April 1952. The San Francisco Treaty marked the end of the occupation; and came as a birthday present for the Emperor, much appreciated by the Japanese people.

THE ECONOMIC MIRACLE

1952–4; hostility towards American policies

Largely due to US dollar aid and the efforts of the Japanese people to rebuild their shattered economy, Japan had regained its pre-war levels of production by 1953. Her Gross National Product grew by over ten per cent annually. Nevertheless, there was some hostility towards the US.

Why?

◊ There were now numerous US bases in Japan. Japanese parents were concerned that they were corrupting young people who lived in the surrounding areas.

◊ The Japanese were appalled by the 1954 Bikini incident.

Read this extract:

> A Japanese fishing boat had been casting its nets on the edge of the zone where the Americans conducted their hydrogen bomb test at Bikini Atoll in March 1954. When the twenty-three crew put into port near Tokyo they were all suffering from radiation sickness. Moreover, their fishing catch was also found to be radioactive, obviously unfit for human consumption. Then came the panic. Some of the fish had been sold! This panic spread throughout Japan, fuelled with understandable fury against the US nuclear tests. The resentment was as great as it had been back in 1945 – when the two atomic attacks on Hiroshima and Nagasaki took place.

Japan survives inflation

Despite this setback in Japanese–American relations, the US continued to invest dollars in the massive programme of economic recovery. This investment, plus the profits Japan made during the 1950–53 Korean War, enabled the people to survive two peaks of inflation:

(a) 1947–9
(b) 1953–5

By 1955 Japan was once more an industrial nation. Vast zaibatsu such as Mitsui and Mitsubishi were employing thousands of people at home and abroad. Many hundreds of highly profitable small enterprises, geared to the developing markets of the western world and to South East Asia, were committed to:

(a) modest wage increases
(b) modest price increases

so that inflation could be kept to a minimum.

Japanese industry generally was willing to take modest profits and to invest the maximum capital in new, efficient production methods and a great deal of research and development. Japanese policies contrasted significantly with those of another industrial giant – Britain. This is why small enterprises such as Honda could grow and finally out-produce the traditional motorcycle manufacturers and eventually crush such distinguished names as Norton, Triumph and BSA.

Japan – a world leader

By 1964 Japan was able to host the Olympics in Tokyo.
By 1970 she led the world in the manufacture of:
cameras; transistorised radios; televisions; motor-cycles; commercial vehicles.

Japan was the world's biggest shipbuilder; and only fractionally behind the US in the new 'sunrise' industries:

> electronic technology – pocket calculators and business computer systems.

Perhaps more than any other nation involved in the 'electronics revolution', Japan was conscious of involving fully her keen and enthusiastic workforce in retraining and upgrading, so they would not be forced into early retirement or redundancy when the 75,000 planned microprocessor robots were introduced. Japan knew that her industrial leadership in the 'third industrial revolution' had to be maintained in:

(*a*)   Asia (where she produced ninety per cent of the television sets and almost all the motor-scooters).
(*b*)   Africa
(*c*)   United States
(*d*)   Western Europe

where by 1980 her lead in automobile manufacture and consumer electronic products was undisputed.

Defence

Another reason for Japan's high level of profitability was her miniscule investment in defence. In 1954 Japan had formed a non-nuclear Self-Defence Agency and maintained small, modern Ground, Maritime and Air Self-Defence Forces. But they made very little demands on the average Japanese worker – again a major contrast with the British – who could earn well over £800.00 a month in a Nissan car factory and yet pay only twelve per cent tax. Under the *1960 Treaty of Mutual Co-operation and Security with America*, Japan committed herself to payments for *'bilateral security'*.

Up to 1981 this was costing her a mere one per cent of her Gross Domestic Profit.

However, in 1981 Japan agreed to accept defence responsibilities for defending her major sea-lanes from the southern ports – Kobe, Osaka, Yokohama and Tokyo – into the mid-Pacific. By then Japanese firms such as Shin Meiwa were delivering anti-submarine patrol flying boats to the Maritime Self-Defence Force; while the Air Self-Defence Force was using the Mitsubishi F-1, the first properly designed supersonic fighter interceptor to be designed in Asia.

Japan has often scrambled her fighters to intercept Soviet reconnaissance aircraft, especially near the 'disputed islands' north-east of Hokkaido and in the narrow strait separating Japan from Sakhalin. Japanese fighters in fact scrambled after the disaster to Flight 007 – the South Korean Boeing 747 shot down by a Russian fighter in Soviet air space over Sakhalin while it was flying from Anchorage to Seoul (1 September 1983).

Japan in space

Japanese scientists began testing small rockets in 1955. By the late seventies Japan had two space centres:

Kagoshima Space Centre (opened 1963)
Osaki Launch Site (developed 1969 onwards).
In 1975 and 1977 Japanese rockets (partly composed of US rocket stages) put two satellites into geostationary orbit:
Kiku 1 (1975)
Kiku 2 (1977).

CHANGES IN JAPANESE POLICIES DURING THE EIGHTIES

The Japanese Prime Minister Yasuhiro Nakasone was very conscious that Japan's policies over the forty years of peace after the Second World War could be summed up as 'export or die'. Japan was now the most successful exporting country in the world. Japan had the strongest economy and paid the highest wages. Could this go on for ever? Would the rest of the world be content for this to happen? Prime Minister Nakasone thought not and was greatly influenced by a report from the Bank of Japan: the 1985–6 Maekawa Report. This recommended that:

◊ There should be a 'dearer' yen on the international money markets.
◊ There should be a drive to increase domestic consumption of Japanese manufactures.
◊ There should be far more overseas investment.
◊ Japan should import more coal and more food.

A stronger line towards the Soviet Union
The disputed islands off Hokkaido In 1945 the Soviet Union occupied four islands (Kunashiri, Etorufu, Shikotan and Habomai). Japan has always claimed that these islands were Japanese sovereign territory. When the Soviet Foreign Minister, Mr Shevardnadze, visited Japan in 1986 he was told by the Japanese that the islands remained a 'basic problem'. Moscow's line has always been that there is no way that any part of these four islands can be returned to Japan – they now form vital defence links and are packed with Soviet armoured units, interceptor fighters and assault helicopters.

A build-up of Japanese defences In 1986 a Japanese White Paper recommended that Japan should be able to repel a conventional Soviet invasion and that Prime Minister Nakasone should be allowed to exceed the one per cent of Gross National Product spending on defence. (One per cent is £8.7 billion – approximately half of Britain's defence budget). In 1986 Japan had 350 aircraft, 150,000 soldiers and 164 naval vessels; its weaknesses were
(a)   A lack of airpower.
(b)   A lack of anti-submarine air/sea weapons.

A greater role in world affairs
Japan began to play a distinctive role in world affairs in the mid-eighties, taking a moral stand on important world issues, e.g.

History 1: World History since 1914

1 *Famine in Africa:*
Bob Geldof's 'Live Aid' concerts and 'Band Aid' record sales made a great impact on the Japanese people. Their concern was shown in their huge donation to help feed Africa's starving millions: a cheque for 192,651,847 yen to the Band Aid Trust secured through the satellite transmissions operated by Fuji Television Network, the Nippon Broadcasting System and the Fuji Network System.

2 *Sanctions against South Africa:*
Japan banned imports of pig-iron and steel (along the lines recommended by the EEC). Additionally, Japan banned the issue of visas to South African tourists; and discouraged Japanese tourists from going to South Africa, where they were classed as 'honorary whites'.

Map questions
On the map of Japan:
1 Name the four disputed islands.
2 Name the port of H in Hokkaido.
3 Name the four major ports in Honshu, K, O, T and Y.
4 Underline the names of the two cities that suffered nuclear attack in 1945.
5 Underline with a double line the capital of Japan.

Multiple-choice questions
1 In 1945 the US Supreme Commander of the Allied Powers was
  ☐ General Eisenhower
  ☐ General Patton
  ☐ General MacArthur
  ☐ Admiral Nimitz

2 The name of the Treaty that marked the end of the Allied occupation of Japan in 1951 was the
  ☐ Treaty of Paris
  ☐ Treaty of Washington
  ☐ Treaty of Tokyo
  ☐ Treaty of San Francisco

3 The hydrogen bomb explosion that horrified Japan in 1954 took place at
  ☐ Mururoa Atoll
  ☐ Tarawa Atoll
  ☐ Okinawa
  ☐ Bikini Atoll

4 Japan's defence expenditure never exceeded
  ☐ 1%
  ☐ 3%
  ☐ 5%
  ☐ 10%
of her Gross National Product.

Asian contrasts: China, Vietnam and Japan

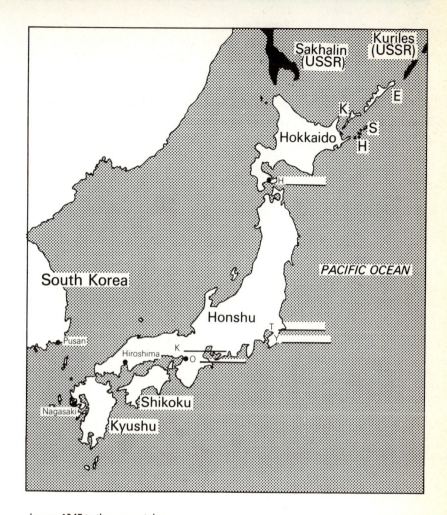

Japan: 1945 to the present day

5   Japan's armed forces are known as the
    ☐ Self-Defence Agency
    ☐ Imperial Armed Forces
    ☐ Non-nuclear defence units
    ☐ Japanese Reserve Forces
6   The Soviet Foreign Minister who visited Japan in 1986 was
    ☐ Mr Gorbachev
    ☐ Mr Molotov
    ☐ Mr Kosygin
    ☐ Mr Shevardnadze
7   Japan's Prime Minister in 1986 was
    ☐ Mr Nakasone
    ☐ Mr Yashida
    ☐ Mr Abe
    ☐ Mr Gotoda

Essay topic
You are discussing with a Japanese friend the ways in which Japan has managed to become the most advanced technological country in the world. Outline the argument you would use either

(*a*)   to explain why Japan should import far more foreign goods, especially the industrial products of Britain; or

(*b*)   to suggest that Japan should spend more of her resources on defence.

CHAPTER TWELVE

SCIENCE AND TECHNOLOGY

CONTENTS

- **Some critical issues in our interdependent world** — 295
  Introduction   295

- **Land and air transport** — 298

- **Space flight and communications** — 302

- **Radio and television: microelectronics and IT** — 307

- **Nuclear power: military and civil** — 308
  Military use   308
  Civil use   312

Science and technology

1 SOME CRITICAL ISSUES IN OUR INTERDEPENDENT WORLD

INTRODUCTION

After 1914 most people in the world were obsessed with the importance of their own self-determination and their rights to enjoy:

- political freedom
- social freedom
- economic freedom

and, above all:

- the right to create their own countries and exercise the privileges of sovereign independence.

This sounded splendid and, by and large, most people won their political independence by 1980. Today, a host of nations range in size from

(a) the billion Chinese living in the People's Republic of China to
(b) the 45,000 West Indians living in St Kitts-Nevis, independent in 1983.

Yet it is quite remarkable how little opportunity these new states have had to exercise their new-found sovereign power. This is because they have gradually come to realise, largely as a result of two World Wars, the population explosion, the terrible danger of nuclear war, poverty, famine and disease, that the risks run by one nation state rapidly become the risks run by every nation state.

This is the nature of global interdependence. Sovereign states have to understand that the world's peoples are all dependent on one another. This wasn't fully appreciated by political leaders before 1945. However, since then we have grown accustomed to the idea of interdependence as far as the risk of nuclear war is concerned. Perhaps we are less conscious of the other areas in which we are similarly interdependent.

MEDICAL ADVANCE

Thanks to the advance of medical research, modern drugs and surgical methods can cope with many 'killer' diseases.

- Penicillin, accidentally discovered by Alexander Fleming in 1928, is an antibiotic substance that will kill bacteria without damaging the cell tissue. Under the pressure of the Second World War, scientists discovered ways of mass-producing penicillin from which millions would benefit.

◊ Yaws can be cured with penicillin.
◊ BCG vaccine has virtually wiped out tuberculosis in both the advanced and developing nations.
◊ DDT spray has eliminated the malarial mosquito in many parts of the world.
◊ Medical skill is beginning to cope with cataract problems (curing blindness in developing countries) and with leprosy.

THE POPULATION EXPLOSION

The population explosion has taken place in both advanced and developing countries – and especially in those developing countries often called the 'Third World' and, more recently, the 'South'. People live longer and this fact, due to medical advance and improvements in our environment, is termed a 'modern death rate'. However, the 'South' has a primitive birth rate allied to the modern death rate, and it is in the 'South' that the population explosion has become alarming, pushing our numbers up from three billion (3,000 million) to over four billion in 1980. A recent report by UNFPA (United Nations Fund for Population Activities) stated that growth rates have begun to decline but that total population figures continue to rise. The world's food and energy resources are finite – it is vital for mankind not to exceed present population figures.

Why do people have large families?

◊ Social custom in some parts of the world demands that families should be large.
◊ Many parents have more children to counter high infant mortality rates.

UNFPA and the affluent North must try to help the over populated South to:

◊ reduce infant and child mortality;
◊ encourage family planning;
◊ foster the advantages of having a small family, e.g.:
(*a*) immediate prospect of healthier babies;
(*b*) improvement in the status of women once liberated from the drudgery of large families;
(*c*) a chance of reducing poverty, the greatest blight among peoples of the South.

THE PROBLEM OF POVERTY

In 1980 the Brandt Report defined the problem of poverty:

Permanent insecurity is the condition of the poor . . . Flood, drought or disease affecting people can destroy livelihood without hope of compensation.

Brandt pointed out that this was the condition of about one-third of humanity. They must be helped through investment, development and research, especially for irrigation, water management and the construction of suitable transport systems. The overwhelming need was to step up production on the farms in poverty-stricken areas and to give more people guaranteed employment and adequate living conditions – if only to stem the drift to the cities in the less-developed South.

Similarly, the affluent North must understand that it is to their advantage that poor people do not cut down trees for firewood or depend on animal dung for fuel. The rain forests and the more temperate zone's woodlands are vital for the environment. Animal dung is better used to aid soil fertility.

Brandt pointed out that the massive help needed is not beyond mankind's present resources: mankind 'never before had such ample technical and financial resources for coping with hunger and poverty'. It could start by reducing expenditure on armaments in order to improve health and thus reduce poverty: 'The military expenditure of only half a day would suffice to finance the whole malaria programme of WHO, and less would be needed to conquer river blindness which is still the scourge of millions.'

Funding development needs
Inevitably UN resources have been divided between dealing with

- short-term effects of warfare, natural disasters (famine, drought, earthquake, locust plagues)
and
- the long-term and expensive programme of convincing people to reduce family size and improving the conditions of family life (sanitation, drinking water, jobs, markets for the sale of products, good roads, lorries).

Not enough money was coming in from rich nations to fund this work. Yet the facilities existed:

- Bretton Woods Conference, 1944 (New Hampshire, USA) began the work.
- It set up the International Bank for Reconstruction and Development (usually called the World Bank).
- It created the IMF (International Monetary Fund) to provide loans to countries on condition they followed policies that would reduce their overseas debts.
- In 1947 the western nations set up the Organisation for European Economic Co-operation (OEEC) to administer the Marshall Aid funds; in 1960 it changed its name to the Organisation for Economic Co-operation and Development (OECD).

These organisations had to realise, however, that to send food relief to hard-pressed countries was simply not enough.

ENERGY

Man has had ready access to fossil fuel for centuries – coal, oil, natural gas seemed limitless. Then events during the 1970s made people realise that these fossil fuels were
(a)   expensive
(b)   finite, i.e. they would run out one day.
Renewable energy sources were the most attractive:

- *geothermal power*, using the heat from the earth.
- *solar power*, using heat from the sun.
- *wind and wave power* – harnessing these forces to run turbines and create electricity.
- *synthetic alcohol fuels*, derived from plants, e.g. ethanol from sugar-cane (successfully pioneered by Brazil).
- *controversial civil nuclear energy* (see page 312).
- *hydro-electric power* – a great potential in Asia and South America.

2 LAND AND AIR TRANSPORT

LAND TRANSPORT, 1914–39

Before the First World War the automobile revolution was well established. Henry Ford had already perfected the techniques of mass-production of motor cars and the most efficient ways of employing large numbers of unskilled workers on the assembly lines. In Britain, for example, there were over 200,000 cars on the road in 1914. Tar-spraying was widespread and the reliability of motor transport (cars, vans, lorries) made it of incalculable importance in the history of twentieth-century land transport.

However, most people were not car owners and up to 1939 depended on public services (trains, trams and buses) for everyday use. The cheapest form of transport was the electric tram (single-deckers until about 1930, after which the double decker was common). Trolley buses were favoured by many cities after 1930. Inside cities, and in rural areas all over the world, buses and coaches (often powered by diesel engines) brought a new mobility to ordinary people. The most dramatic change in rail transport took the form of electrification, though almost everywhere railways were showing very poor profits and often made a loss.

Read this account of the importance of the motor car in America:

> *Apart from the mobility and status it gave American families who could make the down-payment on a $300 Model T, the motor car created dozens of new industries and literally millions of jobs. Road-*

building doubled between 1920 and 1929; garages, filling stations, hotels and eating-houses mushroomed around the new highways. The rubber industry boomed as the demand for wide pneumatic tyres increased every day. The electrical industry turned out millions of spark plugs, generators, wiring systems and starter motors and even developed automatic transmissions. The oil industry flourished, as did paint firms, glass manufacturers and steel and aluminium producers.

1 Does the passage suggest that most American families did *not* buy their motor cars outright?
2 Do you think the effect of the new automobile industry in America was similar to the British experience?
3 What do you think the main difference between the US and Britain was, in terms of the development of the motor car?
4 Name the British motor manufacturers who had the sort of impact that Henry Ford made in America.
5 This is a thoroughbred British motor car built during the thirties. Can you detect its make from the style of the radiator? Is the firm that made it still in existence?

Military uses of land transport

During the First World War the ordinary motor car had been used as a staff car, as an armoured car and as a mobile base for an anti-aircraft gun. Lorries had transported troops and supplies to the battlefronts; tracked vehicles had hauled huge howitzers into position while the tank itself had made its first appearance in warfare.

AIR TRANSPORT, 1914–39

When one remembers that it was the Wright brothers who made the first powered, sustained and controlled flight at Kitty Hawk in 1903, it is surprising that the USA did not lead world growth in civil aviation after 1918. One reason was that long-distance trains were faster and certainly safer and more comfortable than the ex-Army bombers and training aircraft of First World War vintage. Americans realised that aeroplanes were ideally suited for the transport of mail, and Boeing Air Transport and National Air Transport took over this service in the twenties when Americans were sending millions of airmail letters every year. Regular passenger services in America began in 1927, using mainly Ford 4 AT Trimotors, affectionately dubbed 'Tin Lizzies' by the thousands who used them up to 1934.

Britain tried to link her Empire using airships but the two disasters (the R-38 over Hull and the R-101 over Beauvais, 1921 and 1930) ended the experiment. Britain concentrated on fixed wing aircraft, the most famous of which were the majestic Heracles class of four-engined biplanes. In 1936 Short Bros. constructed the new flying boats capable of flying to Australia. For the privileged few, world-wide air travel had become a reality by 1939.

Military uses of air transport

Zeppelins, fighters, bombers, reconnaissance aircraft and aeroplanes capable of operating from warships had all featured in the battles of the First World War. Military research and development did not stop, and new types of warplanes appeared in:

        The Manchurian Affair, 1931–3
        The War in Abyssinia, 1935
        The Sino-Japanese Incident, 1937
        The Spanish Civil War, 1936–9

Best known of the new types of aircraft were the dive-bomber (the Ju-87 Stuka) and the fast, medium bomber (the German Dornier). Britain concentrated on single-seater interceptor fighters (the Spitfire and Hurricane). The design of racing aeroplanes, especially the Schneider Trophy seaplanes, had developed the air-cooled radial engine and the liquid-cooled in-line engine to a very high level of power and reliability. Aircraft were destined to dominate the Second World War.

1. Who designed the Supermarine S6B, winner of the last Schneider Trophy race in 1931?
2. Name the outstanding aircraft engine of the 1929–31 period.
3. Name the country that produced the famous Wasp and Cyclone engines.

The state of technology on the eve of the Second World War

Naval aircraft, flying from aircraft-carriers, eventually replaced the battleship. Ground-attack aircraft, working closely with the armies, made the blitzkrieg possible. Transport aircraft could move entire

Science and technology

the ME-163 Komet

the V-2 supersonic rocket

the V-1 'Doodlebug', or Flying Bomb

The ME-163 Komet rocket-propelled interceptor could climb to 30,000 feet in 2 minutes 36 seconds. It carried two 30 mm cannon.

The V-1 'Doodlebug' or Flying Bomb, also had a one-ton warhead. The tiny airscrew on the nose acted as an air-log and after a given period of time altered the elevator so that the bomb dived on its target. The change of altitude cut off the pulse-jet's fuel supply so that the engine stopped. This had never been intended by the Germans, but it gave civilians below a chance to judge whether or not the bomb was going to fall on them!

The V-2 Supersonic Rocket took less than 30 seconds to reach MACH-1. Its warhead weighed a ton. The 'V' stood for Vergeltungswaffen – reprisal weapon.

divisions and a great deal of heavy equipment from one battle-zone to another, and provide surprise and punch by towing gliders packed with airborne troops or by dropping parachute soldiers. Strategic bombers terrorised civilians, pinpointed precise targets, obliterated entire cities and eventually carried the two nuclear weapons to Hiroshima and Nagasaki. Tanks made land warfare mobile; radio provided the voice contact so greatly missed during the First World War; radar located targets obscured by night and fog; rockets and pulse-jets powered supersonic V2s and low-flying 'doodlebugs'. Most of the scientific research for these weapons took place between 1918 and 1939.

LAND TRANSPORT AFTER 1945

After 1945 the lorries and motor cars dominated the transport scene in most parts of the world. Mass production of family and 'executive' motor cars became monopolised by huge multinational car companies such as General Motors of America and Nissan of Japan. Many relatively small firms went to the wall and in several countries motor car *assembly* (using parts from many other countries) became the fashion rather than motor car *manufacture*.

AIR TRANSPORT AFTER 1945

Immediately after the war most countries used converted bombers and transports that had seen service during the Second World War. These aircraft all had piston engines. But the future lay with the jet engine, pioneered by researchers in Germany, Britain and Italy before 1939. Several German jet aircraft, e.g. the Me 262 twin engined fighter-bomber, had seen service during the war and by the fifties jet engines were reliable power units. The three Comet disasters delayed development but in 1958 one of the most remarkable jet transports ever built came into service – the Boeing 707. In 1968 the first of the wide-bodied jets appeared (the Boeing 747 – sometimes called the 'eighth wonder of the world') and in 1976 the supersonic Concorde came into service.

3 SPACE FLIGHT AND COMMUNICATIONS

Early rockets

Germany, the Soviet Union and the United States led the world in rocket development.

Read the following accounts:

> A group of German enthusiasts had founded the Society for space travel (VfR – Verein für Raumschiffart) in 1927. Their first rocket launch was on 23 July 1930; and in 1932 their work aroused the interest of the German army. Its Weapons Department set up an

Science and technology

experimental rocket section commanded by Captain Walter Dornberger; his young civilian assistant, Wernher von Braun, was put in charge of the liquid-fuel rocket development at Kummersdorf. There he built the A-2 rockets and test-fired two of these from Borkum island, sending them up 1.5 miles (2.4 km). In April 1937 von Braun moved into the top secret research station at Peenemunde on the Baltic coast. He discovered that the main problem was directional control: and he had solved that by 1939 on his A-5 rocket. On 3 October 1942 his first V-2 left the launching pad on Peenemunde Island.

1. Why was the German Army interested in rocket development?
2. Who said 'Today the space age is born' on 3 October 1942?
3. What was the name of Germany's secret rocket research station?
4. Where was it located?

Russian experiments were largely devoted to the development of rocket missiles, particularly the 'Little Katies' – Katyusha multi-barrelled rocket projectiles. The Americans were mainly interested in rocket-propelled aircraft. However, after the Second World War both countries began to prepare for the exploration of space.

ROCKET DEVELOPMENT AFTER 1945

Both superpowers had captured stocks of V-2s – and a number of German rocket scientists. Dornberger and von Braun went to the USA. The Russians made little use of the Germans: they repatriated most of them in 1951. That year the Russians announced they were preparing to launch artificial satellites; other Russian scientists were meanwhile working on the first ICBMs. America had started Project Orbiter designed to launch a satelite during the International Geophysical Year, 1957–8. However, President Eisenhower cancelled the Orbiter rocket and gave the Navy the Task of developing Project Vanguard. At a crucial moment, America fell behind in the space race.

Sputnik, 1957

Sputnik is Russian for 'traveller' and it went into orbit as Planet Earth's first artificial satellite on 4 October 1957. The second Sputnik followed on 3 November 1957.

Explorer I

In 1958 Explorer I (carrying instruments designed by Dr James Van Allen) discovered that Planet Earth is surrounded by radiation belts – known as the Van Allen belts nowadays.

Man and woman in space

The year 1958–9 was an astonishing one for successful rocket technology. America's Atlas I became the world's first communications satellite (1958). Russia's Lunik 1 went into orbit round the Sun; Lunik

2 crashed on the Moon; Lunik 4 took photos of the hidden side of the Moon (1959). In 1961 Alan Shepard flew a sub-orbital 'lob'; Russia's Yuri Gagarin made the first manned space flight on 12 April 1961 in Vostok 1. Valentina Tereshkova made 48 orbits in Vostok 6 in 1963.

Men on the Moon

In 1958 President Eisenhower created NASA (National Aeronautics and Space Administration). President Kennedy promised to put a man on the moon by the end of 1969. So Project Apollo was born. Three astronauts died in the flash-fire on the launching pad in 1967, and shortly after this a Russian was killed testing the new Soviet spacecraft Soyuz 1. Apollo 11, with three US astronauts, successfully put the launch module Eagle on the moon's Sea of Tranquillity (1969). By then the nations interested in space travel had signed the 1967 Outer Space Treaty offering help to stranded or endangered astronauts.

Space stations, probes and shuttles

President Nixon and President Brezhnev co-operated in 'the world's most ambitious experiment in space co-operation': the link-up between a Soyuz capsule and an Apollo spacecraft. This took place in July 1975 and symbolised the progress the two superpowers were making in their Skylab and Salyut space stations. Soon it became quite common for manned and unmanned spacecraft to shuttle back and forth once the big space complexes were in orbit. These were not without incident:

- America's Skylab 4 began to disintegrate after its last astronauts left in 1974. It made nearly 35,000 orbits before falling into the Indian Ocean (1979).
- In 1983 two Soviet cosmonauts faced a propellant fuel leak problem in Salyut 7. The space station wallowed and when the Russians tried to send up a relief crew the rocket exploded on the launch pad. Fortunately the Russian cosmonauts repaired Salyut 7 with fittings sent up by Cosmos 1443 and Progress 18. They returned to Earth in their Soyuz T-9 after 150 days in space.

Meanwhile, America had launched its two Voyager space probes:
(a)   Voyager 1 reached Jupiter (1979) and found the previously unknown moon Io.
(b)   Voyager 2 passed through Saturn's rings, reached Uranus 1986 and headed for Neptune (scheduled for 1989).

The re-usable space shuttles

Space shuttle Columbia blasted off from Cape Canaveral in 1981 and orbited Earth thirty-six times. It lost some of its heatproof tiles and its second flight had to be cut short that year. Its third was a total success (1982) demonstrating that its three companion shuttles (Challenger, Discovery, Atlantis) could be used to service space stations and to

Science and technology

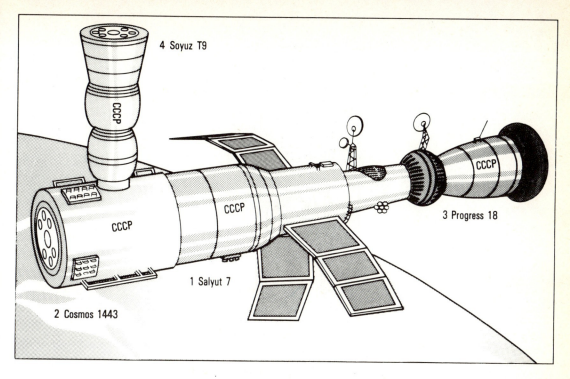

The Salyut 7 incident, 1983
The Salyut 7 was a 47-ton space complex composed of: (1) Salyut space station. (2) Cosmos unmanned space craft. (3) Progress unmanned/manned supply vehicle. (4 Soyuz cosmonaut ferry

launch satellites. However, when Challenger tried to send two commercial communications satellites into geostationary orbit (February 1984) the rockets on the satellites failed – a serious setback partly compensated for by astronauts taking 'free' spacewalks via their special 'backpacks'. Then in 1986 disaster struck Challenger. Twelve seconds after launch the space shuttle disintegrated, killing the entire crew. After this, President Reagan decided to abandon the space shuttle programme for the time being. He was now more interested in ASAT (Anti-Satellite Systems) proposed in his famous Star Wars speech in March 1983. ASAT technology did not in fact contradict the major Outer Space Treaties:

1963 Partial Test Ban Treaty: prohibited the testing and deployment of nuclear weapons in outer space (though the three nuclear powers with their own space programmes – China, France and India – had not signed this).

1967 Outer Space Treaty: prohibited the placing of nuclear and other mass destruction weapons in outer space.

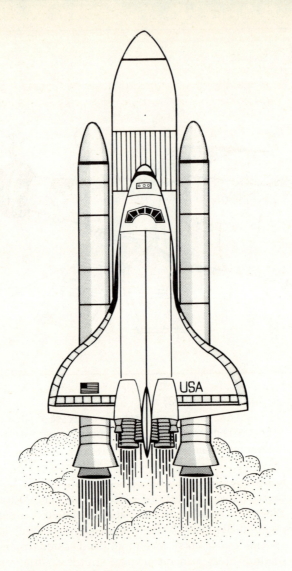

The space shuttle Columbia

1972 SALT-1: prohibited the placing of anti-ballistic missiles systems in outer space.

There was no international law to forbid a space shuttle with an ASAT system from retrieving someone else's satellite!

Space communications

In 1945 Arthur C. Clarke discovered that if a satellite were placed 22,300 miles (38,880 km) above the Earth it would appear to remain stationary because it would take twenty-four hours to complete an orbit – precisely the same time Earth takes to complete a single rotation.

Science and technology

1 What is this orbit called?
2 Name the first artificial satellite.
3 Name the first communications satellite used to relay television programmes in 1962.
4 This was the year after the US President had urged all countries to 'participate in a communication satellite system in the interests of world peace and closer brotherhood among people throughout the world.' Name the President.
5 Many nations joined Intelsat in 1964. What does Intelsat mean?
6 What is the Russian equivalent?
7 Europe has its own Communications Satellite, ECS-1. Name the rocket that sent it into orbit.

Communication satellites have many uses:

◊ Low altitude military satellites have zoomed over Middle East battlefields and beamed back colour pictures of the conflict.
◊ The British Task Force in the Falklands maintained links with London via a communications satellite.
◊ Over half of humanity watched the 1980 Moscow Olympics and the World Cup football matches via satellite – the world had become a 'global village'.

Think of four other important uses to which communication satellites are put. Look at the weather forecast on television tonight for a clue.

4 RADIO AND TELEVISION: MICROELECTRONICS AND IT

Public radio broadcasts did not begin until 1920. Commercial radio began in the US that year; and in December the 5,000-watt radio station at Königswusterhausen broadcast a concert to radio amateurs all over Europe. On 14 November they could tune into London's Radio 2LO; and over the next forty-eight hours Manchester and Birmingham transmitters came on the air. By the end of 1922 the British Broadcasting Company* was in charge of all radio programmes in the UK. In the US, electrical firms set up transmitters and broadcast news, sport and popular music, and soon newspapers and even department stores had their own transmitters. By 1923 600 were in existence and their owners made their profits by selling radio receivers to the public. By 1929 most of these companies had been bought up by the 'Big Three':

*Became the British Broadcasting Corporation in 1927.

    American Telephone and Telegraph (ATT)
    General Electric
    Westinghouse

They created 'prime listening time' in the evenings by broadcasting movie soundtracks, vaudeville acts and big orchestral bands. Those in control of radio had an important vehicle for propaganda. Lloyd George and Stanley Baldwin were two British Prime Ministers who knew this. Name two European dictators who exploited the propaganda value of radio to the full.

Television transmissions began in the thirties. John Logie Baird is usually credited as the first to send a clear picture (1925) but very few people owned television sets before the Second World War. BBC1 began transmitting in 1945; the Independent Television Authority dated from 1954; BBC2 arrived in 1964 and was the first to transmit colour pictures (1967). By 1970 ninety-two per cent of British families owned television sets and by the 1980s television was almost universal, enhanced by the new video systems.

The microelectronics revolution has contributed to the way in which electrical goods have been brought within everybody's purchasing power – part of the general revolution concerning IT (Information Technology).

IT is defined as: 'the handling of vocal, pictorial, textual and numerical information by means of a microelectronics-based combination of computing and telecommunications.'

Development
1940   Dr Marvin Kelly discovered the conducting qualities of silicon.
1948   Dr Brattain invented the transistor, an electronic switch that was later miniaturised and etched on a piece of silicon called a 'chip'.

These developments led to the miniaturisation of electronic computers. The first had been bulky e.g.:
(*a*)   ENIAC (Electronic Numerical Integrator and Calculator) built in America in 1946.
(*b*)   Manchester University's Mk.1 built in 1951.

Then the use of the transistor enabled the computer to become the vital part of the microelectronics revolution, leading to:
(*a*)   the personal computer;
(*b*)   the word processor;
(*c*)   electronic publishing on television: in 1977 BBC Ceefax and ITV Oracle began teletext services and by 1982 half a million teletext sets had been sold/rented in Britain.

List the electronic equipment in your home/school/college.
   How many examples of this equipment make use of a computer?
   Where was the equipment made?

5 NUCLEAR POWER: MILITARY AND CIVIL

MILITARY USE

During August 1945 the Japanese people living in Hiroshima and Nagasaki became the first to experience the horrors of nuclear attack.

In both cities, the devastation went on for several hours in the firestorms that followed the atomic explosions (these were air bursts). Thousands died immediately and then the survivors had to face another horror – radiation. This led to many subsequent diseases; while the 'black rain' containing radioactivity that fell after the firestorms contaminated the rivers, water supplies and pasture land. Fish and animals as well as people became contaminated and the effects would plague survivors for the rest of their years. Total deaths from the two attacks now reach about 190,000 according to Japanese sources.* Such was the awful example of the military use of nuclear power.

*Hiroshima and Nagasaki: a report commissioned by the Mayors of the two cities and published in Japan, 1981.

Deterrence

Both superpowers assembled huge nuclear arsenals during the 1960s to deter one another from making the first offensive strike. This policy of deterrence appeared to maintain world peace – but at a colossal price. Moreover, there was always the risk of a nuclear accident. Accidents did in fact occur, though none had resulted in the accidental discharge of a nuclear missile.

Examples of nuclear accidents

- US B-52 bombers, spearhead of the US Strategic Air Command, have been involved in at least three accidents:
  (a)   1958: one nuclear bomb fell into the back garden of a house in South Carolina.
  (b)   1966: 4 nuclear bombs fell out of a bomber when it collided with its refuelling aircraft.
  (c)   1968: when a B-52 crashed in Greenland its nuclear bombs fell into the sea.
- The Soviet Union has suffered at least nine accidents to its flotillas of missile-carrying nuclear submarines. These accidents included collisions, fires and radiation leaks, one example of each being described below:
  (a)   1984: *collision* – a Victor I class submarine collided with a US aircraft carrier near Japan.
  (b)   1986: *fire* – a Yankee class submarine caught fire in the Atlantic.
  (c)   1981: *radiation leak* – several Russian seamen were poisoned by a radiation leak in a Soviet submarine operating in the Baltic.

Nuclear proliferation

This is a term used to describe the tendency for more and more countries to possess nuclear weapons. The three original nuclear powers were the USA, the Soviet Union and Britain. They were joined by France, China and India, all of whom have exploded nuclear devices. Israel, according to statements issued in 1986, also had nuclear devices and there were reports that Golda Meir, the Israeli leader, ordered a nuclear alert during the War of Yom Kippur.

Pakistan, Egypt, South Africa and West Germany have the capacity to produce nuclear weapons.

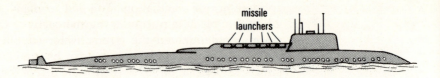

A Soviet Delta class submarine, a re-designed version of the Yankee, capable of carrying 12 missiles. Deltas came into service in the early 1970s; Delta IIs and Delta IIIs were the biggest submarines in the period 1973–83. The US Ohio class (Tridents) are slightly bigger

Multiple-choice questions

1   The headquarters of the Soviet Red Banner Pacific Fleet (1986) is at
   ☐ Murmansk
   ☐ Sevastopol
   ☐ Leningrad
   ☐ Vladivostok

2   The main US nuclear submarine base outside American territory (1986) is in
   ☐ Japan
   ☐ Turkey
   ☐ Britain
   ☐ Norway

3   A Commonwealth country that left the ANZUS Defence Treaty because of objections to the arrival of US nuclear vessels was
   ☐ New Zealand
   ☐ Canada
   ☐ Australia
   ☐ Britain

4   American B-52 bombers are also called
   ☐ Flying Fortresses
   ☐ Superfortresses
   ☐ Stratofortresses
   ☐ Badgers

DEFENCE: BRITAIN AND THE SUPERPOWERS

1948   Labour government allows US B-29s to use British bases at beginning of Berlin Crisis.

1955   Conservative government states it intends to join nuclear club – but it had no missile to carry its new H-bomb.

1958   60 US Thor missiles arrive in Britain – but Americans held the key to the warhead.*

1960   US begins operating its first nuclear submarine equipped with Polaris.

1961   Britain buys Polaris.

1963   All Thor IRBMs returned to US. Britain writes-off its Blue Steel stand-off weapon carried by V-bombers.

1975/6   Soviet Union updates its missile systems and installs the triple-warhead ICBMs called SS-20s. Five NATO countries (including Britain) ask for Pershing IIs and Tomahawk Cruise missile to balance Soviet threat. NATO decides to install these in 1983 (its 1979 decision) unless the Soviet Union reduces its nuclear weapons targeted on the West.

1983   First Cruise missiles arrive at Greenham Common. Britain hoped to start work on expensive Trident replacement for Polaris. Determined to maintain up-to-date nuclear deterrent. In fact, real problem was that Polaris was a product of fifties technology. The Russians could counter this. Therefore Trident was needed for the 1990s.

1986   F-111s strike Libya from British bases.

First Trident submarine (destined to carry 16 or 24 ICBMs) under construction.

*These were Intermediate Range Ballistic Missiles.

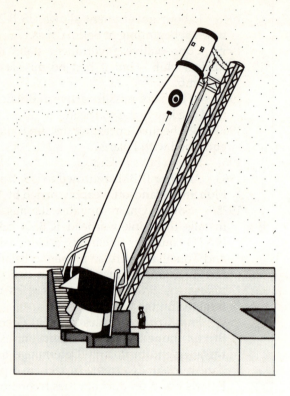

A Thor missile

CIVIL USE

THE HAZARDS OF CIVIL NUCLEAR POWER

Civil nuclear power, to which the world may have to turn when the finite supplies of fossil fuels run out, causes arguments among environmentalists and politicians all over the world.

There are two main problems:

◊ The danger of a nuclear accident and its effects on the environment.
◊ The difficulty of disposing of nuclear waste.

There have been several nuclear accidents since 1945:

1 Three Mile Island (located between Harrisburg and York) in the USA, 1979. This was a Babcock and Wilson PWR pressurewater reactor. There was a leakage of radioactive materials in the reactor containment building where the level of contamination was 30,000 reams per hour. A count of 400 reams per hour can kill a person within a matter of days. There were no fatalities at Three Mile Island.

2 Windscale (renamed Sellafield) in Britain has had more than its fair share of accidents – about 300 since 1950. A fire in No.1 plutonium production reactor during 1957 caused a serious radioactive leak. Silo B38 leaked radioactive caesium and strontium 90 in 1976 (this might have been going on since 1972). During 1983 a radioactive slick forced the authorities to close Sellafield beach after a faulty discharge of radioactive waste into the sea.

3 Chernobyl 1986: this was the worst nuclear accident to date. The Russians acknowledged that it dealt a crippling blow to the Soviet economy with over ninety-five square miles around the reactor unfit for any further use due to contamination. The cost of dealing with this tragic incident was over two billion roubles (£1.9 billion). 135,000 people had to be evacuated; 31 people died; 2000 were admitted to hospital. The precise cause of the incident remained uncertain in the autumn of 1986 – it may have been a combination of human error and antiquated nuclear technology.

Nuclear waste
Dumping of nuclear waste is a problem for all nuclear powers. The London Convention (1972) was supposed to limit low-level waste to certain oceanic zones. By 1982 it was obvious that the rules were being broken and tiny states such as Naurau and Kiribati in the middle of the Pacific were beginning to object to their role as 'nuclear dustbins'. So did many British people during 1986 when NIREX (the government nuclear waste agency) wanted to dump waste at Bradwell-on-Sea (Essex), Elstow (near Bedford), Fulbeck (Lincolnshire) and Killingholme (Humberside).

1. Construct a dialogue between two arms negotiators, one Russian and one American, anxious to reduce the stockpile of nuclear weapons on Planet Earth.
2. List the arguments in favour of nuclear power. Identify one western nation that has decided eventually to dispense with civil nuclear energy. Find out how it proposes to face the problem of limited fossil fuels.
3. After the problem of military and civil nuclear use, what do you think is the next most urgent problem facing mankind? If it is among the following, put them in order of priority:
    The population explosion
    World health
    Drug abuse
    Poverty
    Food shortages (include famines and droughts)
    Other natural disasters such as earthquakes.
4. Do you agree with the Brandt Report that military expenditure should be cut and the money diverted to aid the peoples of the South?
5. What do you understand by the term 'South'. Is it the same as the 'Third World'? Are all 'Third World' countries poor? List some examples that you consider to be very rich indeed.

6 Explain the meaning of the following terms:
   Sputnik   Van Allen belts   NASA
   geostationary orbit   re-usable shuttle   ASAT

ANSWERS TO MULTIPLE-CHOICE QUESTIONS

P. 85–6

1. Yen
2. Zaibatsu
3. Immigration
4. South Manchurian Railway
5. Kwantung Army

P. 104–5

1. All except Wilson
2. All except the Bulge (fought in 1944)
3. All except Plessey
4. Food prices had slumped on world markets

P. 117–18

1. State unemployed relief, old-age pensions, Public Works programmes
2. The NRA
3. The Tennessee Valley Authority
4. All except Harry Hopkins
5. The CCC did all these things apart from building new bomber factories
6. Edgar J. Hoover
7. 1935 and 1937
8. Without payment

P. 158–9

1. Winston Churchill
2. The Atlantic Charter

3 Freedom of Speech
4 The General Assembly
5 Trygve Lie
6 ILO
7 Brtain, USA, USSR, France and Nationalist China

P. 174

1 The neutron bomb
2 Vienna
3 1979
4 1985

P. 183–4

1 Angola
2 Lord Lugard
3 Nigeria
4 Kenya, Uganda, Tanganyika
5 Germany
6 Burma

P. 209

1 Bob Marley
2 Joint Endeavour for Welfare, Education and Liberation
3 Ronald Reagan
4 Sir Paul Scoon
5 Nine
6 Jamaica

P. 231–2

1 Yassir Arafat
2 UNIFIL
3 1970
4 Golda Meir
5 The USA
6 New Jersey
7 Islamic Jihad
8 Iraq
9 Tunisia
10 Saudi Arabia

Answers to multiple-choice questions

P. 244–5

1. Jim Crow Laws
2. Lincoln
3. NAACP
4. Jesse Jackson
5. Los Angeles
6. 'Political will' in the White House
7. Vietnam

P. 255–6

1. The removal of the pass laws
2. Oliver Tambo
3. Steve Biko
4. Dumping grounds
5. Shridath Ramphal

P. 290–92

1. General MacArthur
2. Treaty of San Francisco
3. Bikini Atoll
4. 1%
5. The Self-Defence Agency
6. Mr Shevardnadze
7. Mr Nakasone

P. 310

1. Vladivostok
2. Britain
3. New Zealand
4. Stratofortresses

INDEX

Agadir crisis 15
Agrarian Reform Law 274
Agricultural Adjustment Act (Triple A) 111
Algérie Française 186
Amin, Idi 191
Andropov, Yuri 176
Anglo-Irish Agreement 66, 125
Anti-Comintern Pact 76
apartheid 249, 250, 253
Arafat, Yassir 227, 230
Armscor 254
Aswan 220
atomic attacks 53, 151–2, 162, 287, 302, 308
Attlee, Clement 159
Azikiwe, Nnamdi 188

Baldwin, Stanley 307
Balfour Declaration 215–16, 218
Bandung 276
Bantu 246
Barbarossa 51
Battles
 Marne 1914 19
 Ypres 1914 19
 Somme 1916 19
 Verdun 1916 19
 Jutland 1916 23
 Vimy Ridge 1917 23
 Messines 1917 23
 Ypres 1917 23
 Kaiserschlacht 1918 26–7
 Cantigny 1918 102
 Château-Thierry 1918 102
 St Mihiel 1918 102
 Argonne 1918 102
 Kuanchang 1934 265
 Dunkirk 1940 127–8
 Britain 1940 52
 Moscow 1941 52
 Coral Sea 1942 139
 Midway 1942 139
 El Alamein 1942 137
 Kursk 1943 131, 135–6
 Ichi-go 1944 268
 Falaise Gap 1944 147
 Arnhem 1944 147
 Bulge 1944 147
 Philippine Sea 1944 149
 Leyte Gulf 1944 149
 Iwo Jima 1945 150
 Okinawa 1945 150

Bay of Pigs 167
BBC 307
Begin, Menachem 226, 228
Belloc, H. 182
Ben-Gurion, David 217–18, 222
Benelux 177
Beneš, Eduard 123–4
Berlin Olympics 113
Bevin, Ernest 218
Bhutto Zulfiqar Al 200
Biafra 189
Bikini incident 287
Bismarck, Prince 15
Boers 246
Botha, L. 248
Botha, P. 254
Brandt, Willy 171
Brandt Report 296–7, 313
Brattain, Dr 308
Braun, Werner von 303
Bretton Woods 297
Brezhnez, President 170–2, 174–5, 226, 304
Brusilov, Alexei 43
Burma Road 148, 268

Carter, President Jimmy 174–5, 277
Carrington, Lord 193
Casablanca Conference 138
Catro, President Fidel 168, 207
Ceefax 308
Chamberlain, Neville 123, 125
Chapei 265
Checkpoint Charlie 162
Chernenko 176
Chernobyl 313
Chiang Kai-shek 87, 116, 148, 263–5, 267–70, 276
China Aid Bill 269
Chindits 183
Chou En-lai 275
Churchill, Winston 52, 138, 155–6, 197, 220
Chu Teh 269
Clay, General 160
Clarke, Arthur C. 306
collectivisation (USSR) 46–7
Comecon 176–7
Coolidge, President Calvin 103
Corfu incident 94
cruise missiles 311
Crystal Night 64

Dak Son 282
Daladier, Premier 123–4
D'Annunzio, Gabriele 90
Defence of the Realm Act 36
De Gaulle, General 185–6
Deng Xiaoping 276, 278
Diem, President 280
Dornberger, General 303
Dresden 141
Dual Alliance 15

Eaker, General 139
Ebert, President 59
Eden, Sir Anthony 220
EEC 177
Eisenhower, General Dwight 145, 155, 166, 293, 303–4
Elizabeth II 278–9
ententes:
 Cordiale 15
 Triple 15

Falklands 307
Farmer, James 241
Federal Bureau of Investigation 115
Final Solution 65
fireside chats 110
Fleming, Alexander 295
Flying Tigers 116
Ford, Henry 298
Ford, President Gerald 283
Franco, General 75, 115

Gagarin, Yuri 304
Gang of Four (China) 275
Gandhi, the Mahatma 195–8
Gandhi, Indira 199–200
Garvey, Marcus 205–6
Geldof, Bob 290
George V 17
Giap, General 279
Goering, Hermann 127
Gorbachev, Mikhail 176
Gramsci, Antonio 90–1
Great Purge 50–1
Greenham Common 311
Guantanamo 168
Gulf War 229

Hada, General 268
Haile Selassie (Ras Tafari) 131, 208

Harding, President Warren 103
Harris, 'Butch'/'Bomber' 139
Helsinki Conference 172
Himmler, Heinrich 57
Hirohito, Emperor 152–3, 284, 286
Hitler, Adolf 51–3, 55–65, 110, 121–5, 129–30, 135, 139–40, 147–8, 217–18
Ho Chi Minh 171, 279–81
Hoare-Laval Pact 79, 96–7
Honda 287
Hoover, President 106–7
Hoovervilles 108
Hopkins, Harry 111
Horikoshi, J. 284
Hossbach Memorandum 122
Hua Guofeng 275
Hundred Days 110
Hundred Flowers 274

Irgun 217
Irmino coal mine 48

Jackson, Jesse 244
jazz 237
Jim Crow laws 106, 236, 238
Jinnah, Mohammed Ali 195, 197
Johnson, President Lyndon 241, 243, 280–1

Kaiser Wilhelm II 15, 17, 33, 59
Kamenev, Lev 46–7
kamikazes 150–1
Kaunda, President 195
Kapp Putsch 59
Kellogg–Briand Pact 56
Kelly, Dr Marvin 308
Kennedy, President John 167–9, 280, 304
Kenyatta, Jomo 187, 190
Kerensky, Alexander 44
Krushchev, Nikita 162, 167–9, 276
Kim Il-sung 163
King's African Rifles 190
King, Martin Luther 239, 242
Kosygin, Alexei 170–1
Kreisau Circle 148
Ku Klux Klan 103, 106, 236
Kulaks 46–7

Land Act 1913 248
Lari Massacre 190

Index

Lateran Agreements 94, 215
Lawrence of Arabia 31
Lebensraum 121
Ledo Road 268
Lend-Lease 116, 145
Lenin, Vladimir 43–5, 272
Lettow, Vorbech von 32
Ley, R. 62
Liebknecht, K. 59
Lin Piao 268, 275
Little Rock Nine 211
Lloyd George, David 25, 307
Locarno 56
London Convention 313
London Ultimatum 59
Lubbe, Martinus van der 58
Lucy Ring 136
Ludendorff, General von 59
Lugard, Lord 182
Luxembourg, Rosa 59

Maekawa Report 289
MacArthur, general 163–5, 285–6
Maginot Line 126
Malcolm X 242
Manchuria 84–5
Mandela, N. 252, 254
Mandela, W. 254
Mao Tse-tung 148, 266–8, 272–6, 279
March Revolution 1917 43
Marley, Bob 208
Marshall Plan/Aid 159–60, 177, 297
Matsu 270, 276
Matteotti, Giacomo 92
Mau-Mau 190
Mein Kampf 57
Meir, Golda 226, 309
Memel 66
Mugabe, Robert 193
Munich Conference 123–4
Mussolini, Benito 66, 90, 92–7, 128
My Lai 281

NAACP 237–8
Nakasone, Prime Minister 289
Nasser, Gamal 219–22, 224
Nehru, Jawaharlal 195, 197, 199
Neutrality Acts 115
New Jewel Movement 208
Nicholas II, Tsar 16, 34
Nixon, Richard 226, 243, 277, 281, 304

Nkomo, Joshua 193
Nkrumah, Kwame 187–8
Non-Aggression Pact 1939 51, 76, 125
Nyerere, President 190

Obasanjo, General 189
Obote, President 191
Ojukwa, General 189
Operation Badr 225
Operation Barbarossa 130
Operation Moses 230
Operation Sea-Lion 129
Oracle 308
Orlando 90
Ostpolitik 171

Pact of Steel 76
Palestine Liberation Organisation 223–4, 227–9
Paris Peace Conference 71
Paris Peace Talks (Vietnam) 281
Parks, Rosa 239
Paulus, Friedrich von 135
Pearl Harbor 132–3, 268, 279
Pétain, Marshal 129
Pinnacles 208
Polish Corridor 125
Pretoria-Luanda Accord 260

Quemoy 270, 276

race riots (USA) 242
Rastafarianism 208
Reagan, President Ronald 176, 230
Red Guards 274–5
Reichstag Fire 58
Ribbentrop, Joachim von 124
Rome-Berlin Axis 76
Rommel, Marshal 130, 135, 138, 145
Roosevelt, Eleanor 237
Roosevelt, President Franklin D. 109–14, 117, 133, 138, 151, 156, 206, 237, 268
Rossing Mine 259
Round Table Conference 197
Rowlatt Acts 195
Royal West African Frontier Force 183
Ruhr (occupation) 54, 56

Sadat, President Anwar 224–6
Scheer, Reinhard von 23

Schlieffen Plan 16
Schneider Trophy 300
Schuschnigg, Kurt von 65
Schirach, Baldur von 62
Second New Deal 112
Sellafield 313
Sharpeville 252–4
Shastri, Lal Bahadsur 199
Shepard, Alan 304
Shevardnadze, Eduard 289
Siegfried Line 126
Sino-Soviet Treaty 273
Smith, Ian 192
Social Security Act 112, 195
Soweto 253
Speer, Albert 139
Spinoza, General 194
Stalin, Josef 46–53, 57, 78, 117, 155–6, 160–2, 166, 272–3
START talks 176
Star Wars 176
Stern gang 217
Stresa Front 95
Stresemann, Gustav 55–6
Suez Canal 218–21
Sukarno, Achmad 202
Sun Yat-sen 263
Suzman, Helen 254
SWAPO 249,260
Sykes-Picot Agreement 90, 215
Syngman Rhee 163

Tachai 273
Taiwan 270, 276
Tamils 201
tanks: First World War 33
    Second World War 136–7
Tan-Zam Railway 278
Templer, General 202
Tereshkova, V. 304
Tet Offensive 281
Thag La 276
Thatcher, Margaret 193
Three Mile Island 312
Tito, Marshal 160
Tobruk 130
Tomlinson Report 251
Tonking Gulf Incident 280
treaties
    London 1913 16
    Bucharest 1913 16
    Versailles 1919 31, 37–8, 45, 57, 61, 66–7, 73, 102, 121
    Berlin 1921 102–3
    Washington Naval 1922 73–4, 85

Non-aggression 1937 88
San Francisco 1951 286
Rome 1957 177
Indus Waters 1960 199
Partial Test Ban 1962 170, 305
Outer Space 1967 305
Nuclear Non-Proliferation 1968 170
Sea bed 1971 171
Basic 1972 171
SALT 1 1972
Soviet-Afghan 1978 175
SALT 2 1979
Israeli-Egyptian 1979 226
Triple Alliance 15
Trotsky, Leon 46
Truman, President Harry 151, 155, 162, 165, 218, 269
Truman Doctrine 159, 173
Tshombe, President 194
Turnhalle Conference 260
Tutu, Bishop Desmond 254

U-boats 28–9, 142–3, 181
Uitlanders 246–7

Van Allen Belts 303
Vichy France 129
Vietnamisation 281
Vorster, B. J. 260

Wagner Act 112
Wall Street Crash 57
Walvis Bay 259
Wannsee Conference 65
War Powers Act 1973 (USA) 283
Weimar 53, 57–8
White Rose Society 148
Wilson, President 71, 101–3
Windhoek 260
women (First World War) 36
Wounded Knee 293
Wright brothers 300
Wuhan 275

Yalta Conference 52, 157
Yamamoto, Admiral 133
Yashida 286
Yenan 267

Zaibatsu 83, 286
Zeppelins 33–4
Zia, President 200
Zimmerman Telegram 200
Zinoviev, Grigoriy 46